"It is not often we have the opportunity to read the insights of a veteran missionary who served in several frontline and leadership positions on the field, followed by service as a seminary missions professor. You may not agree with everything in this book, but read it with an open mind. Be ready to learn from a practitioner/professor whose global experiences may be different from yours. Consider his every suggestion for doing the Great Commission more effectively. You cannot read this work without turning your eyes to the nations."

—**CHUCK LAWLESS**, senior professor of evangelism and missions, Southeastern Baptist Theological Seminary

"In a day in which it is often assumed that 'everything is missions,' Don Dent forces us to dust off the once honored tradition of biblical scrutiny. In *Finding Direction to Redeem the Nations,* he reminds us that the One who gives the assignment also defines the assignment, and he challenges his readers to consistently expose their missions assumptions and ambitions to the inconvenient light of Scripture."

—**IAN BUNTAIN**, director, World Missions Center, Southwestern Baptist Theological Seminary

"Don Dent's *Finding Direction to Redeem the Nations* is a valuable resource to any believer, regardless of where they may fall on the spectrum of missions. I firmly believe that anyone who reads this book will be drawn into greater worship of our God who has had a plan to use his people to be a blessing to redeem the nations to himself, and to join him in His mission in the unique role he has created for them."

—**CHERYL BARRETT**, director, For the Nations

"Every mission trainer, every pastor who sends mission teams, and every aspiring missionary needs this book."

—**E. RANDOLPH RICHARDS**, provost, Palm Beach Atlantic University

"In *Finding Direction to Redeem the Nations*, Don Dent provides a panoramic view of the Great Commission through the lens of a field practitioner. From the field to the classroom, Dent continues to impact and influence generations of missionaries and mission leaders with common sense missiology gained from years of living among the nations, tribes, peoples, and languages he has sought to reach with the gospel. Along the way, Dent debunks a lot of modern-day thinking on missions and what it means to engage in the Great Commission in strategic and effective ways."

—**TODD LAFFERTY**, EVP/COO, International Mission Board

"In every generation, the church faces global pressures that influence kingdom labors. And in every generation, the church needs resources to guide toward more excellent ways. Don Dent's work is one of those resources! Blending biblical foundations, historical lessons, missiological principles, and powerful stories gleaned from years of mission experience, Dent has produced a book that is informative, insightful, and engaging. This book is not a lofty academic treatise; rather, this work plants our feet on the ground—where the nations are found!"

—**J. D. PAYNE**, professor of Christian ministry, Samford University

"Don Dent has written a superb book on key missiological issues that every mission leader and practitioner should contend as they steward their amazing resources for the nations. I heartily commend this book to missionaries, mission teams, mission organizations, and local churches engaged in the mission of God. May God use this book to ignite a fire in the hearts of his people as they seek to employ these best practices in hopes that the next movement of God will take place among their people or place."

—**STEVEN M. ELLIS**, executive pastor of mission and church planting, First Baptist Church Rogers, Arkansas

"*Finding Direction to Redeem the Nations* is an important book that anyone interested in God's global mission needs to read. Don Dent brings a lifetime of experience and a fiery passion to the page. Dent exposes the reader to the needs of the word, the biblical call to take the gospel to the unreached, as well as the areas of struggle faced by our US churches. It would be hard for anyone to read this book and not be challenged, not only to think differently but to act differently."

—**Scott Hildreth**, director, Center for Great Commission
Studies, Southeastern Baptist Theological Seminary

"The twenty-first century has brought many challenges and opportunities to the mission of God's church among the nations. Clarity of purpose has never been more needed in order to avert misconceptions and fulfill the mission that Jesus started. In this timely book, Don Dent draws from a lifetime of experience and a wellspring of biblical knowledge to help churches navigate this all-important task that has been entrusted to us."

—**George G. Robinson IV**, professor of global disciple
making, Southeastern Baptist Theological Seminary

"In *Finding Direction to Redeem the Nations,* Don Dent helps us overcome many misconceptions that have resulted in ineffectiveness in missions. In doing so, he charts a course towards more effective cross-cultural disciple-making in the twenty-first century. This book is a must-read for those preparing for or already active in carrying the gospel to the nations."

—**Kelly Malone**, professor of intercultural
studies, Southwest Baptist University

"*Finding Direction to Redeem the Nations* is a solidly biblical analysis of Christ's mission to his people. Don Dent has filtered this message through a life spent on mission with God to help us all distinguish between the mission that Christ mandated and the misconceptions that plague it."

—**David Garrison**, executive director (retired), Global Gates

"The excellent insights in this book could help churches, mission candidates, or missionaries overcome multiple misconceptions in order to become powerfully effective in missions. A number of mission issues are discussed in a clear, concise, well-woven way and supported both by excellent research and powerful stories from actual events. I will be recommending this book to all our mission personnel."

—S. KENT PARKS, CEO, Beyond

"Another 'missions book' for missionaries and keen members of the church's missions committee? Not hardly. Every Jesus-follower needs to read this book because all believers need to understand our Lord's global purposes today and participate in some way appropriate for their lives. This timely message is a page-turner."

—DANIEL SINCLAIR, author of *A Vision of the Possible: Pioneer Church Planting in Teams*

Finding Direction to Redeem the Nations

Finding Direction to Redeem the Nations

Navigating Missions Misconceptions

Don Dent

Discussion Questions by Chesed Dent

WIPF & STOCK · Eugene, Oregon

FINDING DIRECTION TO REDEEM THE NATIONS
Navigating Missions Misconceptions

Wipf & Stock
An Imprint of Wipf and Stock Publishers
199 W. 8th Ave., Suite 3
Eugene, OR 97401

www.wipfandstock.com

PAPERBACK ISBN: 978-1-6667-8412-1
HARDCOVER ISBN: 978-1-6667-8413-8
EBOOK ISBN: 978-1-6667-8414-5

VERSION NUMBER 11/21/23

For Chesed and Rob,
precious missionary kids, coworkers, and collaborators

Contents

List of Figures

Introduction

As a new missionary in Indonesia, I often went out exploring on foot to meet people, get to know the city, practice language, try new foods, explore where to buy things we needed, and share a simple-language testimony. After several hours it would be time to end my adventure and head home. So, I would guess at a compass direction and ask several people if I could get home by walking that way. This often resulted in heading in the wrong direction and it took some time for me to learn not to ask a local, "Can I get to Hegarmanah this way?" Wanting to please, they would always say "Yes" even if they knew that was not the best way to go or had no idea where I was talking about. I needed directions and to learn how to ask the questions that would help me get to my destination. Today many Christians are involved in "missions" activities that will likely not get them to their desired destination due to a plethora of missions misconceptions that misdirect them. This book is about learning to ask the right questions.

Mission and misconception? These two words are in conflict. "*Mission*" = a clearly defined objective. The word is commonly used in such diverse fields as business, science, education, religion, government, and the military, but it consistently refers to *a clearly defined objective*. "Mission" originally came from Latin and meant "sending." It was first used to describe the sending of Jesus and the Holy Spirit to accomplish God's purpose. Each was sent on a mission determined by the sender. Over time the corollary usage of Jesus sending out his followers to the nations to accomplish a clearly defined objective became the norm. The contemporary broad usage of "mission" has misled many Christians today to think of their church's mission as something separate from the clearly defined objective the word "mission" originally described. I will use the term "missions" for action the global church takes to accomplish the specific mission Jesus assigned us, to take the gospel to all the nations. The Bible defines that mission and provides a pattern of how the early church successfully did it.

"*Misconception*" = mistaken, wrong, or inaccurate idea or understanding. There are presently so many misleading and confusing ideas about missions that they can be described as a mishmash, a mixed-up, muddled mess. This is a maze that is difficult to navigate. Tragically, the confusion depletes resources, diverts attention, dilutes results, distracts focus, and dissuades participation. In other words, the muddled mess of misconception mishmash negatively impacts those involved in missions, and has eternal consequences for the peoples waiting to hear about the Savior.

Misconception 1
Missions is whatever we want it to be.

It is not coincidental that misconceptions have taken root when there is a low level of biblical knowledge among Christians, the well-intentioned idea that everybody is a missionary is so popular, missions is judged by how happy it makes us, and postmodern relativism that is uncomfortable with the gospel-revealed Jesus and his Commission to us is common in our pews. We neglect to assess what Christian missions should be and how we carry it out. For many, missions has become whatever we want it to be. If our objective is actually Christian missions, shouldn't we go back and consider how Christ defined it?

My purpose in writing is to identify the *what, why, how,* and *who* of missions. The mission we are examining is the one that the Father, the Son, and the Spirit gave to his church, and especially to those he sends to the nations. This examination necessitates that we identify and counter a number of missions misconceptions that hinder or obstruct accomplishing God's purpose. For that reason, some parts are difficult because we must consider why some popular concepts are problematic.

The three sections of this book explore themes that appear in all the Great Commission statements in the Gospels and Acts. In each of those definitions of this mission, Jesus emphasized a) his authority to initiate this mission because of his crucifixion and resurrection, b) what the core mission task looks like, and c) his presence and power for those who join him.

Each chapter includes references to Scripture and most include an examination of Scripture passages. If you desire to do Christian missions, it is critical to examine the Scriptures to determine what you should believe and practice. Many chapters will also refer to missions history because we can often see scriptural patterns of God's work across the centuries. I am also including in every chapter examples and stories from my own missions experience. These stories are not included because I was an exemplary missionary. In reality, I may not have been the best missionary on any team that I served on during my thirty years overseas. My stories are included because they testify to God's grace and make the subject matter more personal and practical. I hope they will be helpful to you because if I can learn these things, then you can.

I am thankful to Francis Dubose, Baker James Cauthen, and John Mark Terry, my missions professors, for teaching and guiding me. My wife, Anne, and I had the privilege to learn from numerous missionary mentors in two countries in our first decade of service as missionaries. In our mid-career years we had the richest learning environment imaginable as we worked alongside hundreds of missionaries in Southeast Asia and the Pacific Rim. Watching, listening to, and reading reports from over one hundred missionary teams broadened and deepened my missiological understanding. When we moved in later years to South Asia, we learned so much from younger colleagues who were doing far more fruitful ministry than we had even dreamed of! I am deeply grateful for these opportunities to learn from colleagues, so I pray that I can pay this debt forward to other generations from around the world. This book was made possible by the many missions advocates, practitioners, and professors who graciously advised me during the writing phase. Thank you also to the trustees, leadership, faculty, and students of Gateway Seminary who encouraged me as I put my thoughts on paper. Special thanks to Jim Wilson for his continual coaching.

I pray that this book will help churches, individuals called to the nations, ministry schools, student groups, missions teams, and anyone passionate about missions to navigate the misconception maze and find direction to carry out Christ's Great Commission. It is a guide for those who would dare to live decisively to fulfill the destiny of nations for the glory of their Savior. Thankfully, God is raising up such envoys in various environments around the world. It is my prayer that this book will assist these "little ones" to find direction to accomplish what God is calling them to do, to redeem the nations.

Section 1

Missions in God's Perspective

THE ONE WHO PURPOSED mission from the beginning, paid the price to make it possible, and authorizes us to join him is the only one who can define what that mission is.

The five[1] Great Commission statements all emphasize the authority of the crucified and risen Savior to send the disciples to the world to accomplish the mission he has purposed.

- "All authority has been given to me in heaven and on earth." (Matt 28:18)

- "He reproached them for their unbelief and hardness of heart, because they had not believed those who had seen Him after He had risen." (Mark 16:14)

- "Then He opened their minds to understand the Scriptures, and He said to them, 'Thus it is written, that the Christ would suffer and rise again from the dead on the third day.'" (Luke 24:45–46)

- "Jesus came and stood in their midst and said to them, 'Peace be with you.' And when He had said this, He showed them both His hands and His side. The disciples then rejoiced when they saw the Lord." (John 20:19–20)

---

1. The oldest manuscripts of Mark do not include 16:9–20 and most scholars today doubt it includes the words of Jesus. I include it here because it is in most of our Bibles and it reflects an early church understanding of the Great Commission Jesus had given. It also follows the three-part pattern of the other four—authority, assignment, and assistance.

1

- "To these He also presented Himself alive after His suffering, by many convincing proofs, appearing to them over a period of forty days and speaking of the things concerning the kingdom of God." (Acts 1:3)

The four chapters in this section explore the most foundational concepts of missions from God's perspective as revealed in Scripture. These include what missions is according to Jesus and why it should be important to us.

Chapter 1—God's Purpose for the Nations

God has an eternal plan to redeem all the nations that is mentioned repeatedly throughout the Bible. Mission is a clearly defined objective and Christian missions is the clearly defined objective that Jesus gave his followers. So, what does that mission look like?

Chapter 2—God's Intention for the Least of These

There is a common misconception about missions as doing helpful things for "the least of these." This understanding is based on misinterpretation of Matthew 25. Jesus sends the least of his brothers to the nations, who must take them in so they can hear the message of salvation.

Chapter 3—God's Passion for the Nations

In a surprising passage, Jesus shows God's passion to redeem all the nations and his disgust when his people actually obstruct his mission. Christ's followers should seek to make missions a priority in their own lives.

Chapter 4—God's Push to the Nations

Jesus said it is God who pushes workers out into the harvest. We explore six fundamental biblical convictions that motivate Christian missions. If believers actually believe these convictions, they should be highly motivated to join God in his purpose.

Chapter 1

God's Purpose for the Nations

Misconceptions about Missions?

- Several years ago, I was teaching and advising students at a national collegiate conference. Many students had recent missions experiences and were seeking the Lord's direction for their lives. On the last night of the conference, the plenary speaker spoke passionately about God's purpose to reach all nations. He challenged the students to submit their lives to impact the world. He then summarized the challenge by telling them to be friendly to those they meet, but then stated, "You will not even have to share the gospel with anyone." The conference abruptly ended on that note. I sat stunned and broken-hearted that in that opportune moment the speaker had stirred that crowd of missions-minded collegians to go and do far less than Christ commanded. Is this missions or misconception?

- Missionary friends and I attended an English worship service while visiting a neighboring country in Southeast Asia. During the service a missionary led a "missionary moment" and made an emotional appeal for funds to bless the hundreds of villages surrounding the city. We knew that most of those villages were unreached tribal groups, so her appeal caught our attention. She then explained her plan to bless those villages. She held up a beautiful, expensive, white

Victorian doll and explained her hope to import hundreds of them to give to little girls in the villages. She shared how such a doll had been important to her as a child in Britain. The congregation prayed and then took an offering for the dolls. After the service, members explained that the church was very missions-minded and regularly did such projects. Although sincere, the appeal for dolls seemed to fit a pattern of missions activity that is more directly connected to the emotions of the givers than the needs of the recipients. Is this missions or misconception?

- Mexico is a popular destination for church missions teams from Southern California, where I live. The most common project is to send a team to build a house for a Mexican family. What an awesome way to care for people and lead into gospel conversations! I assumed this was usually tied to holding children's programs, visiting in homes, a community celebration to publicly share the gospel, etc. However, most teams do not share their faith or reach out personally to the community. They build a house without witnessing for Christ, praying with people, or challenging the power of Satan in any direct way. It is a well-intentioned service project, but without gospel conversations it seems human-powered, naturalistic, even materialistic. In many cases, a team of non-believers with construction skills could do this better than a church group. Humanitarian projects without a clear gospel witness are wasted opportunities— oh, what it might have been! Is this missions or misconception?

Misconception 2
There is no standard for evaluating missions except what we like to do.

IS THERE NO STANDARD *by which we should define and evaluate Christian missions endeavor?* In a lot of well-intentioned cases, it appears not. The painful truth is that much of what passes for Christian missions today is permeated with misconceptions. These misconceptions are common, confusing, and contradictory. The result is a missions mishmash, a maze of messed-up, mixed-up messages that misguide our thoughts and efforts.

All Nations in God's Purpose

Misconception 3
The God of the Old Testament was only concerned about Israel.

Before examining the mission Jesus gave his disciples, we first need to put his words in the context of God's eternal purpose for the nations revealed throughout the Old Testament. There are many references in the Old Testament to God's redemptive concern for all the nations and their ultimate response to him. For instance, when Yahweh is described as the God of Abraham, Isaac, and Jacob, we are reminded that he established a covenant with this family line that included a direct promise to bless all the families of the earth through them (Gen 12:2–3). God began this covenant relationship with Abraham (Gen 12) and then reaffirmed it with him two more times (Gen 18 and 22). He chose Abraham for a special relationship, to make from his family a great nation, and to bless Abraham so he would be a blessing to others. All three times God talked to Abraham about the covenant, he clearly affirmed that blessing all the nations through his family was an integral part of it. Then God reconfirmed that covenant relationship with Isaac (Gen 26) and Jacob/Israel (Gen 28). To both of them God specifically stated his purpose to bless all peoples through them. So, the initial covenant with his chosen people is confirmed in every case to be about much more than just the one nation of Israel. God chose a peculiar people for the particular purpose of blessing the whole world approximately two thousand years before Christ was born.

Israel often forgot that they were to be the means of blessing all those non-Jewish nations. However, those who were listening carefully to his voice affirmed again and again that they knew God's purpose for all nations. Here are just a few examples.

The exodus is one of the great nationalistic events in the history of Israel. God saved his people from injustice and slavery. Yet, God declared to Moses his broader purpose: "The Egyptians shall know that I am the Lord, when I stretch out My hand on Egypt and bring out the sons of Israel from their midst" (Exod 7:5). Moses declared this broader purpose to Pharaoh, the Egyptian king, approximately 1,300 years before Christ:

> For this time I will send all My plagues on you and your servants
> and your people, so that you may know that there is no one like
> Me in all the earth . . . for this reason I have allowed you to re-
> main, in order to show you My power and in order to proclaim
> My name through all the earth. (Exod 9:14, 16)

After the Israelites left Egypt, God showed them what it meant to be his holy people in the sight of the nations (Deut 4:6). He gave them the law to direct how to live, worship, and approach him. Parts of the law set up a place for God's presence to reside in their midst. During the dedication of the ark of the covenant in Jerusalem approximately one thousand years before Christ, King David called on the nations to praise God:

> Sing to the Lord, all the earth, Proclaim good tidings of His
> salvation from day to day. Tell of His glory among the nations,
> His wonderful deeds among all the peoples. . . Ascribe to the
> Lord, O families of the peoples, Ascribe to the Lord glory and
> strength. Ascribe to the Lord the glory due his name; Bring an
> offering, and come before Him; Worship the Lord in holy array.
> Tremble before Him all the earth. (1 Chr 16:23–31)

In fact, Israel's praise was filled with references to the nations and God's purpose:

> O clap your hands, all peoples; Shout to God with the voice of
> joy. For the Lord Most High is to be feared, A great King over all
> the earth. (Ps 47:1–2)

> God be gracious to us and bless us, and cause His face to shine
> upon us—That Your way may be known on the earth, Your sal-
> vation among all nations. Let the peoples praise You, O God; Let
> all the peoples praise You. Let the nations be glad and sing for
> joy; For You will judge the peoples with uprightness and guide
> the nations on the earth. (Ps 67:1–4)

> There is no one like You among the gods, O Lord, nor are there
> any works like Yours. All nations whom You have made shall
> come and worship before You, O Lord, and they shall glorify
> Your name. (Ps 86:8–9)

Isaiah's visions around 700 BC about God's purpose and the coming King are filled with references to God's purpose for the nations:

> The Lord of hosts will prepare a lavish banquet for all peoples
> on this mountain; a banquet of aged wine, choice pieces with
> marrow, and refined, aged wine. And on this mountain He will

swallow up the covering which is over all peoples, even the veil
which is stretched over all nations. He will swallow up death for
all time, and the Lord God will wipe tears away from all faces,
and He will remove the reproach of His people from all the
earth. (Isa 25:6–8)

Turn to Me and be saved, all the ends of the earth; For I am God,
and there is no other. I have sworn by Myself, the word has gone
forth from My mouth in righteousness and will turn back, that
to Me every knee will bow, every tongue will swear allegiance.
(Isa 45:22–23)

He says, 'It is too small a thing that You should be My Servant
to raise up the tribes of Jacob and to restore the preserved ones
of Israel; I will also make you a light of the nations so that My
salvation may reach to the end of the earth. (Isa 49:6)

Around 530 BC, Daniel had a vision of an exalted figure coming to
bless the nations:

And behold, with the clouds of heaven One like the Son of Man
was coming, And He came up to the Ancient of Days and was
presented before Him. And to Him was given dominion, Glory
and a kingdom, that all the peoples, nations, and men of every
language might serve Him. His dominion is an everlasting dominion. (Dan 7:13–14)

Even Malachi, the last book of the Old Testament, written about 433
BC, affirms a future where the nations worship God:

For from the rising of the sun even to its setting, My name will
be great among the nations, and in every place incense is going to be offered to My name, and a grain offering that is pure;
for My name will be great among the nations,' says the Lord of
hosts. (Mal 1:11)

So, from this brief survey we see that before Israel became a nation
and throughout its history, the God of Israel declared his undeniable purpose to draw all the nations into relationship with himself.

How Jesus Defined Mission

God's purpose was ultimately revealed in the ministry of Jesus and the
commission he gave to his disciples. Jesus called the twelve disciples so

they could be with him, and then he could then send them out to preach and heal (Mark 3:14). Jesus was preparing his disciples for missions, but he was increasingly specific about it towards the end of his time with them. Matthew records that Jesus highlighted what that mission was all about when he began to speak about *panta ta ethne*, "all the nations."[1] This phrase points back to the covenant with Abraham in which God promised to bless the whole world through their relationship. Although we have seen several ways to refer to the whole world, *panta ta ethne* only occurs three times in the Septuagint, the Greek translation of the Old Testament. We find it in Genesis 18:18; 22:18; and 26:4, which all restate the promise in Genesis 12:3 that God chose his people in order to bless all the other peoples. This specific phrase emphatically identifies all nations as beneficiaries of God's redeeming purpose. The fulfillment of the promise is assured in Revelation 7:9.

Matthew 28:18–20 is the best-known statement of the mission Jesus has given his church, but before we look at it, let's consider it in the context of his other *panta ta ethne* statements. In the final major teaching discourse on the Mount of Olives in Matthew 24–25, Jesus uses *panta ta ethne* three times and each time he introduces a specific aspect of this mission to all the nations. *Together these four statements provide a clearly defined objective for what Jesus intended missions to be.*

1. *Matthew 24:9—The pursuit of panta ta ethne will be difficult and costly, even risky, resulting in hatred, persecution, and martyrdom.*

    "Then they will deliver you to tribulation, and will kill you, and you will be hated by all nations because of My name."

The last teaching section in Matthew, chapters 24–25, begins with questions from the disciples about coming disasters and his coming as King. The rest of these chapters is the answer Jesus gave to their questions. Jesus pulled their attention away from the typical apocalyptic signs to point them to global missions to all the nations. The greatest troubles the disciples will face are not natural or political ones, but the costs of carrying out his purpose for all the nations. It is a surprising way to introduce his provincial followers to his concern for all peoples. Obviously, Jesus was not concerned about modern marketing techniques, because beginning with the high cost is not how we would expect to sell

---

1. Jesus introduced global missions after the disciples had realized he was more than a good Jewish rabbi; the disciples knew that Jesus was "the Christ, the Son of the living God" (Matt 16:16).

the disciples on their life work. Before they even knew what this pursuit was all about, Jesus told them it is difficult and costly, even risky, and will result in hatred, persecution, and death for some.

Jesus repeated a warning he gave earlier in Matthew 10:17–22, when rejection and persecution were expected from fellow Jews as the disciples went on mission. In fact, the words of warning are precisely the same: "they will hand you over" and "men will hate you because of me." Jesus then explained that this pushback will also be the response of all the nations, so it is not just local ministry that will be costly, but global missions as well.

> Misconception 4
> God can't expect us to sacrifice or take risks to join his mission.

This great cost will not be the general difficulties of life or social/cultural misunderstandings, but specific hatred and suffering due to being associated with the name of Jesus. It is persecution resulting from witness. Mission history and contemporary experience affirm that persecution is the most common reaction to the gospel entering a new people group, especially when some begin to trust and follow Jesus. Satan does not easily let go of those he intends to drag to hell. So, *Jesus taught that missions is by its very nature costly and risky.* Not all who go on mission experience persecution and martyrdom, but we must be ready to sacrifice to complete the task Jesus gave us.

2. *Matthew 24:14—The pursuit of panta ta ethne will involve proclaiming the gospel of the kingdom.*

"This gospel of the kingdom shall be preached in the whole world as a testimony to all the nations, and then the end will come."

Jesus emphasized that his mission would prioritize proclaiming the good news of him to every people group on earth. Jesus came teaching how to enter the kingdom, how to live in the kingdom, and who the King is. After the disciples took up this mission, their message focused on Jesus the King, because the two necessary elements of a kingdom are a king and those who acknowledge him. So, the good news of the kingdom is that the King has come to be your Savior. It is truly news and it is truly good! And it must be told in order to be heard.

Matthew again used *panta ta ethne* to emphasize the global extent of this proclamation, but he then added further emphasis that all the nations also means "to the whole world"—mission to all the nations and to the whole world. The extent of the gospel proclamation was to be everywhere the disciples could conceptualize, and beyond.

Where the church has been long established, we often consider proclamation or preaching to be the job of a few leaders. Proclamation is not just some formal public event, but simply telling people that Jesus is Savior and Lord. In the early church, anyone who stated their belief that Jesus is King was declaring the good news of the kingdom. Many churches have largely lost this characteristic element of our faith. A common misconception expresses itself in "missions" activities that do not prioritize, or even include, sharing the good news. These activities may accomplish genuine good and have missional intent, but *without the clear sharing of the good news of what Jesus has done through his death and resurrection, it is not missions as Jesus defined it.*

These days we often hear the supposed quotation of Francis of Assisi, "Preach the gospel, and, if necessary, use words." I use quotation marks because someone said this, but it was likely not Francis. This statement appeared in a biography written centuries after his death. Francis came to Christ miraculously as a redeemed adult reprobate and he thought everybody ought to hear about Christ's love. In fact, he trained his Franciscans specifically to do evangelistic preaching. If Christ himself, who lived a perfect life, assisted thousands, and performed astonishing miracles, needed to use many words, who today could imagine they do not? Paul raises the same issue in Romans 10:14, "How can they call on Him in whom they have not believed? And how will they believe in Him whom they have not heard? And how will they hear without someone to proclaim."

Jesus stated that this proclamation of the good news to all the nations is the marker to watch in terms of the second coming. The common signs of wars, famines, and natural disasters are only the beginning of birth pangs, reminders that the day is coming soon and one must get ready. God's eternal purpose will not be accomplished until all the nations hear. The indisputable prerequisite to Jesus' return is our obedience in declaring the good news to all the nations.

3. *Matthew 25:31–46—The pursuit of* panta ta ethne *will determine judgement for all.*

"But when the Son of Man comes in His glory, and all the angels with Him, then He will sit on His glorious throne. All the nations will be gathered before Him; and He will separate them from one another, as the shepherd separates the sheep from the goats; and He will put the sheep on his right, and the goats on the left."

As we have seen, this last teaching section of Matthew (chapters 24–25) focuses on Christ's second coming. The recurring theme is that the end is coming and mankind must be ready for his judgement. Jesus also makes it clear that between that moment of teaching and his appearing, the disciples are to be on mission to all the nations, while facing persecution as they declare the good news of Jesus to the whole world.

In 25:31 Jesus picks up on the theme and wording from 24:30–31, where he identified himself as the heavenly Son of Man from Daniel 7:13–14, coming to establish a kingdom for all peoples. Everything Jesus says between 24:31 and 25:31 emphasizes how critical it is for the disciples to be alert, faithful, and ready because all will be held accountable.

As the Son of Man, Jesus will judge *panta ta ethne* and separate them into the sheep, who are blessed of God to receive the kingdom, and the goats, who are cursed into eternal fire. With the use of "all the nations" once again, Jesus ties the expectation about his coming in judgment in Matthew 25:31–46 to his other *panta ta ethne* statements in 24:9, 14; and 28:18–20. *This coming judgment is directly related to the disciples' costly mission to proclaim the good news of the kingdom to all the nations.* The judgment of the nations in which they will be separated into the righteous and the unrighteous hinges on this mission and their response to the messengers. Matthew 25:31–46 is an unprecedented warning to the nations about coming judgment. This passage is not some sort of parable, but a warning about a real event to come. Those of us who know Christ, as well as all humanity from every nation, will stand before him under judgment; the interaction between his messengers and the nations is critical for their verdict. It is both an unusual and striking passage because of its obvious global importance, its personal implications, and the dramatic imagery of the narrative. We will examine a tragic misconception arising from the misinterpretation of this passage in the next chapter.

4. *Matthew 28:18–20—The pursuit of panta ta ethne will result in disciples from all nations.*

"All authority has been given to Me in heaven and earth. Go therefore and make disciples of all the nations, baptizing them in the name of the Father and the Son and the Holy Spirit, teaching them to observe all that I have commanded you; and lo, I am with you always, even to the end of the age."

In the original language, one of the first things that jumps out in this passage is the use of "all." Jesus has *all* authority to send the apostles to make disciples of *all* nations by teaching them to obey *all* that he has commanded, and he will accompany them *all* the days. The statement is an emphatic, comprehensive commission to the apostles ("sent ones").

Jesus had sent the disciples on mission before, but those instructions specifically said to avoid the nations in order to focus on Israel (Matt 10:5–6). Perhaps that is why toward the end of his ministry he described their mission four times as to all the nations. They had to realize Jesus is more than a local prophet or even the Messiah of Israel alone; Jesus is the Lord of all and that demands a global mission to declare it.

"Make disciples" is the primary command, but "going," "baptizing," and "teaching" are associated participles that are integral elements of that imperative. For example, Matthew uses the same participle for "going" in connection with a command to tell in 11:4 and 28:7. Simply put, when Jesus tells them to make disciples, he then defines what that means in the same sentence. These are not separate things; they clarify the main mission. *According to Christ's description of missions, making disciples is the objective and involves going, baptizing, and teaching.*[2] From this point on, the disciples are the "sent ones," which assumes geographic movement.

When Jesus commanded that we go and make disciples, he was talking about speaking truth to assist non-believers to become followers of Jesus. The first step in that process is what we usually call "evangelism." Once again, proclaiming the good news is central to the commission of Jesus. Jesus expects us to tell lost people about the good news about him for the purpose of leading them into a committed relationship with him.

Baptism is one of the first steps in making disciples and should follow quickly after faith. This implies that people understand they are undergoing a conversion from an old way to a new way of life. That is what baptism meant in Jesus' day and it is what it still usually means in other faith systems. Baptism means that becoming a disciple is not just a private or personal act; it has community implications. Jesus' description

---

2. See France, *Matthew*, 420; and Keener, *Matthew*, 400.

of baptism also indicates that the new disciple understands and affirms his belief in God the Father, Jesus the Son, and the Holy Spirit. In other words, it includes affirming basic Christian doctrinal teaching.

When Jesus said to go, proclaim the kingdom, make disciples, baptize believers, and teach them to obey, he never mentioned the word "church." However, the New Testament makes it clear the disciples/apostles understood that these actions would result in new churches. In Acts, everywhere people become disciples, they gathered into churches. So, church is the biblical product of making disciples, baptizing, and teaching obedience. It is also where the members continue to learn how to walk in that obedience, but we should avoid allowing that process within the church to replace the whole mandate to the world.

What we often call "discipleship," the training of youth from Christian families, is covered in the directive to teach them to obey, but it cannot take the place of evangelism. Some believers say they are into discipleship but not evangelism; this is only a partial obedience to Christ's mandate. Discipleship is about obedience and about how we live. Many churches do not focus on teaching people to obey. We teach with hope that people will slowly understand, but we rarely emphasize or ask them about their obedience. We rarely hold disciples accountable by asking about their walking in holiness or about sharing with those who do not believe. That would be too personal or intrusive! This is likely one reason that over the past sixty or seventy years, the American church has lost about half of each generation that has grown up in our churches.

Is this the norm for Christianity? Not everywhere! I was recently in a church of new converts overseas and watched the pastor go around the room of seventy-five people and ask them whom they shared the gospel with that week and then listed all those they committed to share with the next week. Guess what happened the following week? He went around the room and asked them again if they shared with those they said would hear! I could not help but wonder how many members would even come back the following week in a typical church. That kind of obedience to talking about Jesus has resulted in tens of thousands of new churches in that area in less than a decade. What would happen if this was the norm for most churches? Our habit of disobedience hinders our accomplishing the Great Commission. In missions, making disciples is best done through intensive discipling of new believers in order to establish a new pattern of life in obedience to Christ.[3]

His/Our Task in Simple Terms

As we noted earlier, business, education, religion, politics, and the military all talk about a mission; different applications that all point to a clear objective. So, what is the distinctive objective in Christian missions? According to Jesus, Christian missions is our activity to accomplish the purpose of God and is characterized by:

1. The obligation to push out to the whole world and to all ethnolinguistic peoples

2. Taking risks, paying the cost, and accepting the possibility of persecution

3. Proclaiming Jesus as King to all nations

4. Going in awareness that judgment of all mankind hinges on this task

5. Making disciples as the goal of missions, which will be successful in every people

Misconception 5
We can do missions without evangelism, discipleship, and church planting.

If whatever we call "missions" does not act, look, smell, sound, and feel like this definition of the mission Jesus gave us, then it is not Christian missions. Jesus is the only one who can mandate and define this global mission.

Whenever we are planning or assessing our missions involvement, we must use the metric Jesus gave us to measure it by. In today's terms, the core tasks and best metrics of missions are evangelism, discipleship, and church planting (which includes leadership development) among every people group in the world.

3. Dent, "Decisive Discipleship."

Finishing This Task

This is a historic time to focus on our commissioned assignment to the nations. Missions is under attack from progressives who accuse missionaries of cultural aggression, colonialism, and racism. You can certainly find examples of that in history, but it has not been the norm. The translation of the Bible, or portions of it, into over three thousand languages has been instrumental in buttressing the language literacy, ethnic identity, and cultural history of multiple peoples. Missionaries were often in direct opposition to European trading companies and colonial regimes that looked down on the same peoples the missionaries worked to lift up. In fact, Christian concepts about God's creation and love of all peoples helped inspire independence movements in many countries.[4] Missionaries sacrificially laid the foundation of education and medical services in numerous countries. And, in spite of their inadequacies, missionaries passed on the seed of the gospel to local peoples, which has resulted in extraordinary multiplication of local churches in Latin America, Sub-Saharan Africa, China, and beyond. The 10 percent of the world's population today who are evangelical Christians are scattered through more countries, people groups, and languages than at any time in history. God has blessed the mission enterprise even as Christendom has fallen apart.

Misconception 6
Since there are churches all around the world, the missions task is complete.

Yet, the task remains unfinished and a challenge for this generation. In the post–World War II era, many denominations and missions agencies were withdrawing from missions. They could identify churches in many countries and thought the task was done. In 1974, Ralph Winter revolutionized missions thinking by reminding evangelical Christians that Jesus sent us to reach ethnic peoples, not just countries, and that the greatest missions challenge was cross-cultural evangelism of people groups with little witness.[5] Up to that time, most sending groups had

---

4. See Woodbery, "Missionary Roots of Liberal Democracy," regarding the connections between Protestant missions and contemporary healthy democracies.

5. The original title of his paper was "The Highest Priority: Cross-Cultural

viewed the world in terms of countries. They could place one missionary in India and color it on their map; plant one church in Uganda and consider the task accomplished! God's purpose is a lot more specific than approximately two hundred political countries today; God's love and purpose extends to every ethnolinguistic people.

Today there are approximately 11,723 identifiable people groups in the world with a combined population of 7.8 billion people. 7,063 of those people groups, with a population of 4.6 billion, are unreached peoples who have little access to the gospel.[6] In other words, over half the people in the world today are not only lost, but very unlikely to hear about Jesus from a witness from their own people and language. Jesus sending his disciples to cross those ethnic, cultural, and language gaps is the only way to accomplish God's purpose for all the nations.

If you, or your church, have had little interest in global missions, would you reconsider your part and begin to pray about this task that Jesus has given us? How can we say we love Jesus and care nothing about what he commanded us to do? If you are involved in missions that is not aligned with the task defined by Jesus, would you pray about realigning your efforts with the one who gave himself and is coming again to judge the nations?

Evangelism," but it is now published as "The New Macedonia: A Revolutionary New Era in Mission Begins."

6. Statistics are regularly updated at peoplegroups.org and joshuaproject.net.

Questions to Consider

1. The book started with a few examples of real-life mishmash missions. As you read those stories and consider your own experiences, can you identify any potential mishmash experiences in your own life? What might have made them mishmash?

2. What do you think about the idea that everyone is a missionary?

3. Why might it be important to recognize God's heart for all nations throughout the entire narrative of the Bible? Were there any examples of this that you had not thought of before or see now in new depths? Can you think of others that were not mentioned?

4. Four *panta ta ethne* statements are discussed in this chapter that give direction for how Jesus defined missions. What insights do these statements give to some of the ways you have seen missions taught or lived out?

   • Matthew 24:9—The pursuit of *panta ta ethne* will be difficult and costly, even risky, resulting in hatred, persecution, and martyrdom.

   • Matthew 24:14—The pursuit of *panta ta ethne* focuses on proclaiming the good news about Jesus as a testimony to all nation.

   • Matthew 25:31–46—The pursuit of *panta ta ethne* will determine judgement for all.

   • Matthew 28:18–20—The pursuit of *panta ta ethne* will result in disciples from all nations.

5. Have you responded to Jesus' command and invitation to go and make disciples? How are you taking part in that and who is holding you accountable to it? Whom are you holding accountable?

6. What does it mean for you and your local church to reconsider your part in this task? Are your efforts aligned with Jesus?

Chapter 2

God's Intention for the Least of These

ONE OF THE WORST examples of contemporary missions misconception is related to the third *panta ta ethne* passage in Matthew that we briefly explored in the last chapter. In Matthew 25:31–46 Jesus talks about separating the sheep and goats when the Son of Man comes. This judgment will be based on the reception the nations give to "the least of these brothers of mine." Tragically, "the least of these" has become a theme for a very popular approach to missions that misinterprets Matthew 25:31–46 and ignores 24:9, 14; and 28:16–20.[1]

I believe in humanitarian ministry as an important part of the Christian life. Anne and I have personally contributed tens of thousands of dollars to feed the hungry, rescued a young woman from the snare of prostitution, forced a transfer for an abused foreign maid, and paid numerous medical bills. I have marked contour lines on an Asian farmer's sloping farmland, helped a struggling family start raising rabbits for food because they were being starved out for their faith, distributed food to disaster victims, given people medicine, tested wells for water quality, reached out with the gospel to hundreds of young victims of

---

1. Hesselgrave, *Paradigms in Conflict*, 270. Hesselgrave hits the nail on the head with this mission trend. He states, "This brings us to Matthew 25:31–46, one of the most misinterpreted, misunderstood, and misapplied passages in the entire New Testament."

sexual trafficking, paid an aging widow's rent, done triage for hundreds of people coming to medical clinics, and searched alongside tsunami survivors looking for the bodies of their loved ones. These were humanitarian projects and personal opportunities to meet needs we saw around us while serving as missionaries.

Many of my missionary coworkers used their professional skills as educators, doctors, nurses, engineers, agriculturalists, public health workers, community development specialists, and disaster responders while sharing the good news with those they helped. Not surprisingly, some of the best evangelists were doctors and some of the most productive church planters were agriculturalists. You have likely not heard of them because they were not seeking fame and because the news media rarely talks about gospel-centric humanitarian work. In contrast, many who advocate ministry to "the least of these" today lack focus to obey the commission of Jesus to proclaim him to all peoples.

Misconception 7
Evangelicals should only be concerned about spiritual needs.

That is not to say that the teachings of Jesus do not compel us to help the needy. Jesus lived and ministered in a religious environment that assumed practical concern for those in need because it is affirmed in the Law and the Prophets. So, when Jesus talked about giving to the poor, he assumed the righteous will do so and focused on their attitude and manner of humanitarian action. Matthew 6:2 is a good example: "When you give to the poor do not sound a trumpet." Even his statement "You always have the poor with you" in Matthew 26:11 is a quote from Deuteronomy 15:11 that commands the people of God to freely open their hands to those in need. Treating others as we would hope to be treated is an important teaching of the Master. Loving your neighbor as yourself has a high bar in the illustration of the Good Samaritan, who paid much, and risked more, to help a stranger in crisis. So, helping others is legitimate and important Christian ministry; it is just not, by itself, missions. Missionaries should be personally generous and take intentional action to help the needy with wisdom. Compassionate ministry integrated into courageous verbal witness is powerfully effective. However, meeting human needs is not the critical core of the missions task and it is not what Jesus meant in the "least of these" passage in Matthew 25.

Reconsidering How We Read "the Least of These" in Matthew 25:31–46

> But when the Son of Man comes in His glory, and all the angels with Him, then He will sit on His glorious throne. All the nations will be gathered before Him; and He will separate them from one another, as the shepherd separates the sheep from the goats; and He will put the sheep on his right, and the goats on the left. (Matt 25:31)

As we have seen, Matthew 25:31–46 is the final piece of the last teaching section of Matthew (chapters 24–25) focused on his second coming. Verse 31 points back to 24:9, 14, where Jesus introduced the disciples to the mission to all the nations. The verse also picks up on the theme and wording from 24:30–31, where Jesus identified himself as the heavenly Son of Man coming to establish a kingdom for all peoples (see Dan 7:13–14). In Matthew 24, Jesus states that the nations will mourn his appearing and the elect will be gathered. Matthew 25:31–46 dramatically portrays the nations and the elect being judged on that day. They will be judged on the basis of their reception of "the least of these brothers of mine."

There have been numerous interpretations of Matthew 25:31–46, primarily hinging on the meaning of "all the nations" and "the least of these my brothers." "All the nations" has at times been interpreted to refer to non-Jewish Gentiles, all those who are not Christian, or all peoples. "The least of these" has been understood to refer to the disciples, missionaries, Christians, or any needy person. This passage has traditionally been used to advocate for unlimited charity, especially through the church. Recent studies have raised concern about this interpretation based on the two phrases in question.[2]

This passage holds three keys for interpreting what Jesus meant within the context of the Matthew's account.

---

2. Gray, *Least of My Brothers*, 8–9.

First Key to Interpretation

Christ's coming in judgment in Matthew 25:31–46 must be seen in light of his three other *panta ta ethne* statements in 24:9, 14; and 28:18–20. This coming judgment is directly related to the disciples' costly mission to proclaim the good news of the kingdom to all the nations and make disciples. The judgment of the nations in which they will be separated into the righteous and the unrighteous is determined by this mission and the nations' response to the messengers. Matthew 25:31–46 is an unprecedented warning to the nations about coming judgment; the interaction between his messengers and the nations is critical for their verdict. The word for "nations" (*ethne*) is gender neutral, but "them" in verse 32 is masculine, which signifies that the scope of Jesus' judgment extends to every people group, but the actual pronouncements of judgment are to individuals among those nations. This passage is critically important for all peoples and every single person.

Second Key to Interpretation

Whom was Jesus referring to when he said "the least of these my brothers?" In verse 40, Jesus announced that judgment is based on "to the extent that you did it to one of these brothers of mine, even the least of them, you did it to Me." There have been broad and narrow understandings of who are "the least of these my brothers" throughout history, but during the twentieth century it became more popular to identify "the least of these" with poor people in general.[3]

However, Jesus used three phrases that clearly point to the disciples/ apostles as the objects of the nations' actions.[4]

- In Matthew, Jesus only used "my brothers" in reference to his disciples/apostles who do his will and take up his mission (see 12:49–50 and 28:10). Jesus often taught about proper relationships and morality by referring to "his brother" or "your brother" (5:22, 23), but he never used "my brothers" in that generic way. Those who refer

---

3. Gray, *Least of My Brothers*, 350.

4. These three phrases together contradict Cranfield's assertion that "There is absolutely nothing here to indicate that it was because they were Christians that these brothers were hungry, thirsty, strangers, naked, sick and in prison." Cranfield, "Who Are Christ's Brothers?," 135. Cranfield also misses the difference between "brothers" in general and the restricted use of "my brothers" (p. 128).

to "the least of these" without including "my brothers" may define the term in any way they want, but completely miss what Jesus intended. Partial quotes can easily become misconceptions.

- When Jesus called them "these" brothers, it would have been obvious to those present that he was referring to the disciples who were standing or sitting there beside him. It was not "those" brothers somewhere else in time and space; it was "these" brothers right there with Jesus at that moment.

- "The least of these" echoes Jesus' use of "little ones" in 18:6, 10, and 14 to describe his followers. Believers are normal, humble people who are to be valued because they are precious to God. The "least of " is also reminiscent of 10:42, where Jesus promised a blessing to those who gave the sent ones, even the "little ones," a cup of water.[5] Note the parallels in 10:40 and 18:5, where Jesus states that those who receive these humble representatives, receive him.

In this context, the correct reading of "the least of these, my brothers" is that Jesus is referring to his disciples sent on mission to proclaim the good news to the nations, whose judgment is based on how they respond to the messengers.[6] The messengers are sent out, but the nations have to take them in to hear their good news.[7]

Third Key of Interpretation

The passage includes an unusual and striking structural formula, with six actions repeated in exact order four times in the conversation between

---

5. Green, *Gospel According to Matthew*, 206: "Gentiles who have not encountered Christ himself will be judged on the basis of their behavior towards him in the persons of his disciples. That 'least' means these, and not suffering humanity in general . . . is borne out by the 'little ones' of 18:6, 10, 14 . . . and above all by 10:42 of which the whole scene is really an extended dramatization."

6. Hagner, *Matthew 14–28*, 746. "All the nations of the world—that is, every individual in those nations—are to be judged on the basis of their treatment of disciples of Jesus . . . To treat the disciple, the bringer and representative of the gospel, with deeds of kindness is in effect to have so treated Jesus."

7. Note echoes of this passage in Hebrews 10:32–34, where the believers sided with the sent ones by joining in their persecution and helping them in prison. See also 3 John 5–8, where the church is encouraged to treat the sent brothers and strangers in a manner worthy of God.

the Judge and the judged.[8] The specific order is, "For I was hungry and you gave me something to eat; I was thirsty and you gave me something to drink; I was a stranger and you invited me in; naked, and you clothed me; I was sick, and you visited me, I was in prison, and you came to Me." All mankind will be judged on whether they helped the brothers of Jesus who had those needs.

This structural formula is precisely repeated because it lines up with specific instructions that Jesus had given his disciples when he first sent them out on mission. We have already noted the connection between Matthew 25 and Matthew 10, but let's look at chapter 10 more carefully. In Matthew 10 Jesus instructed the sent ones on how they are to go out on mission, and in Matthew 25 he warned the nations that their judgment will be based on how they receive such messengers. How the disciples are to go out and how the nations are to receive them are in direct, parallel alignment (see table below).

Matthew 10 and Matthew 25 Comparison	
Matthew 10:1–42	Matthew 25:31–46
Directions to the sent ones about how to go on mission	Warning to the nations about their reception of the messengers
10:7—"preach, saying, 'The kingdom of heaven is at hand.'" 1. 10:9–10—the worker is worthy of his meals 2. 10:42—whoever gives a cup of water will not lose his reward 3. 10:11—inquire who is worthy and stay at his house until you leave 4. 10:10—do not acquire a bag, or two coats, or sandals 5. 10:17–18—they will scourge you in their synagogues 6. 10:17–18—they will hand you over to courts, you will be brought before governors and kings	24:14—"this gospel of the kingdom shall be proclaimed in the whole world as a testimony to all the nations." 1. 25:35—"For I was hungry and you gave me something to eat" 2. 25:35—"I was thirsty, and you gave me something to drink" 3. 25:35—"I was a stranger, and you invited me in" 4. 25:36—"naked, and you clothed me" 5. 25:36—"sick, and you visited me" 6. vs. 36—"I was in prison, and you came to me"
10:14–15—the response of the audience determines their judgement	25:32—"All the nations will be gathered before Him, and He will separate them . . ."

8. Hagner, *Matthew 14–28*, 750.

10:40—"He who receives you, receives Me, and he who receives Me received Him who sent Me."	25:40—"Truly I say to you, to the extent that you did it to one of these brothers of Mine, even the least of them, you did it to Me."

So, Matthew 25:31–46 should be interpreted within the context of the rest of the Gospel. The very specific parallels with chapter 10 mean Matthew understood Jesus to have tied the two teaching sessions together. In Matthew 10 Jesus gave instructions to the disciples about how to go out on mission; in Matthew 25 he looked to the future in reference to how the nations received those he sent. In Matthew 25 we also see reference to the fulfillment of his warning to the disciples that their mission will result in their suffering, as he had earlier explained the first time he mentioned pursuing all the nations in 24:9. According to Matthew 25, they will need help when sick from scourging and in great need in prison.

Matthew 25:31–46 must also be interpreted in light of the Great Commission in 28:16–20. In his book on this passage, Sherman Gray states,

> Looking at the larger context, it would seem that 25:31–46, in a proleptic (anticipatory) fashion, is integrally related to the Great Commission that occurs a few chapters later (28:16–20) where the disciples are sent to the very same people (*panta ta ethne*) that are to be gathered before Christ at the end of time. The two scenes have to be taken together; the judgment that takes place in 25:31–46 cannot be viewed apart from the events described in 28:16–20.[9]

Those taking or not taking the six decisive actions were not even aware that the recipients were actually representing Jesus at the time. *Judgment is not based on mankind's response to the Son of Man appearing in the clouds, but on their response to unremarkable, ordinary envoys sent to bring them his message on the ground.* Rejecting the messengers has tragic eternal consequences. Jesus was warning the nations about their reception of the messengers and their message, while also encouraging the messengers about the eternal implications of their proclamation for all those who have not yet heard. It is ironic, and consistent with how Satan twists truth, that these words are now used to advocate service without proclamation. Many people miss the point that Jesus does not send us to assist the less fortunate from a position of strength and wealth;

---

9. Gray, *Least of My Brothers*, 8.

Jesus calls his messengers to become the least of his brothers proclaiming the good news to all nations. That is much costlier and eternally effective.

A variety of popular books, worship songs, large events, missions organization websites, blogs, and popular speakers talk about taking loving action on behalf of "the least of these."[10] This approach affirms painting buildings, holding babies, distributing socks in a tropical village, handing out shiny new toys unavailable in that place, and giving people food with little explanation. Sadly, teams often ignore the most loving action of giving people the chance to believe in the atonement of Christ and gain peace with God and eternal life. They say that by giving a needy person a sandwich you bring them and yourself into God's family. Tragically, this interpretation results in doctrinal and missional confusion. The misinterpretation of this one passage ignores whole sections of Scripture that clarify how to be right with God and how to do missions with Jesus.

Unbelieving biblical critics like to point to this misinterpreted passage as one of the few authentic pieces of the Gospels—"See, Jesus just wants us to be nice." Everybody can get onboard with missions that avoids the risk of proclaiming the life-giving and controversial gospel.

Although helping needy people is admirable and should characterize Jesus' followers, it does not save them or us! Good deeds do not wipe away, negate, or counterbalance the guilt and shame of our sin. All of us, wealthy or poor, are sinners separated from God and are helpless without the atoning sacrifice of Jesus. Jesus said that we must "believe" (John 3:16), Paul said it is "through faith" (Eph 2:8), and Peter said we "come to repentance" (2 Pet 3:9) in order to enter into salvation.

Misconception 8
When we help the least of these we serve Jesus and them. This is the most acceptable form of mission in our modern world.

---

10. DeYoung and Gilbert, *What Is the Mission of the Church?*, 162. "Matthew 25 has become a favorite passage for many progressives and younger evangelicals . . . And few biblical phrases have gotten as much traction as 'the least of these.' Whole movements have emerged whose central tenet is to care for 'the least of these' a la Matthew 25 . . . But in popular usage of the phrase, there's almost no careful examination of what Jesus actually means by 'the least of these.'"

In addition to this theological error, helping the needy without clear and courageous gospel witness rarely results in disciples. At various times in history, missionaries have backed away from simply declaring the good news of Jesus in order to do just humanitarian work. The result has almost always been more comfortable lost people without hope and without God in the world. In contemporary America, Christians who openly share the gospel are considered out of fashion, narrow-minded, judgmental, prejudiced, and evil. No wonder so many Christians today are enamored with the politically correct humanitarian project approach that has little risk and no gospel. Many "believers" in postmodern America are comfortable in their personal faith in Christ, but lack conviction or courage in sharing the only hope with others. Not surprisingly, this is not the first time such a trend has worked against missions as defined by Jesus.

A Cycle of Misinterpretation and Misconception

Social Gospel Mission (1920s–30s)

Protestant Christianity achieved some remarkable social advances in the nineteenth century. The abolition of slavery, widespread education, and multiple social services helped throngs of people seeking better lives, health, and fulfillment in an increasingly impersonal, crowded, and degraded environment. The nineteenth century also witnessed an amazing missionary spread of the gospel to new places and peoples, sometimes because of, and quite often in spite of, European exploitation and colonization of much of the world.

During the 1920s and 30s, a growing cultural shift within mainline Christianity resulted in missions that was more focused on good deeds than good news. Two factors for this shift deserve mention here. One factor was an increasingly naturalistic worldview that denied miracles and the uniqueness of Jesus the Savior. The second was the cultural embarrassment that World War I, one of the most deadly wars in history, was waged between "Christian" nations. Western missions, which was often tied to Western pride, largely lost its gospel voice and impetus, especially in state and liberal churches.

A recognizable misinterpretation of Matthew 25 was a popular rallying cry for this new form of Christian missions. Walter Rauschenbush, considered the father of the Social Gospel, commented on Matthew 25:31–46:

In his wonderful picture of the Messianic judgment there is not a word about sacrifices, prayers, fasting, food laws, or purifications. The Messiah's mete wand (measuring rod) is social sympathy. Some have felt hunger and sickness and loneliness of their fellows; some have not. That alone decides on their fitness for the kingdom of brotherhood. The mercy which Jesus demands here is not the dole of charity, but the sense of solidarity which makes all human life part of our life. He asserts that solidarity for himself is holding that whatever is done to the weakest member of humanity is done to himself.[11]

Liberation Mission (1960s–70s)

In the 1960s and 70s a new revolutionary movement spread through newly independent countries, especially in Latin America. Liberation theology was purely Marxist ideology with a few haphazard references to Christ thrown in, i.e., the primary problem that men face is economic inequality and Jesus told us to redistribute wealth. As social gospel missions was deeply influenced by naturalism, liberation theology was essentially materialistic. Advocates called for activists to fight against economic and political injustice, including taking up arms, while completely ignoring the spiritual needs of the world. The misinterpretation of Matthew 25 was a perfect proof text for Marxism pretending to be Christian.

This approach replaced Christian missions with radical social action that denied Christ's definition of missions. In an open letter to the people of the Third World, radicalized bishops used the misinterpretation of Matthew 25 to rationalize their stance:

> Of course Jesus warned us that the poor will always be with us (see John 12:8); but that is because there will always be rich people who expropriate to themselves the goods of this world and because there will always be certain inequalities resulting from differing degrees of capability and other unavoidable factors. But Jesus also teaches us that the second commandment is equal to the first, since we cannot love God without loving our fellow humans. We shall all be judged by the same standard: 'I was hungry and you gave me food . . . in so far as you did it to one of the least of these brothers of mine, you did it to me.' (Matt 25:35–40)

11. Rauschenbusch, *Christianizing the Social Order*, 61–62.

> . . . It is our duty to share our food and all our goods. If some try
> to monopolize for themselves what others need, then it is the
> duty of public authority to carry out distribution that was not
> made willingly.[12]

This misuse of Matthew 25 by liberation advocates helped provide a
Christian façade for this Marxist movement:

> To have faith in Christ is to see the history in which we are living
> as the progressive revelation of the human face of God. "Who
> sees me sees the Father." This holds to a certain extent for every
> human being according to the important text of Matthew 25,
> which reminds us that an action on behalf of a human being is
> an action on behalf of God. If you gave food and drink, you gave
> it to me; if you denied it, you denied it to me.[13]

Postmodern "to the Least of These" Mission (2000s–20s)

Today few people seem to realize that this misuse of Matthew 25 is undermining the focus of many on accomplishing the mission of Jesus. It
appears that every forty years or so, Christians have been duped into
disobedience to the commission of Christ while thinking they are creating a new approach to missions that is more socially sensitive, more
contemporary, more politically correct, and more generationally aware.
This is missions that:

- ignores the directive of the Sender,

- talks kingdom but fails to proclaim the King,

- lovingly provides temporary assistance but leaves people doomed
  for destruction,

- results in slightly more comfortable lost people while Jesus values
  poor believers,

- and trades the priority of God's purpose for something less.

A significant portion of each Christian generation for the last one
hundred years has fallen into the same scheme of the enemy to divert the
church from its mission to take the risk to declare Jesus as King in order

---

12. Third World Bishops, "Letter to the Peoples of the Third World."
13. Gutierrez, "Toward a Theology of Liberation (1968)," 74.

to make disciples in preparation for the judgment of the nations. Our ignorance of his schemes leaves the nations still waiting on some humble envoy to bring them the good news.

Redeeming a World Filled with Outrageous Injustice!

Lin and Lu,[14] now twenty-three and twenty-two, arrived home after ful-filling a contract signed by their parents for them to work in the city for ten years. Their parents had received two hundred dollars and a color television at the signing. The agent had kept his word and helped them get back home when the contract was complete. Nobody asked about their life in the much hotter, crowded megacity, but their family and a few friends were thrilled to open the small gifts the two young women had brought them. Ma showed them the altar where she had made offerings every morning for their blessing.

When they left the village, it seemed such a good idea to the family. Agriculture was mostly subsistence level and the girls had already done the five years of local schooling. Although they knew a lot about running a household, it had been too soon to think about marriage and a family. Many of the teenaged boys and young men left the village to find work and keep the village alive. If the girls had stayed home, they would have just been extra mouths to feed.

In the coming weeks, some of the young men who had found sea-sonal work elsewhere came home for a few months with hard-earned cash. Perhaps then young men, who had not seen them since they were girls, would be interested in settling down together. At least that was the dream they had shared since childhood. They adjusted to the cooler cli-mate and slower pace of village life as they waited with anticipation for the men to return to the village.

Lin and Lu never mentioned it, but each had around five hundred dollars of savings to pay for a nice wedding and start a new household. In their village, it was enough for a face-saving, family-honoring celebra-tion. Neither talked about another souvenir they brought from the city. They had known for several years they were both HIV positive, although they little understood what it meant. For ten years their food, lodging, salary, and protection—in fact, their whole lives—had been experienced

---

14. I do not know these two young women. This story is adapted from a true ac-count published in a national newspaper in Asia.

inside the locked wing of a house. They had serviced the sexual desires of an average of seven men a day, six and a half days a week, fifty-one weeks a year, for ten years. Each girl was sold by her parents to 22,950 men for half a color television and a hundred dollars. Yes, they looked to the future with some anxiety, but surely the future had to be better than the past?!

It is so outrageous that it is hard to believe such a story could be true. However, it is repeated for thousands of girls in places like Bangkok, Calcutta, and Ontario, California. If that does not enrage you, then something is wrong with your humanity and your spirituality. The Spirit of God hates the work of the destroyer and murderer Satan. Man's rebellion against God, in direct opposition to the kingdom of God, often includes spiritual idolatry, social injustice, and sexual immorality.[15]

Progressive critics of Christianity and missions today do not want you to know about the humanitarian impact of our faith. While slavery was still widespread around the world, it was Christians in places like London and Boston who fought the battle to legally abolish slavery for the first time. During that same era, missionaries led the fight to end the common practice of *sati*, the burning of young widows on the funeral pyres of their Hindu husbands, as well as the tortuous, cruelly disabling binding of the feet of young Chinese girls.

Misconception 9
Advocating politically for social justice is the best way to address evil around the world.

The small early church was in no position to publicly protest common injustices in the Roman Empire. However, their mission included bringing trafficked individuals into a redeemed relationship with God and into a loving community. The testimony of that is found in 1 Corinthians 6:9–11 and Romans 16:14–15, where the power of Christ's redeeming work has begun transforming society one person, and small group, at a time. In spite of the law, human trafficking thrives because of lost parents, "businessmen," judges, policemen, and clientele.

15. This pattern of an "unholy trio" goes back to the fall of man in Genesis 3. It is denounced in both the Law and the Prophets. See, for example, Ezekiel 22, Amos 2, and Habakkuk 2.

You should speak out and act against injustice in the name of Christ. However, do not forget the injustice addressed by Christ's words in Matthew 25:31-46. Jesus came to destroy the work of Satan through his sacrificial death and resurrection. He died for all! He then gave his disciples the clear mission to take that news to all the nations and make disciples. *The greatest outrage in the world today is that after two thousand years the church has so neglected our mission that half the world will live their lives with no knowledge of this great redemption.* Where is our outrage about that?! It is good to treat the symptoms that we call injustice, but why do we neglect to address the cause? The consequences are tragic and eternal.

In the case of Lin and Lu, it may be too late to save them from ten years of living hell, but it may not be too late to go as simple messengers to rescue them from death to life. Discipling Lin and Lu would not only transform their family and village; it could also help save their people from extinction.

So, help the needy and neglected, but do not be satisfied with giving a little from your position of privilege and abundance. In fact, many humanitarian projects done by wealthier foreign Christians actually don't work and often cause harm.[16] *Jesus calls us to give ourselves as humble and bold brothers and sisters who help the King redeem his people among every people group on earth.* This is a much costlier way, but it is the only way to accomplish the purpose Jesus gave his followers.

Questions to Consider

1. What has been your understanding of the relationship between humanitarian aid and missions? How has this chapter either supported that or brought in new considerations?

2. Read Matthew 24–28, taking the following passages into specific consideration: 24:9, 14; 25:31–46; 28:16–20. How does considering these passages in a larger context and in relation to each other affect the way you understand these passages?

---

16. If you are not aware of this problem, you should read Lupton, *Toxic Charity.* "Contrary to popular belief, most mission trips and service projects do: weaken those being served, foster dishonest relationships, erode recipients' work ethic, deepen dependency" (p. 16).

3. Respond to the idea that instead of followers of Jesus assisting the less fortunate from a position of strength, we are actually called to become the least of his brothers.

4. As you consider your own discipleship or teaching that has impacted your faith, do you need to recognize how a history of cyclical misunderstandings and teachings have impacted your own perspective on what missions means? Is there anything that needs to be corrected either in you or by you as you disciple others?

5. Is there anything you and/or your local church need to do in order to realign your approach to humanitarian aid with an appropriate understanding of missions? Has your aid to those in need been strategic for gospel proclamation, or is that something that needs to be brought back into the central focus?

Chapter 3

God's Passion for the Nations

My flight landed at the airport in an Islamic republic around 9:00 p.m. I had come to walk and pray alongside my colleagues who felt led to stay and minister during a crisis of significant turmoil and danger. For my colleagues it was even more personal than that; friends had been gunned down in their city, where every third vehicle was filled with armed men and anger seethed barely beneath the surface.

The last stop inside the terminal was a row of money changers, so I headed there once I cleared immigration and my luggage cleared customs. It was after 10:00 p.m., so there was only one money changer still open, but I needed local currency for any miscellaneous expenses I might have the next morning. A sign informed me that the exchange rate was ninety cents on the dollar, well below official published rates. With resignation I handed the money changer a hundred-US dollar bill and counted the local currency he exchanged for it. I calculated twice and it appeared to be eighty-one-dollars' worth of local currency!? I counted again and then complained that he had miscounted. He casually told me the listed rate did not include the 10 percent service charge for changing money. An exchange rate of ninety cents on the dollar amounted to ninety dollars and a 10 percent service charge on that was now eighty-one dollars. He was the only changer open and deep down I realized this was a racket I could not escape. Frustrated, I asked for my money back and he gladly handed me seventy-three US dollars. A 10 percent service charge again to change it back! Wow, he had made twenty-seven dollars in under two minutes. Eventually, I convinced him to give back the original eighty-one dollars' worth of local currency and I made a mental note to be more prepared when arriving late at night. Even if you know what is coming, it is sometimes hard to avoid a racket when it is a monopoly, especially if it is a trap for foreigners. In spite of the public relations signs in the airport, and in contrast to the many times I felt completely welcome in the countries I have visited, my entry this time did not make me feel so "Welcome to Nooradinabad!"

Jesus Raised a Ruckus in the Temple

> And He entered the temple and began to drive out those who were buying and selling in the temple, and overturned the tables of the money changers and the seats of those who were selling doves; and He would not permit anyone to carry merchandise through the temple. And He began to teach and say to them, 'Is it not written, My house shall be called a house of prayer for all the nations?' 'But you have made it a robbers den.' The chief priests and the scribes heard this, and began seeking how to destroy Him . . . (Mark 11:15–18)

The Gospel accounts of Jesus raising a ruckus in the temple point to an event that is certainly a curiosity. When I think of this event, two facts grab my attention even before I look deeper into the story.

- An account of this event appears in all four Gospels. In the Synoptic Gospels the story is during Passion Week, but in John it appears early in his ministry. I believe it is the same story in John but it is placed thematically instead of sequentially.[1] So, the four Gospel writers, who each wrote from slightly different perspectives on Jesus, all decided their story needed this story. They have my attention because there is something significant revealed about Jesus here.

- The story is also unusual because what Jesus did was completely surprising, to the people who experienced it and to us. Jesus acted dramatically in a way that seems at first to be out of character. He seems angry and somewhat violent. This does not fit the words of

1. Borchert, *John 1–11*, 160–61. "But the familiar argument of two cleansings is a historiographic monstrosity that has no basis in the texts of the Gospels. *There is only one cleansing of the temple in each Gospel*."

Wesley's old hymn, "Gentle Jesus, meek and mild, look upon a little child." This Jesus is indignant and definitely not mild-mannered or meek-spirited. What in the world is going on and why is it so important that we understand this story to know who Jesus is?

What Did Jesus Actually Do?

The accounts are all similar, but a review of all four provides a list of actions that probably go beyond our initial imagining of this event. Having looked around the temple the day before, Jesus entered and started a riot. Well, sort of. Jesus raised quite a ruckus: he seems to be the only one who took dramatic action and it appears everybody else was just in shock. So, what did he actually do?

1. Jesus pushed over the tables of the money changers, making a big crash and spilling perhaps thousands of coins across the floor. Imagine that happening in your local bank or at church. Talk about getting everybody's attention! (Matt 21, Mark 11, John 2)

2. He made sure all the coins were spilled on the floor by pouring them out of whatever leather bags or clay pots they were in. Don't tell me the crowds in the courtyard were not interested in picking up a few (John 2).

3. He turned over the seats or benches of those selling doves for sacrifice. Can you see sellers sprawled on the floor looking to see where the doves are? (Matt 21, Mark 11)

4. He prevented Levites, Jews, and foreigners from carrying merchandise through the temple. Perhaps this included fresh fertilizer for a garden, bundles of hay, wood and oil for sacrifice, cages of doves, and bags of coins. If it were today, we might expect kosher pizza delivery for those manning the tables, plus T-shirts and mugs from our coffee shop. Jesus forcibly shut down a very busy temple bazaar, so imagine what it took to do that! (Mark 11)

5. He drove out of the temple all who were buying and selling there. Surprisingly, the Greek verb is *ekballo*, the word usually used for forcing out a demon. It does not always mean violence, but it does mean pushing something out that otherwise will not go. There were many people in the temple, but Jesus picked on those most involved

in the economic activities, who were some of the powerful people there. (Matt 21, Mark 11, Luke 19, John 2)

6. He made a scourge of cords and also drove out a considerable number of sheep and oxen. A cattle drive? That means he used the whip to make enough sound and probably to hit a few animals to startle them and get the herd moving. Try to imagine what the animal keepers were doing! I can almost hear, "Move 'em on, head 'em up, head 'em up, move 'em on, move 'em on, head 'em up, rawhide!" (John 2)

The Temple

Of course, this craziness took place in the temple in Jerusalem. The temple of Yahweh was the center of the faith of Israel, the site of the sacrificial system that was dedicated one thousand years before and would continue on that spot for another generation. It was filled with music and praise, reading and teaching of the Scriptures, offerings, and sacrifices of live animals. Levites serving as priests, worship leaders, gate keepers, and scribes were everywhere. It was a busy place. Thousands of Jews, from Judea and the diaspora, flocked to it to worship God and participate in festival celebrations. This was also the place where God was drawing the nations to come learn about him.

It was also Herod's temple. Yes, it was *that* Herod the magi were warned to avoid! Herod had rebuilt it as extravagantly as he could in an attempt to buy favor with the Jews, who largely hated him. Temples were often the most impressive structures in ancient cities, and this one was the centerpiece of the Holy City and the goal of all those Passover pilgrims. There really was no other reason to visit Jerusalem.

Ancient temples were also massive commercial enterprises and served many of the purposes of a modern bank. The Jerusalem temple had assigned guards and accountants handling multiple times more money than any other commercial enterprise in the city.[2] This probably included receiving the temple tax, changing foreign coins, buying and selling approved animals for sacrifice, receiving offerings, keeping accounts of tithes, charging fees for priestly services, accepting deposits, making investments, and giving and taking payment for loans. There

2. See 1 Chr 26:1–28 and Neh 12:25 for biblical references to these officials.

would have been an unusually high number of coins at the tables at this time because of coming Passover and the due date for the annual temple tax.[3] Foreign coins with images of pagan kings were unacceptable and had to be exchanged for temple coins without images; the temple held the monopoly on this exchange. There was no central bank in the city besides this one and, most certainly, the wealthy Jewish class, including the Sadducees, controlled and benefited from this financial system.[4]

We must consider Jesus' actions within this context to begin to understand the implications of what he did. He interrupted the ritual and spiritual activities of the people of God while simultaneously shutting down the biggest commercial concern in the capital city. There is no real equivalent today, but Jesus did something more disruptive than stopping worship in a megachurch while simultaneously forcibly shutting down the largest mall in the city. In Mark 11, this story is actually the third in a series of prophetic dramatic acts taken by Jesus that pointed to his authority—the arrival of the king, the death of the fig tree, and raising a ruckus in the temple. There is certainly something of symbolic significance here.

Much of this temple activity was centered in what was known as the Court of the Gentiles. Everybody walked through this outermost court of the temple complex. Unless they were involved in selling approved sacrificial animals or exchanging money, the people of Israel only walked through this court on their way to their own assigned places for worship. For all others—the nations, Gentiles, non-Jews—this was as close as they could get to the place where God's presence dwelled, because one step across the temple threshold was a death sentence; a sign made this threat clear to all.

It is not surprising that Mark (11:18) tells us that in response to raising a ruckus the religious leaders "began seeking how to destroy Him; for they were afraid of Him." Surely Jesus was aware that his actions would earn the wrath of the leaders of his people. Even in our own country, such action today would be viewed as economic terrorism, a religious hate crime, and an abuse of animal rights, not to mention the rage of those accountants who had to recount the coins. This was not an attempt to take over the temple or reform its worship. It was rather a dramatic demonstration of disgust at what the religious life of the temple

3. Brooks, *Mark*, 185.

4. A good recent source on the economic activity of the temple is Stevens, *Temples, Tithes, and Taxes.*

had become. Rather than a cleansing, it was dramatized judgment. That judgment was coming soon and not one stone would be left. Jesus could not have done anything more provocative than this in-your-face assault on the commercial-religious complex of their nation. It is no wonder that the religious leaders and the powerful ruling class viewed it as Jesus picking a fight. Even then, as Mark 11:18 states, they had to wait for the right moment because of concern about his popularity among the crowds.

A Good Reason

So, what was so important to Jesus that he felt compelled the day after entering Jerusalem with public acclaim to then raise a ruckus, pick a fight, drive a disturbance, commence a commotion, and create a kerfuffle?

The answer to that question is important enough that Jesus himself gave the explanation. Immediately after raising the ruckus Jesus began to teach, "My house shall be called a house of prayer for all the nations." Jesus, standing where the tables were overturned and the coins were spilled out, was quoting a passage in Isaiah that prophesied God would reward foreigners for their desire to know him:

> Also the foreigners who join themselves to the Lord, to minister to Him, and to love the name of the Lord, to be His servants, everyone who keeps from profaning the Sabbath and holds fast my covenant; Even those I will bring to My holy mountain and make them joyful in My house of prayer. Their burnt offerings and their sacrifices will be acceptable on My altar; For My house will be called a house of prayer for all the peoples. (Isa 56:6–7)

Isaiah knew that Solomon had prayed for that kind of blessing to the nations during the dedication of the first temple. From its founding, the temple was intended by God to be a place of revelation and blessing to all nations, so Isaiah was repeating what was already known from the beginning about God's purpose for the temple. Solomon himself prayed at the dedication:

> Also the foreigner who is not of Your people Israel, when he comes from a far country for Your name's sake. . . when he comes and prays toward this house, hear in heaven Your dwelling place, and do according to all for which the foreigner calls to You, in order that all the peoples of the earth may know Your name, to fear You, as do your people Israel . . . (1 Kgs 8:41–43)

In fact, God drawing the nations to Jerusalem in order to worship him is a major recurring theme for Isaiah:

> Now it will come about that in the last days the mountain of the house of the Lord will be established as the chief of the mountains. . . and all the nations will stream to it. And many peoples will come and say, 'Come, let us go up to the mountain of the Lord, to the house of the God of Jacob; that he may teach us concerning His ways and that we may walk in His paths. (Isa 2:2–3)

In the Second Servant Song, Isaiah foresaw a servant raised up to bless all the nations:

> He says, 'It is too small a thing that You should be My Servant to raise up the tribes of Jacob and to restore the preserved ones of Israel; I will also make You a light to the nations so that My salvation may reach to the end of the earth. (Isa 49:6–7)

It is not surprising that Isaiah refers to God as the God of Jacob, because the covenant that God had made with Abraham (Gen 12:3), Isaac (Gen 26:4), and Jacob (Gen 28:14) had repeatedly affirmed that the Hebrew people were chosen to bless all the peoples of the earth:

> "And in you all the families of the earth will be blessed." (Abraham)

> "By your descendants all the nations of the earth shall be blessed." (Isaac)

> "In you and in your descendants shall all the families of the earth be blessed." (Jacob)

So, from the beginning God has chosen a peculiar people for a particular purpose to bless all the other nations. They had to learn to be his people to show the other nations how to obey, honor, and worship Yahweh. God was actively drawing men and women from many nations to come learn about and worship him in this temple. God's intention was to give them joy in knowing and worshipping him, especially in the specific location of the Court of the Gentiles. Perhaps Zechariah best expressed God's plan to reach the nations by drawing them to Jerusalem to worship alongside his chosen people:

> Thus says the Lord of hosts, 'It will yet be that peoples will come, even the inhabitants of many cities. The inhabitants of one will go to another, saying, 'Let us go at once to entreat the favor of

> the Lord, and to seek the Lord of hosts, I will also go.' So many peoples and mighty nations will come to seek the Lord of hosts in Jerusalem and to entreat the favor of the Lord. Thus says the Lord of hosts, 'In those days ten men from all the nations will grasp the garment of a Jew, saying, "Let us go with you, for we have heard that God is with you." (Zech 8:20–23)

What an amazing expression of God's passion to draw the nations to himself and to use his chosen people to assist the nations in finding this God! And the nations were coming, traveling at great expense, facing dangers and discomfort for weeks or months at a time. They had heard of this one great and true God who could not be represented by a mere idol. Back home, many were disillusioned by the pantheon of feuding selfish gods no one could be proud to follow. What they knew of this God of Israel was that he was unlike any other—holy and powerful and gracious. So, they came to learn from the chosen people and worship in that unusual temple.

Then they stepped into the Court of the Gentiles. The locus of God's mission purpose had lost the focus of God's mission passion. The one place God was drawing the nations to seek him was actively functioning with no sense of God's love for all the nations. God's people were too busy going about business as usual, i.e., making money and NOISE!! Yes, there was more than one kind of racket in the Court of the Gentiles, and it was more offensive than my experience arriving in Nooradinabad. The place God set aside to listen to their prayers and to bless them had become a noisy market where they were gouged when they exchanged coins and bought an approved sacrifice. "Welcome to the temple of God Almighty!" God's people, chosen for a purpose, were not only neglecting his mission, but they were also, perhaps obliviously, hindering it. How different the visitors' experience would have been if the Jews' hearts had been in tune with God's passion for these Gentile seekers! Undoubtedly, their religious activities and traditions had gradually and completely covered their eyes and hardened their hearts so that they now were at cross-purposes with God.

Jesus further explained his shocking actions by quoting Jeremiah 7:11, "You have made it into a robber's den . . ."

> Do not trust in deceptive words, saying 'This is the temple of the Lord, the temple of the Lord, the temple of the Lord'. . . Will you steal, murder, and commit adultery and swear falsely, and offer sacrifices to Baal and walk after other gods that you have not known, then come and stand before Me in this which is

called by My name, and say, 'We are delivered!'—that you may do all these abominations. Has this house, which is called by My name, become a den of robbers in your sight? Behold, I, even I, have seen it,' declares the Lord. (Jer 7:4, 10–11)

Jeremiah's words prophesied that the temple would be destroyed because the Jews worshipped God with little concern about obeying God. Jesus quoted Jeremiah

"because it recalls the prophet's denunciation of the false confidence of the people of Judah who think that they can commit the most serious sins since the temple guarantees their safety. . . Jeremiah does not anticipate that the people will repent. . . is not an offer of repentance and restoration but a prophecy of judgment and destruction."[5]

The Jews were busy carrying out part of the letter of the law with no regard to the overall purpose of God. Their activity looked religious, but their hearts were unrighteous and unrepentant. They had mastered the art of using religion for their own purposes. The ruckus Jesus raised with his dramatic actions was an open affront to the religious leaders, but his words of explanation must have been even more insulting. Now the religious elite knew they had to take Jesus out.

"Den of robbers" may not directly refer to the gouging of foreigners by the money changers or overcharging foreigners for spotless lambs by the merchants, but his other actions certainly raise that possibility. Stories from that time mention extortionary prices for buying sacrificial animals in the temple. This is the likely point of Jesus' explanation for raising the ruckus in John 2: "Stop making my Father's house a place of business." The sheep in the temple had previously raised a racket when they had been fleeced. When foreigners entered the temple, it was their turn to be fleeced in the temple racket. Jesus raised a ruckus to renounce the racket!

God created the world and mankind was the most unique part of it because we were created in his image. Man sinned and was cast out of the garden, but God began to work immediately to redeem them. One key act was to choose a people to be his people in order that through them all the nations would be blessed. He gave them a law to follow and then, at their demand, formed a kingdom that was often in rebellion against him. He sent multiple prophets to turn their hearts back to him with the hope that the nations would come worship him also. God then sent his

5. Schnabel, *Mark*, 273.

Son to redeem them, but God incarnate looked around his temple and was disgusted with his chosen ones. Jesus raised a ruckus to renounce the racket that made a mockery of his purpose for the whole world.

> Misconception 10
> It is normal to say I love God and care nothing about what he is passionate about.

So, rather than thinking Jesus raised a ruckus because he momentarily lost his cool, we should recognize that Jesus revealed an integral aspect of God's character in these intentional actions in the specific court purposed for the nations to approach the presence of Yahweh. Rather than acting out of character, Jesus was expressing God's passion for sharing his grace with the nations and his passionate disgust that his people could care less. God is jealous that all nations should come to him and angry with his rebellious, selfish people who get in the way. Chosen by God to be world changers, they settled for being self-focused money changers. On the outside, money changers stay busy, fill the space, maintain a sense of order and organization, preserve the status quo, provide a service, look busy, and keep the religious leaders happy. They also block, hinder, and thwart God's plan to reach the nations.

Our Court Today

We, of course, live in a different era of God's plan. There is no temple in Jerusalem to draw the nations into worshipping God today; no place to buy an approved lamb to offer as a sacrifice for sin. Between his denunciation of the temple activity and the commission to those he sent out, Jesus shifted the locus of missions from the Court of the Gentiles to us, the church.

I think about this story often when I am in church. What would Jesus do in the midst of our religious activities that are mostly focused on ourselves? There are certainly churches who love and support missions sacrificially, families that budget their finances and vacations to impact the nations, and missionaries whose whole lives are focused on raising disciples among a people group. For others, mission to the nations is great as long as we don't let it get out of hand, as long as we have financial excess, as long as it does not get in the way of doing our thing, or as long as it really is somebody else's job. If Jesus walked into church next Sunday, would he see world changers or money changers?

To change our ethos from money changer to world changer takes a miracle in our hearts. Only God can bring about such a radical transformation. If we want to know him well, we have to be open to that change in priority and habit or we may wind up filling religious activity with unmoved hearts. The paradox of loving God and being loved by God means that it cannot be primarily about you, at least for long. How can you say that you love God and care little for the nations that he is passionate to redeem?

I pray for churches around the world, including my church, to live passionately for God's purpose for all nations. In the very least, it would include the following actions.

1. We would actively and intentionally love and help the nations within reach of our churches. Most of us do not have to look very far to find some of "those" people, and we are the people God intended to bless them.

2. We would joyfully proclaim the good news to them that God loves them and wants to redeem and bless them. This would not be difficult if we were passionate about God's global purpose; in fact, it would be inevitable.

3. We would reorder our Christian traditions and busyness in order to prioritize missions. Most churches do very little in regard to his mission to the nations, and few make it a true priority of time, energy, and resources.

4. Churches, small groups, and individual believers would pray for and encourage missionaries. It has never been easier to stay in touch, to send a word of support, and to actually partner with those God has sent to serve the nations long-term.

5. We would develop strategic partnerships with one or more missionaries around the world. This would include short-term opportunities for members to get personally involved.

6. We would give sacrificially to support mission to the nations. As it is, an increasingly smaller percentage of our church funds go to the passionate pursuit of the nations. Jesus told us there is a direct

connection between our treasure and our hearts. It is pretty obvious in most personal and church budgets today that the nations are not our passion.

I encourage you to reflect on the story of Jesus in the temple and think of the present-day church. It seems clear how Jesus would view our religious activities that rarely focus on the nations. It is difficult for me to not compare churches I know well in America with those I have been connected to overseas. In recent years it has been my privilege to stay in contact with missionary colleagues and some of my students who are serving in a place of great lostness and growing responsiveness. That includes meeting and interviewing some of their local partners, who are among those who have planted tens of thousands of new churches in less than a decade. Those house churches are composed of recent converts from several global faiths; the passion of those relatively new believers is what drives the whole movement. These believers are under cultural, social, and political pressure because of their joyful confession of Christ. Their average income is much less than five dollars per day and most house church leaders are unpaid or bivocational. Yet, one network of new churches gives 30 percent of all offerings to church planting in new locations. It is also one of several new church networks that in less than five years began planting churches in several other countries. In stark contrast to self-centered abundance, those churches give abundantly out of their poverty. No wonder that when I am with those believers, Jesus seems to be in their midst and he is not wielding a whip of cords.

> Misconception 11
> God should be satisfied with whatever we contribute to reach the nations.

When the gospel got to you, your church, and your people, who were you supposed to pass it on to?

Questions to Consider

1. The temple had an original design, specific purpose, and function that had been tainted. Consider this in light of your modern experiences with the body of Christ (the new temple) and the local church (the community of the body of Christ). What is the original intent and purpose? Have you experienced rightly focused expressions of these things?

2. Jesus drives out that which is in the temple that should not be there. *Ekballo* is the Greek word used that means pushing something out that otherwise will not go. Jesus' actions were a dramatic demonstration of disgust at what the religious life of the temple had become. What in our church life might need to be pushed out?

3. Respond to this quote: "Chosen by God to be world changers, they settled for being self-focused money changers. On the outside, money changers stay busy, fill the space, maintain a sense of order and organization, preserve the status quo, provide a service, look busy, and keep the religious leaders happy. They also block, hinder, and thwart God's plan to reach the nations." Are there ever temptations in your life to be a money changer more than a world changer? What does your church raise up, train, and send out?

4. Are you open to God changing your priorities if there is an area in your life where you value religious activity with an unmoved heart? What area would you like to honestly consider before the Lord?

5. What nations are in reach of your church? How are you actively, intentionally, and strategically loving them and joyfully proclaiming the good news to them?

6. Are there any Christian traditions and/or busyness that need to be reordered in your personal life or in the life of your church in order to prioritize missions? Consider the below ways that this can be done:

   a. Prayer

   b. Strategic partnerships with one or more missionaries around the world

   c. Sacrificial giving

Chapter 4

God's Push to the Nations

A MISSIONARY FAMILY RETURNED to the US for nine months for rest and family time to rejuvenate from their demanding cross-cultural ministry at an overseas hospital. After serving for several months at a hospital while in the US, the missionary doctor was offered twenty times his missionary salary to stay and head a prestigious department. When he turned down the offer, hospital staff kept exploring what salary or benefit would convince him to stay because they recognized his unusual medical expertise. He quietly assured them he was not holding out for a better offer. So, if not money or prestige, what could push a man into thousands of sleepless nights in med school, internship, residency, and calls to the floor of a hospital where no one is rich or famous?

A young missionary family served faithfully for several years, but the father/husband suffered from a serious, and often painful, health issue and was advised by doctors he should move to a temperate climate. Field leaders were surprised when the young missionaries asked to be reassigned to a more remote tropical location to pursue unengaged peoples. The new location was a several days' journey further away from good medical care and the relief that only a good hospital could give him when his symptoms flared. I admit it was one of the most difficult decisions this field leader faced as to how much medical risk was acceptable in missions assignments. What pushed a young couple with small children to go way beyond anyone's expectation geographically and medically, well beyond what many would consider to be good sense?

I use the word "push" intentionally. We know the words of Jesus, "The harvest is plentiful, but the workers are few. Therefore, pray to the Lord of the harvest to send out workers into His harvest" (Matt 9:37–38). Surprisingly, the Greek word translated "send out" is not a normal word for sending. It is found again just one verse later in 10:1 in its most common usage: Jesus "cast out" a demon. *Ekballo* does not mean "to send," but "to throw out," the same word used for Jesus driving out the buyers and sellers from the temple (a gentler analogy is the shepherd pushing out the sheep to lead them in John 10:40). Jesus knew that the Father must powerfully nudge, push, even cast out laborers into the harvest field beyond their comfort zone. It is God who pushes us to serve sacrificially so the nations might come to him.

Misconception 12
Missions should be voluntary; God would never push someone to go to the nations.

To those who are cast out, this internal compulsion that is the whispering voice of God is undeniable, but to many others it may seem incomprehensible. As Jesus said, we should be praying that God would push out workers into the harvest fields. That includes all believers, who are responsible to contribute as they are able to accomplish the Great Commission, as well as those who are called to go to the nations as a long-term vocation. All need to sense God's compelling push to go, just as Paul talked about the love of Christ pushing him (2 Cor 5:14).

In this chapter I identify biblical truths that push God's people to take up the Great Commission and go out into the harvest fields. These concepts are more than a rationale; they are actually a mandate that demands our action in response to God's plan. But before we examine them, let me tell a story that illustrates how powerfully God speaks to us through his word if we are listening.

Iit and I joined the men's Bible study at our church at the same time. I was a new missionary just arrived in country and he was a new Muslim-background believer who knew little of the Bible. During that first year,

Iit's questions stirred the sedate manner of the class and hinted at unusually deep theological reflection.

After one year the church asked me to use my developing language to teach a Theological Education by Extension class. So, I taught my first course in the national language with fifteen students, including Iit. He struggled with the programmed instruction method of the class, but gave insightful answers to verbal questions.

So, the church asked me to teach Iit individually for a year and we began to meet weekly. For several months I tried to teach Iit a weekly Bible lesson. He listened as I taught, but something was still not right. In frustration I finally asked Iit what God was teaching him. He pulled out a notebook and his already well-worn Bible and began to show me his daily notes from his two-hour Bible study each morning!

At the age of ten, Iit had to leave school and go to work to help his widowed mother. Over the next twenty-five years, his third-grade reading skills atrophied for lack of use. When he heard the gospel and believed, Iit's insatiable desire to understand his new faith pushed him into reading again as he spent hours daily studying his Bible. His notebook was filled with one-page highlights of the meaning of a particular passage, insightful observations, and organized summaries. When he left my house that day, I was humbled by the glimpse into what the Holy Spirit was teaching this man.

For the next eight months, Iit became my teacher. I listened as he passionately shared what God was teaching him; I was hearing biblical insights expressed in completely new ways for me. I was also learning about his culture, because he was showing me how Scripture provided answers to issues of importance in his life. From the beginning I had decided that the Bible would be our only resource for study. Now, as I listened, I occasionally asked questions for clarification and suggested other passages that would be good commentary on the passage he was explaining to me.

The following year, Iit became the bivocational pastor of a house church among his people. With little formal education but deep spiritual insight, he filled a critical leadership need in that growing group. As far as I could find out, this was the first house church among his people group to be led by one of their own.

Our church congratulated me on the excellent results of my teaching, but it was not false humility when I insisted I had almost nothing to do with it except standing in awe of the power of God and his word.

A Personal Commitment

I was raised by devout believers who, along with our pastor, taught me from an early age that non-conforming Protestants such as Baptists are skeptical of tradition—even their own—unless it is regularly tested by Scripture. The Reformation principle of *sola Scriptura* means that only God's revealed word is our ultimate authority and guide for life, doctrine, and ministry. That is why this is a part of my personal credo, but is also a missionary principle.

1. Theology is important, but we should think about it through the lens of Scripture and not vice versa. Every theological system developed in church history was influenced by its cultural context and is imperfect for teaching globally. The context deeply influenced the system of thought, the categories, and the questions answered by that theology. That context is usually foreign to the issues faced by those coming to Christ today from other cultures.

2. The Bible should be the primary source of doctrine and life pattern for new believers and churches. In laying the foundation of the church, missionaries guide new believers to seek theological answers from the Scriptures. On numerous occasions I have been amazed to hear new believers articulate deep spiritual insight from spending time listening to the Spirit transform their minds through reading the Bible.

3. I know that it is impossible for me to be completely objective about my culture and theological assumptions. However, I do believe that intentionally introducing Western theological systems, categories, and debates is usually not helpful for establishing indigenous churches among non-Western Christians, although these can personally inform the missionary. When higher education for leaders is needed in a maturing movement, leaders and churches may benefit from awareness of broader theological systems.

The majority of global Christians today have an affinity for Jesus and the Bible while still wondering why Americans, for instance, are so strange. Missionaries are those who take the gospel from one cultural context to another, and that is accomplished best by minimizing the cultural expression of their home culture. In fact, that is at the heart of the principle affirmed in Acts 15 that accentuates the simple gospel without additional cultural traditions through which to develop indigenous churches. I am comfortable sitting on a bamboo floor in Southeast Asia telling stories from the Bible and talking to local people about how they can learn and live those truths. I am not comfortable with introducing new believers to Western Christian theological systems about which even Westerners cannot agree. In laying the foundation of a people group church, biblical theology comes before systematic theology.

Mere Mission Motivation

So, I am asking you to consider the core convictions found in Scripture that stirred the earliest missionaries, rather than the lens of centuries of subsequent debate about theology. Read Scripture with me and see if these truths are clearly and consistently taught in the New Testament. I will point to six core convictions expressed repeatedly in the New Testament that the authors knew were foundational to taking on the mission Jesus gave to his church. We cannot possibly explore every verse that expresses these convictions, but we will begin with several passages in which all six are expressed. Then I will attempt to define each of the convictions based on key passages that express it.

To get started, I will name each conviction and show you how integrated these concepts are in the New Testament:

- *Eternal Purpose of God to redeem the nations (EP)*

- *Complete Lostness of mankind; we cannot fix what separates us from God (CL)*

- *Universal Intention of grace to all people and nations (UI)*

- *Particular Effect of salvation for some, but not all are saved (PE)*

- *Specific Condition of faith by which we receive the gift of salvation (SC)*

- *Catalytic Action of witness to share the gospel and make disciples (CA)*

> There came a man sent from God, whose name was John.[EP] He came as a witness, to testify about the Light,[CA] so that all[UI] might believe[SC] through him. He was not the Light, but he came to testify about the Light[CA]. There was the true Light which, coming into the world,[EP] enlightens every man[UI]. He was in the world, and the world was made through Him, and the world did not

know him.[UI] He came to His own, and those who were His own did not receive Him.[CL] But as many as received Him,[SC] to them He gave the right to become children of God,[PE] even those who believe in His name,[SC] who were born, not of blood nor of the will of flesh nor the will of man,[PE] but of God.[EP] (John 1:6–13)

"or the love of Christ controls us,[CA] having concluded this,[SC] that one died for all, therefore all died; and He died for all,[UI] so that they who live might no longer live for themselves, but for Him,[CA] who died and rose again on their behalf.[EP] Therefore, from now on we recognize no one according to the flesh, even though we have known Christ according to the flesh,[PE] yet now we know Him in this way no longer.[SC] Therefore, if anyone is in Christ, he is a new creature;[PE] the old things passed away;[CL] behold, new things have come.[PE] Now all these things are from God, who reconciled us to Himself through Christ[EP] and gave us the ministry of reconciliation,[CA] namely, that God was in Christ[EP] reconciling the world to Himself,[UI] not counting their trespasses against them,[PE] and He has committed to us the word of reconciliation. Therefore, as ambassadors for Christ, as though God was making an appeal through us; we beg you on behalf of Christ,[CA] be reconciled to God.[SC] (2 Cor 5:14–20)

For it was the Father's good pleasure for all the fullness to dwell in Him,[EP] and through Him to reconcile all things to Himself,[UI] having made peace through the blood of His cross; through Him, I say, whether things on earth or things in heaven.[EP] And although you were formerly alienated and hostile in mind, engaged in evil deeds,[CL] yet He has now reconciled you in His fleshly body through death, in order to present you before Him holy and blameless and beyond reproach[PE]—if indeed you continue in the faith firmly established and steadfast, and not moved away from the hope of the gospel[SC] that you have heard, which was proclaimed in all creation under heaven, and of which I, Paul, was made a minister.[CA] (Col 1:19–23)

Peter, an apostle of Jesus Christ,[CA] To those who reside as aliens[PE] . . . who are chosen according to the foreknowledge of God the Father, by the sanctifying work of the Spirit,[EP] to obey Jesus Christ and be sprinkled with His blood: May grace and peace be yours in the fullest measure.[PE] Blessed be the God and Father of our Lord Jesus Christ, who according to His great mercy[EP] has caused us to be born again to a living hope through the resurrection of Jesus Christ from the dead, to obtain an inheritance which is imperishable and undefiled and will not fade away, reserved in heaven for you,[PE] who are protected by the power of God[EP] through faith[SC] for a salvation ready to be revealed in the last time[EP] . . . and though you have not seen Him, you love Him, and though you do not see Him now, but believe in Him, you greatly rejoice with joy inexpressible and full of glory, obtaining as the outcome of your faith the salvation of your souls[SC] . . . in these things which now have been announced to you through those who preached the gospel to you by the Holy Spirit sent from heaven[CA]. . . As obedient children, do not be conformed[PE] to the former lusts which were yours in your ignorance[CL] . . . knowing that you were not redeemed with perishable things like silver or gold[EP] from the futile way of life inherited from your forefathers,[CL] but with precious blood, as of a lamb unblemished and spotless, the blood of Christ. For he was foreknown before the foundation of the world, but has appeared in these last times for the sake of you who through Him are[EP] believers in God[SC], who raised Him from the dead and gave Him glory,[EP] so that your faith and hope are in God. [SC] (1 Pet 1:1–21)

The Lord is not slow about His promise, as some count slowness,[EP] but is patient toward you, not wishing for any to perish, but for all to come to repentance.[UI] (2 Pet 3:9)

Eternal Purpose of God

Everything begins and ends with God. His gracious eternal purpose is to redeem mankind from our sin-caused separation from him. His plan was a mystery hidden through the ages, but manifested in Jesus and the church. God sent his Son, the Messiah, to die as a redemptive sacrifice for our sins and empowered him to overcome Satan and rise from the dead. His Spirit draws us to him, stirs us to repent, and gives us new life. Every aspect of our salvation is possible only by God's initiative, power, and kindness.

In the beginning was the Word, and the Word was with God, and the Word was God. He was in the beginning with God. All things came into being through Him, and apart from Him nothing came into being that has come into being. In Him was life, and the life was the Light of men. The Light shines in the darkness, and the darkness did not comprehend it . . . And the Word became flesh, and dwelt among us, and we saw His glory,

glory as of the only begotten from the Father, full of grace and truth. (John 1:1–14)

For those whom He foreknew He also predestined to become conformed to the image of His Son, so that He would be first-born among many brothers; and these whom He predestined, He also called; and these whom He called, He also justified; and these whom He justified, He also glorified. What then shall we say to these things? If God is for us, who is against us? He who did not spare His own Son, but delivered Him over for us all, how will He not also with Him freely give us all things? (Rom 8:29–32)

Blessed be the God and Father of our Lord Jesus Christ, who has blessed us with every spiritual blessing in the heavenly places in Christ, just as He chose us in Him before the foundation of the world, that we would be holy and blameless before Him. In love He predestined us to adoption as sons through Jesus Christ to Himself, according to the kind intention of His will, to the praise of the glory of His grace, which He freely bestowed on us in the Beloved. In Him we have redemption through His blood, the forgiveness of our trespasses, according to the riches of His grace, which He lavished on us . . . (Eph 1:1–8)

Complete Lostness of Man

God created us in his image for fellowship, but mankind's rebellion, dis-obedience, and sin have separated us from our holy God. Our sin has resulted in a corrupted human nature and personal guilt from our own choices. We are spiritually dead, in enmity to God, and deceived by and under the thumb of the devil. Our minds and hearts are darkened. We can in no way overcome or pay off our sinfulness. We are helpless to return to God or to gain salvation ourselves. We are the walking dead and deserve eternal punishment.

He who believes in Him is not judged, he who does not believe has been judged already, because he does not believe in the name of the only begotten Son of God. This is the judgement, that the Light has come into the world, and men loved the dark-ness rather than the Light, for their deeds are evil. For everyone who does evil hate the Light, and does not come to the Light for fear that his deeds will be exposed. (John 3:17–20)

For the wrath of God is revealed from heaven against all ungodliness and unrighteousness of men who suppress the truth in unrighteousness . . . For even though they knew God, they did not honor Him as God or give thanks, but they became futile in their speculations, and their foolish heart was darkened . . . For they exchanged the truth of God for a lie, and worshiped and served the creature rather than the Creator, who is blessed forever, Amen. For this reason, God gave them over to degrading passions . . . God gave them over to a depraved mind, to do those things which are not proper . . . and although they know the ordinance of God, that those who practice such things are worthy of death, they not only do the same, but also give hearty approval to those who practice them. (Rom 1:18–32)

And you were dead in your trespasses and sins, in which you formerly walked according to the course of this world, according to the prince of the power of the air, of the spirit that is now working in the sons of disobedience. Among them we too all formerly lived in the lusts of our flesh, indulging the desire of the flesh, and of the mind, and were by nature children of wrath, even as the rest. (Eph 2:1–3)

Universal Intention of Grace

God loves all the nations and every person. His eternal purpose to redeem us from our complete lostness is for the whole world, all people. The inclusiveness, the universality of God's intention and action, is often surprising, even to his faithful followers. The Bible affirms repeatedly that Jesus died for all people. God was in Christ reconciling the world to himself by offering him as a ransom for all because he desires all people to be saved.

It is not the will of your Father who is in heaven that one of these little ones perish. (Matt 18:14)

For God so loved the world, that He gave His only begotten Son, that whoever believes in Him shall not perish, but have eternal life. For God did not send the Son into the world to judge the world, but that the world might be saved through Him. (John 3:16–17)

And I, if I be lifted up from the earth, will draw all men to Myself. (John 12:32)

He who did not spare His own Son, but delivered Him over for us all . . . (Rom 8:32)

For the love of Christ controls us, having concluded this, that one died for all, therefore all died, and He died for all, so that they who live might no longer live for themselves . . . God was in Christ reconciling the world to himself, not counting their trespasses against them . . . (2 Cor 5:14–19)

For it was the Father's good pleasure for all the fullness to dwell in Him, and through Him to reconcile all things to Himself, having made peace through the blood of the cross, through Him, I say, whether things on earth or things in heaven. (Col 1:19–20)

This is good and acceptable in the sight of God our Savior, who desires all men to be saved and to come to the knowledge of the truth . . . who gave himself as a ransom for all. (1 Tim 2:3–6)

We have fixed our hope on the living God, who is the Savior of all men, especially of believers. (1 Tim 4:10)

. . . so that by the grace of God He might taste death for everyone. (Heb 2:9)

The Lord is not slow about His promise, as some count slowness, but is patient toward you, not wishing for any to perish, but for all to come to repentance. (2 Pet 3:9)

Particular Effect of Salvation

Although God's love is inclusive, not all people are saved. Salvation is the particular effect that impacts some people while others are still lost. Not all are or will be redeemed. When we receive the gift of salvation, our sins are no longer counted against us, we are made a new creation, and we are given eternal life. God's plan is for us to be transformed into the image of Jesus and to be blameless at his coming. Those who do not receive salvation are without excuse and have earned eternal death.

Enter through the narrow gate; for the gate is wide and the way is broad that leads to destruction, and there are many who enter through it. For the gate is small and the way is narrow that leads to life. And there are few who enter through it. (Matt 7:13–14)

Not everyone who says to Me, "Lord, Lord," will enter the kingdom of heaven, but he who does the will of my Father who is in heaven will enter. Many will say to Me on that day, "Lord, Lord, did we not prophesy in Your name, and in Your name cast out demons, and in Your name perform many miracles?" And then I will declare to them, "I never knew you; depart from Me, you who practice lawlessness." (Matt 7:21–23)

All the nations will be gathered before Him, and He will separate them from one another, as the shepherd separates the sheep from the goats, and He will put the sheep on His right, and the goats on His left. Then the King will say to those on His right, "Come, you who are blessed of my Father". . . (Matt 25:32–34)

Therefore if anyone is in Christ, he is a new creature; the old things have passed away; behold, new things have come. (2 Cor 5:17)

But God, being rich in mercy, because of His great love with which He loves us, even when we were dead in our transgressions, made us alive together with Christ (by grace you have been saved), and raises us up with Him, and seated us with Him in the heavenly places in Christ Jesus. (Eph 2:4–6)

But, beloved, we are convinced of better things concerning you, and things that accompany salvation, though we are speaking in this way. (Heb 6:9)

Specific Condition of Faith

It is impossible for sinful men to earn God's favor or to purchase it with good deeds. God's salvation is a gift we do not deserve and cannot buy. However, we must respond to God's choice of us in Jesus Christ. Simple faith in God's faithful promise is the specific condition of receiving this unmerited favor. "Abraham believed God, and it was credited to him as righteousness" (Rom 4:3). Paul described this faith with the words "believe," "confess," "obey," and "call on" (Rom 1:5; 10:9, 13, 14). Whoever hears the truth and believes will be saved.

But as many as received Him, to the He gave the right to become children of God, even to those who believe in His name." (John 1:12)

Whoever believes in Him shall not perish, but have eternal life . . . He who believes in the Son has eternal life." (John 3:16, 36)

For this is the will of My Father, that everyone who beholds the Son and believes in Him will have eternal life, and I Myself will raise him up on the last day. (John 6:40)

For I am not ashamed of the gospel, for it is the power of God for salvation to everyone who believes, to the Jew first and also to the Greek." (Rom 1:16)

If you confess with your mouth Jesus as Lord and believe in your heart that God raised Him from the dead, you will be saved . . . For the Scripture says, Whoever believes in Him will not be disappointed. For there is no distinction between Jew and Gentile; for the same Lord is Lord of all, abounding in riches for all who call on Him; for whoever will call on the name of the Lord will be saved. (Rom 10:9–13)

For by grace you have been saved through faith; and that not of yourselves, it is the gift of God; not as a result of works, so that no one may boast. (Eph 2:8–9)

And without faith it is impossible to please Him, for he who comes to God must believe that He is and that He is a rewarder of those who seek Him. (Heb 11:6)

. . . and though you have not seen Him, you love Him, and though you do not see Him now, but believe in Him, you greatly rejoice with joy inexpressible and full of glory, obtaining as the outcome of your faith the salvation of your souls. (1 Pet 1:8–9)

Catalytic Action of Witness

God's sovereign will includes sending us as witnesses and missionaries so the world will know and possibly believe. People cannot believe unless they have heard and they cannot hear unless we declare the truth. Paul taught that what we do and how we do it makes a difference in whether the lost come to faith and are saved. Essentially, we are obligated to tell everyone the gospel. Paul adapted his life and witness to his audience so that by all possible means he might save some. Without witness, believers are disobedient, but more importantly, the lost have no hope.

. . . but you will receive power when the Holy Spirit has come upon you; and you shall be My witnesses both in Jerusalem, and in all Judea and Samaria, and even to the remotest part of the earth. (Acts 1:8)

How will they call on Him in whom they have not believed? How will they believe in Him whom they have not heard? And how will they hear without a preacher? How will they preach unless they are sent? . . . So faith comes from hearing. (Rom 10:14, 17)

For though I am free from all men, I have made myself a slave to all, so that I may win more . . . I have become all things to all men, so that I may by all means save some. (1 Cor 9:19–22)

Now all these things are from God, who reconciled us to Himself through Christ and gave us the ministry of reconciliation, namely, that God was in Christ reconciling the world to Himself, not counting their trespasses against them. And He has committed to us the word of reconciliation. Therefore, we are ambassadors for Christ, as though God were making an appeal through us; we beg you on behalf of Christ, be reconciled to God. (2 Cor 5:18–20)

For the word of the Lord has sounded forth from you, not only in Macedonia and Achaia, but also in every place your faith toward God has gone forth, so that we have no need to say anything. For they themselves report about us what kind of reception we had with you, and how you turned to God from idols to serve a living and true God . . . (1 Thess 1:8–9)

Some may wonder why I have not included the death and resurrection of Jesus, the critical hinge event of salvation history, as one of these convictions. The reason is that all six convictions are about the cross and resurrection. The eternal purpose of God is expressed most clearly in that event. The death and life of Jesus were necessary because mankind is completely lost with no hope without them. Nothing expresses God's universal intention as powerfully as the cross and resurrection. The particular effect of salvation in a person's life is brought about by their meeting the specific condition of faith in that saving action. And our part in catalytic activity is simply to declare Jesus to have died and risen again for the salvation of the world.

Interestingly, these six convictions form three pairs of paradox. The pairs seem to be contradictory, but both parts are true. To our detriment, human logic sometimes pushes us to emphasize one over the other. We may not be able to completely understand such paradoxes, but we must affirm both sides of each.

1. Whose mission is this?
   Eternal Purpose—It is sovereign God's mission.
   Catalytic Action—It doesn't happen without our obedience.

2. Why is it important?
   Complete Lostness—We are helpless to save ourselves.
   Specific Condition—We can respond to the gospel in faith.

3. How extensive is it?
   Universal Intention—God intended redemption for all.
   Particular Effect—Not all receive salvation.

Missions in light of the *eternal purpose of God* is confident and hopeful. Missions without it is hopeless human endeavor.

Missions in light of the *complete lostness of man* is crucial and urgent. Missions without it is unnecessary and dispassionate.

Missions in light of the *universal intention of grace* is inclusive and global. Missions without it is self-satisfied and ethnocentric.

Missions in light of the *particular effect of salvation* is specific and measureable. Missions without it is fuzzy and undefined.

Missions in light of the *specific condition of faith* is people focused. Missions without it is impersonal and predetermined.

Missions in light of the *catalytic action of witness* is active, sacrificial participation. Missions without it is passive spectatorship.

Misconception 13
Interest in biblical doctrines should have no impact on whether we are passionate about missions.

These core convictions pushed the disciples of Jesus and the early missionaries, including Paul, to spread the good news across their known world. Most suffered for doing so. Even today, it is these core concepts that create passionate concern for global missions. Not all are called to be long-term missionaries, but every believer should be committed to this goal because they share these convictions. In fact, where missions is neglected, it is often due to lack of clarity about one or more of these convictions or to cold intellectual assent without true conviction. Even missionaries who have gone to the nations may find themselves under attack as Satan attempts to undermine one or more of these convictions.

So, What Happened to Those Pushed Ones?

That missionary doctor and his family returned to their ministry at that hospital, where he helped thousands of patients, whose families heard the gospel, and some believed. The long-term result of that ministry is a populous district in which the percentage of residents who are followers of Jesus is approximately ten times the number of any neighboring district. The loving action and verbal witness of that hospital is the primary factor that explains that difference.

That young family who moved to a more remote location had to send the ill father several times on week-long journeys to get medical attention. Rather than quitting or playing it safe, the missionary kept seeking out peoples who had never heard the gospel. One day he heard about an isolated village of an unengaged people group he had been searching for. When he arrived in the village after hours of driving through the jungle, he was welcomed with fanfare. He noted their extreme poverty and commented on the very poor soil and location of the village. The head man's son wrote down his name and the date in a diary and then asked him a question.

"Do you have something valuable to share with us? You see, our forefathers established this village and told us to never leave because one day a stranger would come bearing a great treasure. We have been waiting and watching for generations."

Realizing immediately the hand of God in his sense of direction to arrive in that isolated village, the missionary responded without hesitation, "Yes, I have come to bring you the most valuable treasure in the world." Within a few days that young leader of his people had found the treasure they had so long awaited.

Pushed by the God, who is himself that treasure.

Questions to Consider

1. Have you ever felt "pushed out" by God to do something in obedience to him that might not have seemed to make sense? What was that like? How did others respond? If not you, have you seen this in anyone you know? How did you respond?

2. What stands out to you from these passages and what do you see in the relationship between the convictions identified? Have you ever seen this relationship before? Why does that relationship matter?

3. The six convictions form three paradoxical pairs that seem contradictory but, according to God's word, are true. Human logic sometimes pushes us to emphasize one side of each paradox. What emphases have you primarily heard in your context for the three pairs identified? Or what emphases do you tend to choose?

   a. Eternal Purpose—Catalytic Action

   b. Complete Lostness—Specific Condition

   c. Universal Intention—Particular Effect

4. It is stated that it is these core concepts that create passionate concern for global missions and that when there is a lack of clarity or conviction regarding these, oftentimes missions is neglected. Consider your own context and respond to this. Are these truths being equally taught in your church and body of believers? How is this done well? Where do you see room for this to be done better? Do you need reformat your mind to accept both truths of these paradoxes? How can you better disciple and teach to all these truths?

Section 2

Missions in God's Pattern

How we go about accomplishing the core task of missions is critically important. The biblical record, historical patterns, and contemporary examples of missions provide a pattern of what missions should look like.

Each of the five Great Commission statements reveals Jesus' plan for his mission in different words, but together they paint a powerful picture of what it should look like.

- "Go therefore and make disciples of all the nations, baptizing them in the name of the Father and the Son and the Holy Spirit, teaching them to observe all that I have commanded you." (Matt 28:19–20)

- "And He said to them, 'Go into all the world and preach the gospel to all creation. He who has believed and has been baptized shall be saved.'" (Mark 16:15)

- "Thus it is written . . . that repentance for forgiveness of sins would be proclaimed in His name to all the nations, beginning from Jerusalem. You are witnesses of these things." (Luke 24:47–48)

- "So Jesus said to them again, 'Peace be with you; as the Father has sent me, I also send you.'" (John 20:21)

- "you shall be my witnesses both in Jerusalem, and in Judea and Samaria, and even to the remotest part of the earth." (Acts 1:8)

The five chapters in this section examine major issues in how we should go about the mission Jesus has given us. There are consistent patterns of how missions should be carried out as seen in Scripture, history, and contemporary missions activity.

Chapter 5—Getting There

There are multiple pathways to get to the nations today, but not all are equal in facilitating sent ones becoming effective at accomplishing the Great Commission. Churches and individuals should be wise in choosing the right pathway.

Chapter 6—Short-, Mid-, and Long-Term

God uses various lengths of service for missionaries to impact the nations. Those who want to make the greatest impact with their lives need to work with effectiveness and endurance.

Chapter 7—Context and Crux

Communicating Christ includes both speaking to a specific context and speaking revealed truth about Jesus. Inadequate contextualization may result in a misunderstood or irrelevant message. Overcontextualization may result in something far less than biblical faith.

Chapter 8—Indigenous Churches

Healthy biblical churches grow from their own resources and are not dependent on anything foreign. Missions that does not carefully use outside funding can destroy the spiritual dynamic that powers churches to grow and reproduce.

Chapter 9—Movements to Christ

Jesus taught that the kingdom grows in mysterious and abundant ways. In order to accomplish the Great Commission, missions should seek to facilitate reproduction and multiplication of witnesses, disciples, and churches.

Chapter 5

Getting There

MIKO AND CARLITA FELT God's nudge to the nations in their teens and individually followed the push through years of preparation. He is an educated, skilled, and experienced professional, perfectly situated for thriving in the global job market. She pursued intercultural education, used her musical ear to learn another language, and worked for years with that language group both overseas and in the US. When the couple first met, they were both surprised to find someone with the same internal push to the nations.

They considered going through a missions agency but felt they should try going a non-traditional route. He found a job opening in a key global city, applied, and was accepted. It would have been lucrative and comfortable, but during a visit it became clear that the setup for expatriate workers would keep them isolated from the people of that city . . . no time for language, little daily contact outside the expat community, etc. They wisely concluded that living the expat life would not facilitate their purpose of reaching the nations.

They then explored serving alongside missionaries in a hybrid role in which they would split time each year working with the overseas team and then returning to the US to pick up professional roles here. This may have been a workable, creative model of contemporary missions, but the hybrid nature confused their US supporters and eventually they gave it up.

They have now moved to join a large business in a least-evangelized country where they will have regular contact with local people, including the highest levels of society. The highly-sought-after job offers great pay and perks. I am praying with Miko and Carlita about how they will share the good news with people in this creative-access country. Their story highlights some of the opportunities and the challenges of "getting there."

Not a New Development

Today there are multiple options to explore how to support yourself and gain access to the nations where Christ is not known. Actually, we are getting back to patterns of missions that are recorded in the New Testament and have continued through much of the last two thousand years, although in the nineteenth and twentieth centuries they were less common in a world with "missionary visas."

Paul's trade was leather-working, one of the most portable of his day. It was also one of the best trades for evangelism and discipleship while making a living with his hands. Paul partnered with a business couple, worked long hours, modeled hard work and self-reliance, supported himself and his team, and accepted support from churches established elsewhere.[1]

William Carey never had a missionary visa, went extended periods without money from his missions society, spent months sick and hungry in a mangrove swamp surrounded by tigers and crocodiles, managed an indigo plantation, brought several business concerns to India, and eventually was hired to teach Indian languages to colonial administrators like those who had denied him entrance to British India. The good salary from his day job funded many projects but effectively curtailed his gospel preaching. His diaries show he worked seventeen-hour days in order to fulfill his calling, but it was very costly to his family.

For over a thousand years before Carey, monks were a primary means of Christian missions to pioneer areas. Sometimes they were supported by the church hierarchy, but many formed self-supporting communities in which still-famous cheeses, wines, baked goods, and preserved fruits supported them. The Moravians, those Protestant predecessors of Carey, sent missionaries with just enough money for initial travel and then the

---

1. See Acts 17:17–18; 18:1–5; 20:34–35; 1 Cor 4:12; 9:6–15; 2 Cor 11:7–9; Phil 4:14–19; and 1 Thess 1:9.

missionaries either plied their own trade or sold themselves into slavery to reach the poor. Throughout church history small teams working with a clearly defined objective have been the norm. Among Protestants, missions agencies have been the major channel to get the "pushed out" ones to their work.

Modern Mission Multiple Choice: Support, Platforms, Tents, Markets

Anyone called to the nations for longer than two weeks on a tourist visa needs to carefully consider the best way to get there. Much like beginning a journey across the mountains, it would be wise to consider what type of vehicle is most likely going to get you to the other side. Many never make it, so this is an important issue. From a practical perspective, your "vehicle" needs to address several critical needs before you can even get to the nations, but especially if you intend to stay there.

1. *Income*—how you will support yourself (and family). This, of course, is deeply influenced by job skills, your family status, and the cost of living at your destination.

2. *Legal status*—the basis for your permission to live in that location. You have to identify a need that country will allow you to address, whether in business, education, development, etc. As a matter of integrity, you should do whatever it is that the government has given you a visa to do (but often for less than forty hours a week).

3. *Social identity*—how the local people view you and your purpose. This is more complicated than some people assume; I have seen foreigners develop a legal status that made it very hard for them to spend time with local people and share their faith.

As they think through these three initial issues, potential missionaries may consider a broad range of options for choosing a vehicle to get them to the nations.

Options for Getting There		
Category	**Options**	**Considerations**
Fully supported (by agency, church, or group)	Open identity Creative access	The open-identity supported worker is the traditional missionary. A supported worker using creative access is very good if he/she does what was promised to the government.
Partial support		A worker earns partial support and receives assistance for other needs. May allow more time for ministry than regular employment, but also provide non-traditional identity.
Tentmaker	International corporation Local company Self-employed	This is a great option, but the key is balancing two vocations. Tentmakers must be prepared to work very hard with long hours. A self-employed person, such as a consultant, may have more freedom of schedule and movement.
Aid/NGO		A great option in the right place. Some governments severely restrict. Many public NGOs, even Christian ones, have signed non-proselytization agreements, so no witnessing is allowed.
Marketplace ministry		An expatriate integrates witness into his business activities. This has great potential, but if you can't start a church this way back home, then you probably can't in another culture.
Great Commission company		Usually, a privately owned company that does business, but with a priority of advancing the kingdom. Often requires owners/investors to accept lower profits. With the right partners, this is a great option amidst present global challenges.
Funded startup		A worker is supported for one to three years in order to develop a company or NGO that provides long-term support and access.
Bookends	Young adults/ students Retired adults	These are excellent options for growing a team, but often require good support from leaders. Best when the team makes use of the special strengths of either group.

Having multiple options to explore is a great advantage when there are so many situational variables facing potential missionaries. Some of the more important situational variables are the country and even location they want to serve in, the type of assignment they are drawn to, their personal experience and education, family situation, church or denominational connections, relationship to potential donors or business partners, how deeply their church and its leaders are committed to missions, and differences in preparation required for the various channels. We will look at factors to consider when choosing a pathway to the nations after we examine what effectiveness after you arrive looks like.

The Most Important Journey

"Getting there" certainly starts with finding a means of support, obtaining a visa, and arriving at an airport. In that journey you hope to arrive at the right airport with visa in hand and whatever luggage you brought with you. That is when the real journey to the most important "destination" begins. The journey I am talking about is the long, sometimes unpaved road to missions effectiveness. Before heading overseas, many people have never seen missions effectiveness, so this destination is often an enigma to those who have not made the journey.

> Misconception 14
> There is no practical way or reason to consider what kind of missionary is most likely to be effective.

I am going to describe what the destination of missions effectiveness looks like, based on thirty years of working with missionaries, including fifteen years of leading, learning from, and assessing hundreds of them. My observations are drawn largely, but not exclusively, from my own experience as part of an agency that emphasizes strategic deployment, language and culture acquisition, core missionary tasks, accountability and support, and long-term service. This missionary profile describes the missionaries who usually see the most fruit and make the deepest impact among the people they serve in the areas of evangelism, discipleship, church planting, and leadership development. This journey to effectiveness involves each person developing proficiencies in critical missions tasks in a particular context while pursuing deep spiritual growth. Cross-cultural effectiveness has nothing to do with ethnicity (unless it is the same), age, gender, marital status, personality, professional background, family of origin, or size of your hometown. Life experiences and practical skills can be very helpful, but much of this journey occurs after the missionary arrives in their country of service.

The Real Destination

The person most likely to be effective in reaching the nations develops the following strengths once they arrive in their country of service:

- Has served overseas for seven or more years (longevity)
- Is fluent in the language of those he/she works with (fluency)
- Works a strategic plan for planting indigenous churches (strategy)
- Reports regularly to someone who oversees (accountability)
- Spends significant portion of energy doing the core missionary task (priority)
- Spends significant time with local people (relational)
- Shares the gospel courageously and consistently (boldness)
- Pours their life into local disciples and leaders (investment)
- Has persevered through setbacks and difficulties (endurance)
- Serves on a midsized team of four to eight foreigners that partners with local believers in accomplishing the task[2] (team)

Some who believe that everyone is a missionary or that short-term is the new missions normal may feel this sounds like snobbery. However, this profile is evident in the New Testament, missions history, and even contemporary missions. For example, as a new missionary to Indonesia, I asked Ed, my country director, what effective missionary church planters

2. When I use the word "team" here, in most cases I am not talking about four to eight foreigners who do all their ministry together. This is more like a baseball team (part of the time you take the field together and then you bat on your own) than a basketball team (which should coordinate every movement together). In fact, I have concerns about eight foreigners planting one church together, because it will be harder for it to be truly locally led. There are outstanding outlier teams composed of only one or two foreigners working alongside local partners.

I could go work alongside to learn the ropes. Ed sent me and family to spend time with Greg and Shelley, Clarence and Ruth, Charles and Barbara, and Ken, all of whom closely matched this profile. In later years as a field leader, I gave direction to new apprentices based on this profile. In fact, from regular discussions with field leaders from around the world, this pattern of effective missionary life and work was consistent among thousands of missionaries in many countries.

Published research points to this same profile of the long-term, language-fluent, gospel-sharing, local-leader-raising missionary as the pattern of those who are most effective in evangelism, discipleship, and church planting. Patrick Lai surveyed 450 missionaries in the 10/40 Window and analyzed their responses in light of each's effectiveness in these areas. The research showed that the channel or means of reaching a country was not the most critical factor in effectiveness, but the pattern of life and ministry of the missionary on the ground was absolutely critical.[3] However, the reality is that the channel or pathway we take does influence how we work toward the pattern of effectiveness.

Lai's research identified several important positive factors in mission effectiveness:

- Worked with internationals before moving overseas
- Practice fasting as a personal discipline
- Are adventurous and entrepreneurial
- Have lived among the people for five or more years
- The more fluency in language, the greater the effectiveness
- Involved in local language church
- Have experienced a demonic confrontation
- Actively seeks opportunities to verbally share the gospel
- Have a clear strategy for planting a church
- Most of their partners are from the target people group
- Have monthly accountability

3. Patrick Lai is an experienced missionary, scholar, and advocate for tent-making missionaries. He surveyed 450 missionaries serving in the 10/40 Window during the same years I was seeing this pattern among those I worked with. Patrick's work should be studied by every mission strategist, advocate, and candidate. See Lai, *Tentmaking*; or his summary of findings in Lai, "Tentmaking Uncovered."

- Serve on a foreign team whose maximal size is eleven to twelve (much smaller or larger teams are less likely to be effective)

There are numerous advocates for missions today who do not know or choose to ignore this pattern of the most effective world changers. Most of those advocates have never flown to another country on a one-way ticket and seen the long-term outcomes of numerous approaches to engage the nations.

> Misconception 15
> It does not matter which pathway you take to arrive in your country of service.

A critical issue for someone who wants to make a difference for Christ among the nations is to consider which pathways are most likely to assist him/her to reach the real destination of effectiveness.

There are multiple pathways to get to the nations today, and there are courageous, committed world changers that are serving effectively in each of the categories we look at below. However, the question for most of us should not be whether it is possible to become effective through that channel, but which channels are most likely to help us reach missions effectiveness.

Students and Retirees

These two groups are in an unusual position to contribute to a missions team for a few months or years. Students who want to experience missions during or after college and retirees who are relatively healthy may be freer than most groups to engage the nations. Although they are unlikely to match the long-term profile above, they can make a real contribution to a team that is already at work. Both groups have special opportunities to reach out to people of their own age group. My own student experience of ten weeks in East Malaysia was transformative and confirmed my call to the nations. Retirees may bring professional skills or willingness to provide support ministry to a long-term team.

Funded Startup

Some early Protestant mission agencies used this model; they sent and supported missionaries with the expectation they will start their own businesses. The Foreign Mission Board (FMB)[4] moved away from this model in the nineteenth century, however, when questions kept arising about the amount of time missionaries spent on "the main thing." Today, this is a workable option as long as both sides have clear expectations and the business opens doors to witness rather than closes them. Once a person has learned the language and developed ministry skills, it may be easier to balance running a business while doing missions.

Great Commission Companies

Working with a company that is doing legitimate business, but not solely for the purpose of making money, is a wonderful option. Someone once said, "You cannot serve God and money" (see Matt 6:24; Luke 16:13). So, as long as the business is primarily to support the mission, this is God-honoring. From the examples I have seen, however, the critical task is finding partners/investors who are completely committed to this end. Businessmen are usually better at running a business and making profits; missionaries are usually better at accomplishing the Great Commission. When the two objectives and skill sets get together in this form, it can be a powerful synthesis.[5]

Aid/NGO

I worked with many missionaries whose entry came through aid organizations and who produced much fruit. The aid might be educational, medical, agricultural, community development, justice, etc. However, most major aid organizations have signed anti-proselytization agreements that may severely diminish witness through the organization.[6]

4. The Southern Baptist Foreign Mission Board (FMB), founded in 1845, changed its name to International Mission Board (IMB) in 1997. This agency is an active case study of missions in multiple contexts that can be traced back 175 years.

5. See Rundle and Steffen, *Great Commission Companies*.

6. No truly Christian organization wants to "induce" or "pressure" the people they help to become Christians. Non-proselytization agreements may have had that purpose originally, but many large NGOs now receive public funding and are vehemently

Also, some governments are suspicious of NGOs because they either get involved in politics or simply make the government look bad. If you can find a place where the organization encourages sharing about Christ and the government does not see it as adversarial, this can be a marvelous channel to accomplish the Great Commission.

Marketplace Ministry

This is the appeal to be missional in everyday life, including as an expatriate worker. Practically speaking, it is usually more effective for evangelism than indigenous church planting. Every Christian expatriate should be sharing their faith and some of those gospel seeds will bear fruit. In less developed countries, care must be taken to avoid raising "rice Christians"[7] whose faith is tied to their employment.

Sadly, I know young adults deeply committed to reaching the unreached who pursued marketplace ministry in an expensive city without realizing some of the limitations. Even with years of preparation, most of them have simply settled into being active church members trying to make ends meet. If you feel called to be a businessperson who shares your faith, then doing it among the nations is an exciting option. Being a witness in English can result in believers and disciples, but it is usually not the best way to plant reproducing churches among a specific unreached people group. This is a great opportunity for lay people who want to invest their four to five hours per week in something strategic. If your primary calling is to redeem the nations, then this may not be the most effective option.

Tentmaking

As I have already mentioned, the apostle Paul and later William Carey largely did their mission this way. Many Christian young adults are drawn to this model and we should wholeheartedly encourage them, as long as they know the real cost of the journey. Many tentmakers make little more than tents; the reasons are the practicalities of time, language, etc. Expatriate workers often cost companies a lot in terms of salary, housing, travel, kids' schooling, etc. Companies expect the employee to

opposed to any verbal witness.

7. See chapter 8.

earn all those benefits, so increased work hours per week is typical for highly paid expatriates. Attrition of expatriate businessmen is over 10 percent even with the best efforts for retention and is even higher in some places missionaries serve. So, companies try to place them in comfortable environments with international schools and churches.

Most local companies also expect long hours from foreigners, who are usually more expensive than local hires. If you want to find a job overseas while also accomplishing the Great Commission, you will need to work two full-time jobs and also be prepared to limit your involvement in the expatriate community. The average international assignment for an American overseas is less than three years and is getting shorter. Thousands of committed Christian businessmen go with the hope of being a tentmaker, but they should join a missionary team reaching local people instead of an international church serving expatriate Christians.

I recently heard a missions advocate speak about the large American expatriate community as the key to the Great Commission. As they say, the devil is in the details. The US State Department estimates that there are three to nine million expatriate Americans; let's say six million. Let's guess the average family size is three, so there are two million families or single units around the world. According to recent Barna research, about 7 percent of American adults have a biblical worldview (= 140,000).[8] Of the believing Christians you know, would you estimate that 10 percent are passionate enough about God's purpose for the nations that they would sacrifice time and lifestyle to change the world? That is 14,000. Let's assume about 50 percent of expats actually live within practical reach of major unreached populations (= 7,000). How many of those who do not consider themselves to be missionaries will learn the language, spend most of their time with the unreached, share the gospel boldly, etc.? 10 percent = 700. The reality is that most expatriate workers—even Christian ones—are not really tentmakers. Find those 700 expatriates tentmakers and assist and encourage them in any way that you can. Praise the Lord for those exceptional expatriates that God nudges out of their comfort zone!

Anne and I have known, befriended, ministered to, and been blessed by many hundreds of international expatriates over the years, but the reality is that non-missionary expatriate workers, especially Westerners, have never been, and will not likely be in the future, the major group

8. Barna Group, "Survey Reveals."

reaching unreached peoples. Many expatriate families are incredibly sincere Christ-followers, but the demands of expatriate business life and community limit their reach for the Great Commission. The key group for reaching the nations are those who go for the express purpose of accomplishing the Great Commission and pay the price of the harder journey to reach effectiveness. That group includes expatriate workers, especially non-Americans.

Partial Support

This pathway is designed to mix some self-support with some outside support. For instance, you work part-time as a paid marketer or consultant overseas while getting partial support from a church. If everyone understands the relationship, this is an excellent option that can facilitate reaching mission effectiveness and relieve pressure to earn full support, while providing a legitimate identity and natural contacts. Most of those I have personally known who pursued this pathway did so for five years or less, perhaps because it felt like walking a tightrope. Perhaps it is a great transitional model for getting to the nations and figuring out what to do long-term.

Fully Supported

This is a broad category with lots of subgroups, but I am including anyone who is sent to accomplish the Great Commission with full financial support. Some will be supported by an agency, some by their home church, and some by groups of individuals and churches where they have raised support. Fully supported workers may work in a context where they can openly be a missionary, but many work in a creative-access environment where they have to maintain a secular identity. For that reason, having vocational skills in addition to missions preparation can increase your options for visas. Situational variables significantly impact these full-time workers, but the various differences are not as important as the fact that *this group is most likely on average to reach the goal of effectiveness.*

Of course, I worked for a mission agency for thirty years and I am biased in that direction. No agency is perfect; even those blessed by God are composed of and run by imperfect people. However, an agency may provide training, ethos, direction, logistical support, and member care that facilitates becoming effective. I worked in a country that recognized me as a missionary, in a country where I was allowed to teach Christians, although my main objective was sharing the gospel with an unreached people group (UPG), and a country where I worked as a consultant for an international corporation while also pursuing kingdom purposes. Many missions agencies today have experience with personnel who require creative access to accomplish their purpose. Churches and individuals should choose an agency wisely.

A growing number of churches are sending their own missionaries directly. By definition, only a small percentage of churches can afford to do that and even fewer are capable of supervising their missionaries well from a distance or providing timely care in crisis. Although there are wonderful exceptions, a missionary sent directly by a church will on average stay fewer years and is less likely to reach effectiveness than those who work under the direction of a missions agency. A few years ago, research showed that missions agencies increased in efficiency and effectiveness in helping their missionaries accomplish the task when they increased in size from less than twenty to more than fifty missionaries.[9] Most sending churches are essentially small missions agencies. A healthy balance between strategic direction and member care is essential to maximizing missionary retention and many churches lack the expertise to do both well.

Several years ago, three missionary families sent by a missions agency arrived on their field of service at about the same time as three families sent directly by their church. Within eighteen months all three agency couples had reached a practical level in language fluency and were actively engaged in ministry in that local language. All three church couples failed to reach fluency in language, began working as they could in English, and by the three-year mark had decided to continue their work as best they could from the US. There are outstanding missionaries sent directly by their church, but the percentage is not as high as those sent in partnership through an agency. Churches can make a huge difference in preparing missionaries, maintaining a close relationship with them, and even providing all financial support while working through a missions agency that adds other strengths.[10]

---

9. Hay, Lim, et al., *Worth Keeping*, 39–40.

10. For a detailed study of the role of the partner church and the apostolic team in the New Testament, see Dent, *Ongoing Role of Apostles in Missions.*

An Appeal

I admire anyone who is trying to fulfill a missions calling. If you are already pursuing a people group overseas and find you are not on a pathway that is assisting you to be effective, then please go the second mile and do all you can do to reach that destination. If your pathway seems to drag too heavily against this journey, then seek another one as soon as is practical.

I sometimes wake in the night heartbroken that potentially effective workers are tied up in the maze of misconceptions. So many people are telling the younger generation to go to the nations in any way that they can. Many are making plans to do just that with little thought to the real destination and where their journey needs to take them once on the ground.

It would be tragic for a generation of devoted Christian young adults to go to the nations with a desire to change the world for Christ, but without awareness of the harder and more important journey from the airport to effectiveness. Without that awareness, there is little hope they will achieve the mission that Jesus assigned us. Of all the messages I have heard directed to this younger generation telling them to go overseas, I have yet to hear anyone raise the issue like Jesus did of counting the cost to build a tower (Luke 14:28–30)! If they are not wise, they may move overseas only later to realize they are not in a position to change the destiny of nations.

In recent years, popular appeals have called on young Christians to join a limitless team of expatriate workers who enjoy their profession and want to use their secular education for the Lord. They will stay closely connected to their sending church back home and gain support from the large overseas city team. They do not need to learn a language well because "enough" people in the globalized city speak English. They will serve and support an international English-speaking church while building relationships at the office to sensitively share the gospel.

From a pastor's perspective, this might look like the ultimate missions opportunity for their committed young adults, because it follows the proven pattern of opening another campus twenty miles away. From an informed global missions perspective, however, this model is likely a tragic waste of Great Commission potential. Each line in the previous paragraph highlights a seriously negative factor in missions effectiveness to win the lost, make disciples, and plant indigenous churches.[11] It would be hard to develop a more appealing but less effective means to bring the nations to Christ. *It not only matters whether we do missions; it matters where and how we do missions.*

Church leaders and missions volunteers, please hear me. Do your homework and choose wisely how you send and go to the nations, especially keeping in mind what it really takes to "get there."

Questions to Consider

1. This chapter considers multiple "vehicles" for how missionaries might be sent to the nations. Consider your own connections and networks. Which of these vehicles are represented by the people you know or that your church supports?

2. This chapter offers a profile of someone who is most likely to reach the nations effectively. When you look at that list, what are things that stand out to you? Why? How would prioritizing those things change the way someone might pursue reaching the nations?

3. Respond to the statement, "Research showed that the channel or means of reaching the country, while very strategic and important, was not as critical to missions effectiveness as the pattern of life and ministry of the missionary on the ground." What are areas of your pattern of life and ministry right now that would aid in being effective on the mission field? What are areas that are lacking or are misplaced?

4. A second list for effectiveness (from Lai's research) is included. How is this list the same as the list from the earlier list? How is it

11. See Lai, "Tentmaking Uncovered." The more limitless the team of expatriates (over fifteen), the less effective it will be in accomplishing the Great Commission (pp. 94–95). The quality of the connection with a church back home had very little influence on mission effectiveness in the study (p. 89). Workers who socialize primarily with other foreigners gain no benefit missionally from it but are much less effective missionally because they are not socializing with locals (pp. 86–87, 89). Tentmakers who state they enjoy and are continuing their careers or who want to use their secular education are less likely to be effective missionally (p. 83). Using English instead of learning the local language is one of the strongest factors in cross-cultural ineffectiveness (p. 92). Involvement in an international church has a strong correlation with mission ineffectiveness (p. 90). Workers who expect to build relationships with people before sharing the gospel are highly ineffective missionally (p. 91).

different? When you look at that list, what are things that stand out to you? Why? Is there something on that list that you see as an area you would like to respond to actively in your life?

5. Consider the different pathways listed in this chapter. Are any of them new to you? Or are there any new considerations for them that you had never thought about before? Which might be an option that would be well suited for you?

6. This chapter ends with an appeal to church leaders and missions volunteers: "Do your homework and choose wisely how you send and go to the nations, especially keeping in mind what it really takes to 'get there.'" How do you think you need to respond to this appeal?

Chapter 6

Short-, Mid-, and Long-Term

The Beauty of Short-Term Missions

MY FIRST GLOBAL MISSIONS experience was spending ten weeks in East Malaysia the summer I turned twenty-two. My student partner and I lived with local believers and moved to a different city every week or two. We led retreats and revivals for those dear brothers and sisters and often spoke in local schools about life in America and our faith in Jesus. We joined outreach efforts in cities and encouraged isolated churches deep in the jungle. The people, the food, and the experiences were delightful, although we were constantly making cultural mistakes. We were overwhelmed at the graciousness of the people and at God's grace to use us. That same summer, Anne joined a team of ten students traveling in East Africa to sing and speak at churches and schools. Before she left with that mixed team of guys and gals, I made sure there was a ring on her finger! We wrote letters to each other all summer in hopes of them arriving in the right locations at the right time to share what we saw God doing in and through us.

God used those short-term experiences to whet our appetite to get back overseas as quickly as possible. They were stepping stones he used to lead us to mid-term and eventually long-term missions. And with each stone we became more aware of the incredible invitation and mandate God was pushing us toward, the real cost of what it would take, the skills that would make us more effective, and the rich experience of being part of what God was doing in each of those types of service.

Decades later, when I became a professor of missions at Gateway Seminary, I was concerned about my inexperience in one area—I had never been on a two-week missions trip, much less led one. Several short-term teams had come to work with us overseas and I had seen the benefits that a short-term team could add to our long-term work. I also knew that the value of those teams did not happen without careful planning. So, when I began to plan for short-term trips for my students at Gateway, I did so on the basis of what I had hoped for as a missionary.

- The location would be where the team would engage people with no knowledge of Jesus Christ. I wanted them to be broken-hearted by the depth of darkness.

- We would partner with missionaries so we could see their life and learn from the model of their ministry. Most of us learn more by seeing than any other method.

- If possible, we would work alongside local believers and experience this kind of partnership. The testimonies of such courageous local believers is inspiring.

- We might do other things, but direct evangelism would be the priority. Sharing the gospel is the most important task short-termers can do.

- We would go where more missionaries would be welcome, just in case my students sensed God's call to serve among that people. From one team of ten several years ago, five now serve full-time in that country and two more make regular short-term trips.

These annual trips with my students have become the highlight of my teaching experience. They renew me, transform the students, hopefully encourage the missionaries, and most importantly, rescue men and women from eternal darkness to light. Doing an international missions project together bonds me to my students more deeply than anything else and bonds all of us to what God is already doing in that place.

A Short-Term Trip

On one trip ten students ministered for two weeks in one of the world's great concentrations of lostness. None of the students had ever been to that part of the world before and none had ever done the type of Luke 10 ministry we did by going out in pairs of students and a translator and looking for a "person of peace" to invite us into their home or business where we could share about Jesus. Each was prepared to tell their testimony, share a "Creation to Christ" presentation, or use the visual tool "Life on Mission: 3 Circles" to explain God's plan of salvation.[1] Before you think that seminary students, but not your church members, can do this, note that the three witness tools we used are simple standard approaches that only require a little practice. The skill of sharing the gospel clearly and simply should be a minimum requirement for anyone going on a short-term team. Some students were a bit nervous about such direct evangelism with strangers, but within a few hours each realized that God was opening doors to share about Jesus. In many cases, once inside the home they had complete freedom to share the story of Jesus and often ten to twenty-five family members, neighbors, and friends gathered to listen for one to two hours.

A taxi driver drove a team around one day, visited homes with the team instead of waiting in his taxi, then showed up the next day to ask the team to come share the same story of Jesus with his whole family. That day his family prayed to receive Christ, denounced their religious devotion to other gods, and asked for baptism and discipleship.

Bryant was on his first international trip, but quickly realized his testimony of coming to Christ out of addiction gave hope to several families he visited, because many young men there had started drinking before their teens. He shared the gospel and led several young men to profess faith in Christ and ask the local partner to do follow-up teaching with them.

Katie's team wandered into a small factory and when the thirty workers realized a foreign visitor was there, they took a break. Usually shy, Katie stood and spoke to the group, divided into women on one side and men on the other, and shared "Creation to Christ" and several Gospel stories about Jesus. Her translator/pastor then encouraged them to seek Christ and the group asked him to come back weekly to teach them more.

1. For "Creation to Christ," see https://c2cstory.com/learn/. For "Life on Mission: 3 Circles," see https://lifeonmissionbook.com/conversation-guide.

The students discovered that these extremely religious people had lots of gods and no peace! During our trip we shared the gospel with 640 people and fifty-nine came to faith the first time they heard it. About two hundred others asked the local partners to come back and share more so they could understand this new message. One student summarized, "We had heard repeatedly that the harvest is plentiful, but we had never been to a place where it is obvious that millions might believe if there were only enough people to tell them about Jesus."

Our short-term team partnered closely with missionaries and stepped into their ongoing strategy. The missionaries set the agenda, defined the territory, recruited local partners, and assisted in follow-up after we were gone. Our experience would not have been as meaningful, or even possible, without their partnership. Missionaries had invested in developing relationships and training local partners before they worked with us for those days we shared the gospel. In many of the neighborhoods we walked in, we joined those local believers in laying a gospel foundation for a new church.

Both Acts and Paul refer to short-term missions trips. The Jerusalem church sent members to Antioch on several occasions to check on their faith, offer help, and clarify a misunderstanding (Acts 11:22; 15:24–33). The Macedonian churches sent representatives to carry famine relief to the church in Jerusalem (2 Cor 8). There are also references to churches sending financial, and likely other, assistance to Paul (Phil 2:25). In fact, Paul sometimes refers to these short-termers as "apostles [missionaries] of the church" (2 Cor 8:23; Phil 2:25). Although Paul made a distinction between them and the God-called vocational missionary apostles, he stated that they performed priestly service to God and brought him glory.[2]

Misconception 16
Short-term missions is like politics: one party thinks it is all bad and the other party thinks it is all good. One of those groups is completely wrong.

If your church is not involved in short-term missions, it could be. If your church already sends short-term teams that are not evangelistic,

---

2. See Dent, *Ongoing Role of Apostles in Missions*, 61–62. The book explores the New Testament usage of the word "apostle" for early church missionaries.

encourage them to add sharing their faith to the mission. Short-term missions can revitalize a church and encourage members, although that should never be the main objective. The main objective should be God's people bringing the light of Jesus to those living in darkness.

Sadly, this is in contrast to many short-term missions trips, which help the airlines more than the "beneficiaries" of the project.[3] Some mission trips resemble the series *The Amazing Race*, where rich Americans rush around the developing world begging help from local people they do not know so their team can win the race and one million dollars. That amazing *dis*-grace is the essence of "the ugly American," who is focused on photo ops and their social media profile. Two common reasons that missions trips do more harm than good is that they do little to accomplish what Jesus commissioned us to do (chapter 1) and they use finances unwisely (chapter 8).

Mid-Term Missions

If short-term experiences whet your appetite for more and you sense God pushing you further to the nations, then a mid-term assignment of six to twenty-four months is a great next step. Students and recent grads may be in a good life phase to invest their lives in and experience a deeper level of missions. This is also a great opportunity for those who can retire, perhaps early, from their careers. Mid-term missions is going to require more investment and grit, but it facilitates deeper relationships, cultural experiences, and mission effectiveness. If you make the most of your opportunities, you can actually experience more of the process of discipling potential and new believers.

Anne and I spent our first year of marriage doing student ministry in Singapore. We stepped into a place where God was already working and saw two dozen teenagers trust Christ within a couple of months. We spent the rest of the year discipling this fruit from others' labors. Anne opened the heart of an unbelieving Chinese mother by spending a day with her on her kitchen floor making mooncakes. She gave permission for her two teenaged daughters to be baptized, who were followed by herself and the whole family within a few years. Our ministry included seventy-five teenagers from America, Singapore, and other countries

---

3. "We fly off on mission trips to poverty-stricken villages, hearts full of pity and suitcases bulging with giveaway good, trips that one Nicaraguan leader describes as effective only in 'turning my people into beggars.'" Lupton, *Toxic Charity*, 4.

as they learned to walk with Jesus and care for one another. Unlike our short-term experience, this time we established a home, ate and cooked local foods, learned how to navigate the city, made deep friendships, grew in ministry giftings, and saw lives changed over a longer period. While short-term trips can give great cultural and ministry exposure, it is not until you live in a place for more than a few months that you begin to go beyond the honeymoon phase and to learn more deeply. Away from normal routines and comforts, and unable to say, "my flight leaves next week," the mid-term missionary is given the opportunity to be a part of the people they have moved to share Christ with. This is something the short-termer never has the opportunity to do. And it is often in this longer opportunity to live and work in a context very different than your own that God turns head knowledge into heart and experiential knowledge. This is true both for the joy of the journey and for the hardness of the fight. That year showed me areas of needed growth and pushed me to prepare so that we could be effective in such a place long-term. So, when our term was over, we moved back to the US and entered seminary.

Misconception 17
Short-term trips are the only option for those who love missions but have no clear vocational call.

Mid-termers often fill support roles, at least part-time, or teach English in order to share their faith. Those are good ways to contribute to the missions team and engage the local people. Some teams assign them to learn language and mid-termers have surprised their mentors by how fluent they became. Mid-termers have backpacked gospel packets into isolated mountain villages with many government restrictions—and in at least one valley 1,800 villagers trusted Christ without ever meeting an outside Christian. In another, mid-termers were invited to stay with the village elder of a Muslim unreached people group, and after several weeks of learning from him, he asked them to share their good news with all the elders.

It is common for mid-termers to say their ministry was really developing in the final months of their assignment. Deepening relationships, cultural acquisition, and time for planted seeds to sprout are major reasons. Most realize that they could become far more effective if they came back to serve long-term. That is when God either pushes them to seek long-term missions service or to take their missions experience into their life and careers back home. Multiple pastors, businessmen, teachers, and other professionals approach their life and work in a different way because they followed the Lord to the nations for a while. Most become informed missions advocates in their church.

A seminary leader once commented that there is no other group of students like these recently returned mid-term missionaries. They have experiences, and scars, that few others can relate to. In essence, they raise the bar for the whole preparation system. For those who are pushed and pulled back to the nations, they undoubtedly begin that process with a head start. An open secret in many mission circles is that a large percentage of the most effective mission veterans once served as mid-termers.

Long-Term Missions

Four years after our mid-term assignment, Anne and I moved back to Asia, where we served for another twenty-nine. This time we traveled with a one-year-old and another in the oven. We served as front-liners for eleven wonderful years and then God pushed us into serving as field leaders. It was then that I first met Randy when he was being appointed as a missionary. I had read his short biographical sketch and was intrigued by his story. After sensing God's call to the nations in college, he had finished seminary and moved across country to start an urban church among a different ethno-cultural people. In order to prepare for overseas missions, he had taken on a challenging cross-cultural church-planting project and succeeded. I thought such long-term diligence was exactly what we were looking for overseas.

Randy did very well in language acquisition and was assigned to bring the gospel to a Muslim unreached people group with almost no witness or gospel resources. There were no foreigners living in the area and no national team engaging this people. It looked like a hard nut to crack, but Randy believed this was his work and dove in. In the next couple of years, he got established as an acceptable outsider, registered a unique business that benefited the area, developed relationships with multiple people, including key men of peace, discreetly shared his faith, and worked to get the message into that language. For seven years he reported no believers, disciples, or churches among his people group. Some time after he began to report increasing numbers in all three categories, Randy told me he thought I was going to "fire" him every time he filled out the report with zeros. Today, the fruit among that people includes thousands of believers and hundreds of churches.

Randy's concern really surprised me because I believed he was taking the right steps to get from zero (believers, disciples, churches) to many. He matched the pattern we talked about in the last chapter. Sometimes, especially in such a pioneer situation, the fruit the team should count is faithful action and not the receptivity of the audience. I prayed for and fully expected the harvest would come, although I had to smile when it began at the seven-year mark.

Misconception 18
Long-term missions service is unnecessary because of short-term opportunities.

Missions history records that many famous missions pioneers worked diligently for seven years before they saw their first convert. Protestant pioneers to India (Carey), Burma (Judson), and China (Morrison) all toiled until the seventh year before someone accepted Christ. Dozens of contemporary missionaries have told me their own stories of seven years of labor without many visible results. It sometimes takes years to learn a new language, establish an acceptable identity, learn cultural cues related to sharing the gospel through study and failure, build deep relationships, and sow the seed of the gospel where it has never been heard. Praise the Lord when it happens in fewer than seven years! However, in such an unreached context, Randy's first seven years were not an anomaly; they were closer to a norm. Although missionaries may see fruit within the first year or two, they will not reach their personal maximum effectiveness that quickly.

In his book *Outliers*, Malcolm Gladwell explains why some people excel to the point of becoming a musical virtuoso, world-class athlete, or computer genius. Outliers have developed skills that far exceed their earlier undeveloped level and are far beyond the average person who develops that skill. Gladwell found that the reason their skills developed to such a high level was not as simple as IQ, childhood giftedness, or natural ability, although some measure of these are foundational. Outliers are provided an opportunity to increase their skill level and work extremely hard to take advantage of it to maximize their potential ability. Gladwell's research shows that it takes approximately ten thousand hours of intense focused practice to keep developing a skill like playing the violin or soccer to world-class excellence.[4]

The clearly stated objective of missions should challenge missionaries to pursue highly developed skills like those of a violin virtuoso or a professional soccer player. If a new missionary spends thirty hours a week in the most focused practice activities, and if he/she were able to maintain that lifestyle for at least forty-eight weeks per year (there are visa trips, trainings, illness, vacations, etc.), how long would it take to reach ten thousand hours? Exactly two weeks short of seven years! Throw in two weeks for dengue fever, or whatever, and it comes to exactly seven years.

Why would it take ten thousand hours of focused practice to become the best missionary you can be? You are going to learn a language and culture and then share with a different people group why they should brave the reaction of their social circle for completely changing their worldview in hopes of something they cannot yet see. It humanly looks so improbable that critics around the world sometimes assume we actually pay people to follow Christ!

Getting to even the first levels of effectiveness takes diligence. If you have never done this, imagine that first year of language learning. You have left a job you knew how to do and a broad support system. Simple daily tasks are now more complicated. Back home, non-verbal cues were second nature, but now you miss many of them. You've had to work hard to gain the vocabulary of a three-year-old, but still lag in pronunciation. Aaarrgh!! It may take months to sound as smart as a five-year-old! You never imagined it was possible to make so many language and cultural mistakes. At six months you have progressed a lot, but sometimes just enough to be dangerous. Learners who fall below twenty to twenty-five hours per week in these focused activities, not including a lot of other tasks, usually plateau or regress in language ministry skills. Couples with children can both gain gospel fluency, but it will likely require adjustments in lifestyle. The concentration and stress of it on some days wears at you mentally, emotionally, and physically; some of your normal coping routines are not possible now.[5]

4. Gladwell, *Outliers*. As usual, you need to read the whole book to catch the complexity and beauty of Gladwell's argument.

5. I highly recommend Fidler, *1000 Cups of Tea*. This book encourages language

We worked with new missionaries in a formal three-year apprenticeship that made it easy to set specific goals toward effectiveness and to provide help and accountability to reach them. Our team broke down the large objectives of language, witness, and intercultural relationships into small daily, weekly, and monthly bites. In Gladwell's terms, we were defining the intentional focused practice that develops muscle and mind memory common to outliers. Most missionaries do well in developing these patterns of effectiveness if they persevere, work hard day after day, and build on a series of small victories. Yes, this is approximately the same amount of time that the longest mid-term missionaries serve, so they are leaving just as their skills start to reach apprentice proficiency. For long-term missionaries, this is when things start to really pick up.

Missionaries may see some wonderful victories earlier than seven years in, but they will not reach their maximum potential without those hours of skill development. Those seven years are certainly not wasted, nor are they just preparation; they are increasingly effective and fruitful. Ministry and witness should begin immediately, even in the first few months of learning language. After six to eight weeks of learning many languages, missionaries can be telling simple stories about Jesus to their neighbors. As their language skill deepens, their stories and ministry deepen as well. After the first year or two, language fluency continues to develop as the missionaries spend most of their time in ministry in that language. Teams can facilitate leaps in professional development by providing good mentoring, supporting new members through culture shock, passing along tactical insights, and handing new missionaries an effective language tool for evangelism or discipleship. However, the pattern for developing a person's potential in a particular skill applies to missions as well as music and sports.

Developing deep missionary skills can be complicated by today's misconceptions:

- Some short-term volunteers have accepted the misconception that their level of skill is the new standard. Even some who want to serve long-term are unwilling to invest in the practice it takes to gain missions expertise. I recommend that those who want to maintain a volunteer level of skill should maintain a volunteer mission status; they will never know what they are missing.

---

learners to learn more quickly, more joyfully, and more fruitfully.

- Some missions advocates declare the misconception that "everyone is a missionary." If that means every believer should find and fulfill their personal role in the global missions challenge, then I completely agree. However, some mean there is no difference between serving two weeks, two years, two decades, or two hours per week. In every other field of human enterprise, we know that is simply untrue, so why lower the bar for sent-out ones? I have not yet met a pastor who would also apply the same principle by telling his members they are all pastors too.

- Some people believe the misconception that all missions is equally valuable. They may scoff at the idea of "professional" missionaries, as if being professional is about pride rather than proficiency. We are unlikely to scoff at such pursuit of professional excellence if we are choosing our fantasy football team, are told we need brain surgery, have been framed for murder, or are considering going to the symphony. Perhaps we are more competitive about fantasy football than making disciples of all nations.

Why do we not consider accomplishing the Great Commission the virtuoso skill worthy of spending our lives to attain? The real question is *why we think that Jesus, who bought our salvation and commanded us to make disciples, is not worthy of our very best* to accomplish that task.

Going the Distance

Paul pursued his call to the nations immediately and continued it for the rest of his life. Although ten years of that ministry is the best documented, Paul actually served as a missionary for about thirty years. In Acts, short-term volunteers went on mission and then were released to go home when it was accomplished (Acts 15:30, 33). Paul viewed the service of his apostolic team in a different light. We see this when John Mark went home early from Pamphylia (Acts 13:13; 15:38). Paul did not believe John Mark had accomplished his mission and thus considered him to have deserted the team early. The same response is seen in his remarks about Demas, who deserted him due to his love for temporal things (2 Tim 4:10). Paul understood his missions calling to be vocational and expected some of his teammates to share that same long-term call.

The most productive years for missions service should be after the first seven. There are certainly valid reasons that missionaries leave the field earlier than they originally planned. However, it is sad to see missionaries go home before experiencing the depth of skill that a few more years of intentional practice would have produced. It is also sad to see missionaries with developed skills unnecessarily leave their ministry with the potential of many more years of service.

The challenge of persevering to reach and use the skill set of effectiveness continues beyond those first few years. Thankfully, most missionaries become more at home, learn coping techniques for cultural stress, and develop satisfying relationships. Missionaries may still struggle with desires related to public affirmation, the accumulation of goods, living closer to family, or a more comfortable life back home. In addition, there are people groups where the missionaries have reached effectiveness in sharing the gospel, but receptivity is still very slow. Even excellent missionaries may have to persevere for years to see the harvest. Some give up along the way. So, long-term service is not assured even if they reach the pattern of effectiveness.

Best-selling author Angela Duckworth writes about the importance of sheer determination and stick-to-itiveness in accomplishing difficult goals.[6] She gives evidence that having the grit to not give up easily is more important than multiple other factors. Resilience, diligence, stamina, or just plain bull-dog tenacity trump IQ and natural ability. In simple terms, grit is the opposite of quit. Duckworth developed two simple equations to show why sheer effort matters more than anything else:

"talent x effort = skill"
"skill x effort = achievement"

Or as Duckworth says, "effort counts twice."[7]

Duckworth's first equation, "talent x effort = skill," fits well with the journey to effectiveness covered in the previous chapter. Her second equation, "skill x effort = achievement," is relevant to long-term service. Duckworth's research convinced her that *grit is not innate, develops over time, is influenced by generational experiences, and can grow as you get*

6. Duckworth, *Grit*, 3. Duckworth describes her quest to address a problem faced by West Point military academy. Although only a small percentage of applicants are accepted into the academy, approximately 20 percent drop out before graduation. For years admissions staff had judged each applicant based on a "Whole Candidate Score," which proved useless in predicting who would finish their officer training. Duckworth developed a survey that was highly predictive by asking questions related to what she calls "passion" and "perseverance."

7. Duckworth, *Grit*, 42.

older.[8] Duckworth describes four "assets" of grit, which are relevant for missionary perseverance.[9]

1. *Interest.* This refers to what you are passionate about, what you enjoy doing, and what keeps you engaged in your work. Multiple passions can be expressed in missionary service, including spending time with people, thinking through difficult conceptual problems, serving God, seeing people come to faith, and teaching.

2. *Practice. Grit* overlaps with *Outliers* on this point—pursuing intentional focused practice to develop greater skill both takes grit and builds it. Duckworth points out that gritty people practice longer and harder, and then experience "flow" as a result. In missions that flow is the joy of ministry and can include language fluency, witnessing, discipling new believers, and empowering local leaders.

3. *Purpose.* The grittiest people in tough times are those who believe their work makes a difference. That is why those six motivating convictions in chapter 4 are so critical for mission service. Missionaries may not enjoy rewards other careers offer, but they are making an eternal difference in the lives of those they serve. If that purpose wanes in their heart, missionaries will likely not stay.

4. *Hope.* People who persevere through difficulties and delayed response must have some form of hope to sustain them. Missionaries have multiple forms of that hope. They believe God himself chose them for the task, and this call is critical to endurance and longevity. They know Jesus goes with them in their mission and they are assured there will be ultimate success because all the nations will be represented in the New Jerusalem.

Spiritual resources in these four areas are the reason that missionary attrition is usually lower than that of expatriate businesspeople, who receive more financial and comfort benefits. God works to strengthen the diligent faithfulness required to get the missions task accomplished.[10] Paul wrote about such difficult objectives that require grit and a bit of suffering in Romans 5:3–4, where God uses them to produce perseverance, which produces character, which produces hope.

8. Duckworth, *Grit*, 79–92.

9. Duckworth, *Grit*, 91–195.

10. See, for example, Col 4:17; 1 Tim 4:14–16; and 2 Tim 4:5, 17.

Because grit can develop, is influenced by environmental factors, and may increase with age, a missionary team can contribute to the grit of its members. That is why Paul admonished his younger apostolic teammates toward passionate focus and diligent effort so they would fulfill the ministry God gave them. A team also does that by modeling effectiveness and endurance, by working together with mutual respect, by holding new teammates accountable for those precious practice hours, by celebrating new levels of skill and milestones in length of service, by providing assistance at the low points that every missionary experiences, and by prayer. Missionary retention is tied to a balance of strategic focus and member care as needed.

I admire the young adults who by the grace of God climb out of the cesspool of contemporary culture to serve Christ among the nations. I pray many of them will "get there" within a support system and field team that helps develop grit. When grit gets mixed with the strengths of each generation, it is powerful. We know when the task of global missions will be accomplished—when all the nations are worshipping before the throne of the Redeemer. Until then, the missions task continues and reminds us of one important fact:

Effectiveness x Endurance = Maximum Life Impact

Addendum
Maximum Life Impact: Two Women's Story

CHARLOTTE HEARD GOD'S CALL to missions when her pastor preached one Sunday in 1873 on the "harvest is plentiful." This divine push lasted the rest of her life. Her college sweetheart was drifting in another direction, and she could not wait on him. As a well-educated teacher, her dream was to start a boarding school for girls in China. Before the year ended, Charlotte arrived in Shantung Province.

She jumped into learning Mandarin and experienced joy in the difficult task. As she learned language and culture, she fell in love with the Chinese people. Of particular influence on Charlotte was the ministry of Sallie Holmes, the senior Baptist missionary in Shantung. Sallie ran a school like Charlotte hoped for but spent even more time doing house-to-house evangelism in neighboring villages.

As new missionaries, Sallie and her husband, Landrum, had progressed quickly in learning language and searched for ways to pioneer work in an unevangelized area. They got permission to reside in Shantung, so Landrum was the first Protestant to preach in the province and baptized the first convert in 1860. Their first child, Annie, was born that year and brought great joy to their household.[11]

Landrum's fluency opened doors for him to translate for the US Consul and to talk with leaders of the Taiping Rebellion, which had created chaos and war across much of China. It appeared that doors were opening up, but then lightning struck twice in 1861. Little Annie died of an unknown disease in August. Six weeks later a small village in Shantung asked Landrum to intercede with a band of marauding Taiping deserters who were nearing their village. Landrum approached the soldiers on horseback, dismounted, and was immediately hacked to death. He was the first Southern Baptist missionary to die as a martyr. Sallie lost her baby girl and her twenty-five-year-old husband within a few months.

Heartbroken, Sallie knew God wanted her to serve the people that Landrum had given his life for. She served in Shantung for twenty more years in spite of loneliness that almost overwhelmed her heart. This gritty veteran became a model for Charlotte, who was also a teacher, a single woman, and driven to share the gospel with the Chinese people.

In 1878 Charlotte "Lottie" Moon opened her boarding school for Chinese girls in the small coastal city of Tengchow. Over the next few years Lottie worked hard to run the school, while being drawn more and more into the village trips with Sallie to share the gospel more openly. She had come to China to do evangelism and was beginning to see that the school might not be the best means. After five years Lottie closed her school and committed to doing village evangelism full-time. She and her local partners would visit several villages each day, looking for persons of peace to invite them into their house so they could share the gospel with many local women. This approach resulted in sharing the gospel with large numbers of Chinese.

Lottie hoped to move further inland from the established mission stations and in 1885 God opened the door to move to Pingtu. This area showed an openness to the gospel, but male missionaries had been rebuffed by local officials. Lottie traveled with a native Pingtu believer she knew from Tengchow, who found a house on a primary travel route through the city, and Lottie was home! She was very fluent in the language, stood four-and-one-half feet short, dressed in simple clothing,

11. Brady, *Not Forgotten*; see chapters 11 and 12 on Landrum and Sallie.

and attracted less public attention than any foreign man. She essentially got established before any officials could object. Lottie kept the house simple, ate local foods, and dressed like her neighbors so that people would be comfortable around her. Lottie offered fresh cookies and tea to visitors and quickly attracted curious groups of women and children. She shared Bible stories and taught them songs as Sallie had modeled for her. The young women were especially attentive and Lottie poured herself into bringing them to Christ.

Soon curious men began to hang around and sometimes stand in the back of her class of women. Several men eventually asked her to teach them the way to Life. She could not turn them away, although she did not want to be in authority over them. So, Lottie moved her chair to the middle of a large room to teach her class of women in front of her while a growing number of men listened from behind.

By 1887 Lottie had been laboring hard for a full decade without a break and needed a furlough in the US to replenish her energy and health. As she was preparing to travel from Tengchow to San Francisco, two men arrived after walking 115 miles from Pingtu. They pleaded with her to come back and finish teaching the people, who were longing to hear the words of Life. Lottie canceled her furlough and returned to her house in Pingtu, where every day she shared with curious Chinese in her home and in the villages.

This was her life for the next twenty-five years of effective, enduring service to the Chinese people she loved. In 1889 the first Baptist church in the Pingtu area was formally organized, and in the following years more churches were birthed and thousands of Chinese heard the gospel. Famine hit China in 1912 and Lottie began to starve along with her Chinese friends. Alarmed missionary colleagues put her on a ship to the US, but within a couple of days she died aboard ship. She had been lonely and sickly, but her real heartache was that so many of her beloved Chinese neighbors were dying without Christ.[12]

In the face of incredible challenges, Sallie and Lottie found ways through their diligence to make a difference for the thousands who came to faith. Because she would not pastor the churches that were planted out of her evangelism, Lottie mentored local men to lead them from the beginning. This pattern of church planting was more productive than any of her male missionary colleagues of that time. For a full generation after

---

12. There are several excellent biographies of Lottie Moon. I enjoy Lawrence, *Lottie Moon* because it was informed by those who knew her.

her death, the area around Pingtu remained the most productive field for evangelism for Southern Baptist work in China.[13] Twenty years after her death, a great spiritual revival broke out in Shantung, including three thousand new believers during 1932 in the region where Sallie and Lottie had sown so many gospel seeds.[14] Even now the world's largest missions offering inspired from Lottie's correspondence continues to sustain thousands of missionaries around the world.

Effectiveness x Endurance = Maximum Life Impact

Questions to Consider

1. Have you been on a short-term missions trip before? How did your trip impact you? How did it impact the long-term work that God was and is doing in that place? How do you think that trip was chosen and strategized?

2. Consider the trips you have seen or been a part of in relation to the description of a good short-term trip. Does that list give you any new insights, questions, or things to celebrate from the short-term missions trips you have been a part of?

3. Have you taken part in mid-term missions or known someone who has? What further growth in knowledge and understanding did that provide?

4. Have you ever thought of missionaries needing skills that take ten thousand hours to perfect? How does this change your perspective on training and serving as a missionary?

5. See the list of misconceptions that can complicate developing deep missionary skills. Have you or your church given into any of these misconceptions? If so, how can shift your perspective and what needs to change?

6. Do you personally know any missionaries who have served longer than seven years in their field? What have you seen or heard from them about the work going on? Do you have any new insights into

13. *Southern Baptists and their Far Eastern Missions*, 170. "In this way the foundations were laid for the great Pingtu field, which is, perhaps, the greatest evangelistic field we have in all China."

14. Crawford, *Shantung Revival*, 43.

what they have shared with you after reading this chapter? If you don't personally know anyone in this category, how can you get connected to someone so that you can pray for and support them?

7. Have you ever considered the grit that it takes to serve overseas long-term? Whether you are sent overseas or stay in your local context, grit can be a valuable skill for seasons that need perseverance. How can you pursue grit now so that you are better postured for maximum life impact?

Chapter 7

Context and Crux

Context

GOD LED US TO relocate from our church-planting work in Singapore to Indonesia in 1989. He was drawing us to an unreached Muslim people whose homeland had been colonized by the Dutch soon after their forced conversion from Hinduism in the early 1500s. The harsh colonial attitudes and policies of the Dutch *Kristens* pushed Islam deeper into the hearts of this people.

Our missions agency had worked with local partners in our city for forty years, resulting in sixteen churches with twenty branch congregations among non-majority people in that province, but with no real inroads into the majority people group, who were over 80 percent of the population.

We studied language full-time that first year and balanced time between our Muslim neighbors and a wonderful local church. At the end of that year, I field-tested a gospel presentation using traditional church language, which had been effective in the next province. In our area, I quickly learned that I could hardly begin the evangelistic conversation without being cut off. If I was going to share the gospel with many, something had to change.

Terms. I suspected part of the problem was terminology. The Indonesian church had decided decades earlier that it would not use common

99

Arabic religious terms except *Allah*, for the purpose of distancing itself from Islam. In Muslim minds, Christian religious language was associated with the Dutch church and their harsh regime. I was hopeful because a change in religious terms had resulted in far greater response to the gospel in other countries.

A pastor who was a believer from a Muslim background (BMB) who had come to Christ out of Islam coached me to find better terminology to communicate the story of Jesus. This partly involved the use of Arabic names for Bible characters instead of Dutch names. I tested the difference in terms by making ten attempts to share the gospel presentation using church terms and then ten times using Arabic terms. Seven of ten times using the church language resulted in being cut off before I could even get a good start. Eight of ten times using Arabic names, such as *Isa* for Jesus, resulted in the person listening to the whole biblical presentation. Just mentioning *Isa* often nudged the hearer from skepticism toward curiosity. How could such a small tweak in language result in such a different receptivity from listeners? Perhaps because most Muslims believe that Christians have changed our holy book and a foreign-sounding name raises suspicion we are quoting from that falsified gospel.

Literature. We needed some new literature to help our friends consider trusting Christ. I had learned quickly that even the most open Muslims often needed months to consider faith in Jesus and that many of those who did believe made the decision alone with God. Scripture portions in the available Bible translations sounded too churchy. The tracts translated from other regions of the Muslim world were largely polemic debates over theological concepts. Few local Muslims seemed interested in those extended arguments. We were supporting a Bible translation project that used *Isa* for Jesus and affirmed him as Son of God, but it was going to be several more years before it was finished.

Art. My readings about Islam said that Muslims are easily offended by any kind of art except geometric designs. I found this not to be true among our non-Arab Muslims by accident. A local partner and I had visited a village and left a variety of tracts in several homes, as I was still testing the response to them. When we returned one week later, nobody in the village even remembered the wordy conceptual arguments, but a translated comic-like tract had been read in multiple homes. In that village with few simple reading materials, school children had read the tract to their families while showing them the pictures! Our large Muslim people group was drawn to art.

Story. I knew from my own experience that well-educated people like and remember stories better than a series of propositional statements. I discovered that devout Muslim families were often drawn to stories about Jesus. Don't argue theology; tell Jesus stories! Once they are drawn to Jesus, answer the questions they ask (in story form when possible). Sharing Jesus stories opened many doors in villages and visiting those homes gave me an easy answer about why I was there.

My artist colleague Peter created Muslim-sensitive art for a tract on the "Great Sacrifice" and a booklet on the true life of "*Isa Al Masih.*" Bible stories, Muslim-sensitive art, and non-churchy language became contextual tracts to share the Jesus story with thousands of our Muslim neighbors. When I received the printed booklets, I gave one to a devout Muslim friend, who looked at it for a minute and then asked, "Why are you giving me one of our books?" Several weeks later I saw a group of teenage boys in our neighborhood reading a booklet together, and when I asked them what they were doing, they nonchalantly replied, "Reading the story of *Isa Al Masih.*" These little tracts have continued to be used for decades and they have been translated for use in several countries besides Indonesia.

Such contextualization has been an important factor in the advance of missions work around the world, especially among unreached people groups. Good contextualization helps missionaries rethink how to communicate the gospel, how to live as effective witnesses, and what the church should look like among a specific people. Missionaries should consider these issues and work to address them appropriately.

Biblically Sound and Culturally Relevant

According to Acts 5:17–32, the apostles were thrown in jail for healing and preaching in the name of Jesus in the temple. An angel came that night, opened the doors of the jail, and gave these directions, "*Go, stand* and *speak* to the people in the temple area the whole message of this Life" (v. 20). The messenger of God reminded them of the task Jesus had given: beginning in Jerusalem, taking the risk of persecution, and proclaiming the good news, with realization that the judgement of the whole world depends on this and with confidence that Jesus is going to draw disciples from every ethnicity. It is surprising that they were told to go right back to the camp of the opposition, where they were most likely to get in trouble.

Risky, but, more importantly, it was where the greatest number of people would hear. Once inside the temple, they were to assume a specific posture—"take a stand." No sneaking around or hiding or pulling back from offending some with the gospel. They were about to follow Jesus' example and raise another ruckus in the temple. Obedience to God's messenger to "go–stand–speak" characterized the early church, but many Christians today think the height of their devotion is only to "come–sit–listen." That contrast is tragic for our own faith and for the nations.

Note the two essential elements to be balanced in their proclamation: speak all the words of Life and speak to the people in the temple. First, there was an identifiable, revealed message in words that bring Life. Any compromise, deletions, or omissions miss the target. The English word "crux" comes from the Latin for "cross" and means the most important, and often difficult, issue at hand, so *these words of Life are truly the crux of the matter*; the cross is the most important, and most difficult, part of our message. Paul explained (1 Cor 2:2) that he intentionally focused his message on "Christ, and him crucified." Appropriate contextualization must be undeniably, unapologetically, and whole-heartedly biblically sound and the "sent ones" are responsible to make that happen! Paul affirmed to Titus (1:9) that this message of sound doctrine taught by the apostles must be held firmly by the leaders of those newly planted churches as well.

> Misconception 19
> We know Paul contextualized the gospel, so the further we go, the better it is.

Secondly, that eternal message had to be communicated to a specific audience, in this case the Jews, proselytes, and God-fearers in the temple. *The unchanging eternal message needed to be addressed to a group with their own assumptions and objections in mind.* This involves adapting your communication so the message makes sense in a particular context. Even the eternal truth of God means nothing to an audience if it is in the wrong language or addresses issues that are not relevant to that people. How the message was communicated needed adaptation to culture to have greatest impact. Therefore, appropriate contextualization that honors God and accomplishes our assigned mission must be both biblically sound and culturally relevant. The crux of the message, the cross of Jesus, must be communicated clearly in the context of a particular culture.

Appropriate contextualization travels down a road with guardrails on each side. On one side is the biblically sound guardrail. Crash that guardrail and get mired in compromise and syncretism. In some ways it may look like biblical faith, but it has made adaptations, additions, or deletions that have changed the essential character of the faith. Let's be honest and acknowledge that this is not just a problem where the church is being pioneered. Syncretism is found in established Christianity as well, but we are just more accustomed to our own forms.[1]

On the other side of the road is the guardrail of cultural relevance. Jump that guardrail and get mired in correct doctrine that is mostly incomprehensible or irrelevant to your audience. We may be saying words that make sense to us but not to our audience. Again, this is not just a pioneer missions issue. Established churches may face a challenge in this area to adapt their language and forms to communicate the gospel to young adults today, who are living in an ever-changing culture.

Careful contextualization is even more critical where we are laying the initial foundation of the church, though it may be a few years before all the weaknesses in a foundation come to light. In a Buddhist, Muslim, or Hindu context, we could be guilty of establishing churches that have no cultural relevance in their context . . . they are alien and easily ignored. On the other side, we might establish churches that are at home in their environment, but do not adequately contend against formal religious teachings or free the people from the oppression of folk religion. The result in either case will be failure to bring the maximum number[2] of Muslims, Buddhists, and Hindus to true faith in Jesus. Keeping these guardrails in view helps us stay on the road we need to travel. My most vivid memories of guardrails are from mountain roads where there was a precipice on one side. Crashing through the guardrail would require not a tow truck, but a coroner. I love those roads with hairpin turns that need speed warnings and the critical guardrail may be on alternate sides as you drive the road. Yes, a lot like contextualization.[3]

1. Perhaps the most common syncretism in America is materialism, but it it's not the only threat. See Barna, "Competing Worldviews."

2. See 1 Cor 9:19, 22.

3. God weaves little things into our lives that he later uses for his glory. A college classmate gave me a framed cross-stitch of Acts 5:20. That verse and that girl have been prominent in my heart and home ever since. Just below where that cross-stitch hung

Scriptural Speed Bumps

These seven scriptural questions were helpful guides to me for contextualizing the eternal gospel in a different cultural setting. They functioned as speed bumps as I maneuvered between the guardrails of contextual witness (see 2 John 9 for a reference to "running ahead" of God).

1. **Does it deny the relationship? (Matt 10:32–33)**

   "Everyone who confesses me before men, I will confess . . . I did not come to bring peace."

   True followers of Jesus will clearly confess him as their Lord. Paul said, "If you confess with your mouth that Jesus is Lord . . ." (Rom 10:9). There are times when the term "Christian" may not be the best way to confess your relationship with Christ, especially if the church is considered a political entity, or is morally and theologically bankrupt. In America today, where only about 15 percent of "Christians" have a biblical worldview,[4] I often state my commitment to Christ in other terms. For example, I might tell someone I am a follower of Jesus, but in Indonesia my family told friends that we were followers of *Isa Al Masih*. Believers' identity and personal witness should clearly communicate their Christ-focused devotion. It is critical for the cross-cultural worker to be bold, because boldness begets boldness.

2. **Does it disguise the scandal? (1 Cor 1:17—2:2)**

   "The word of the cross is foolishness to those who are perishing . . ."

   In many contexts there is much that is offensive in Christian culture and history, so non-believers may be put off long before they have a chance to hear and consider the truth. Let us not forget, however, that God Incarnate offering himself as a sacrifice on the cross is scandalous and always has been. The cross is a scandal to Buddhists because it was necessary, to Hindus because it was unique, and to Muslims because it was allowed. The goal of contextualization is to highlight the cross, which is a wonder so surprising that it is scandalous, rather than a thousand other non-essential things.

---

was a Bible with scribbled sermon notes from hearing an Adrian Rogers sermon when I was in high school, which inspired these "speed bumps."

4. Barna has been studying this for a couple of decades and the decline is shocking. See Sherman, "Only 17% of serious Christians have biblical worldview."

Minimizing personal and cultural offense while clearly challenging non-believers with the story of the death and resurrection of Christ is powerful contextualization.

3. **Does it depend on the wisdom of men? (1 Cor 2:4)**

"Not in persuasive words of wisdom, but in demonstration of the Spirit and power"

This question is focused more on the attitude and expectation of the communicator, rather than on the content of the message. Some cross-cultural communicators fall into the trap of trying to figure out that "perfect" presentation, so they rarely share. Yes, we should seek to improve our communication, but we are not ever going to perfect it. The gospel itself is perfect, but our explanation of it will never be. In the end, only consistent, bold, loving, and Spirit-empowered witness is going to penetrate the darkness and lead people to Christ.

4. **Does it deceive the audience? (2 Cor 4:2a)**

"renounced the things hidden because of shame, not walking in craftiness"

When Muslims, Buddhist, and Hindus come to Christ, their communities often accuse Christians of deception of some kind. Christian witnesses must make sure they never give ammunition to these accusers. We may cross cultural bridges, but the gospel should be clear from the beginning and there should never be manipulation or half-truths involved. This is a good reason for missionaries to mention their faith in the first conversations they have with new friends and neighbors. That is how "seasoning every conversation with salt" (Col 4:6) gets started.

5. **Does it distort the word? (2 Cor 4:2b)**

"not adulterating the word of God, but by the manifestation of truth commending ourselves."

Certainly there are sensitive issues that need to be addressed carefully in every context. However, avoiding those topics completely or explaining our belief with hermeneutical gymnastics that doesn't point to the clear teaching of Scripture lays a faulty foundation. If new believers and churches are uncomfortable with specific doctrines or Bible passages, then something is wrong. For example, I encouraged BMBs, who usually have questions about Jesus' divinity, to read John's Gospel because of its simple and powerful declaration of the uniqueness of Jesus and the relationship between the Father, the Son, and the Spirit.

6. **Does it degrade the essence? (Gal 1:6–10)**

"you are so quickly deserting Him who called you by the grace of Christ, for another gospel"

We need to occasionally step back from specific issues or verses and see if the pattern of our teaching leads away from the treasure entrusted to us. This might start out as an innocuous or subtle digression but could lead to a loss of the message we preach. This is especially important in cross-cultural settings since our words or actions can be so easily misconstrued. If believers cannot affirm wholeheartedly the biblical teachings about Christ and how we come into relationship with him, then the foundation is faulty.

7. **Does it dodge appropriate persecution? (Gal 5:7–12)**

"if I still preach circumcision, why am I still persecuted?"

Paul was persecuted because he would not allow Jewish tradition to be integrated into the gospel of grace for all. Though we should avoid unnecessary persecution over peripheral issues, like eating pork among Muslims or beef among Hindus, we must contend for the gospel. The cross is the stumbling stone and we should anticipate a negative initial reaction to the gospel on the part of many listeners. Our proclamation needs to explain and appeal to people, primarily to clarify truth. Appropriate persecution is that which comes from clear and courageous proclamation of the gospel story to a growing number of people. Jesus warned us that the messengers may be persecuted (Matt 24:9) and Paul warned us that those who choose to obey will face such persecution (2 Tim 3:12).

I hope envisioning this simple contextualization pathway will assist you as you speak the crux of the gospel to the context God has called you to.

Controversy and Crisis

For several decades there has been growing disagreement between missions practitioners over the boundaries between biblical soundness and cultural relevance. This has been the most controversial area in missions and, if anything, is dividing us into separate camps with little influence on each other.

Much of the early phase of disagreement used terminology developed by John Travis to describe the types of fellowships that were developing among a Muslim people.[5]

- C1—A church that appears foreign and worships in a foreign language

- C2—A church that worships in the national language, but is clearly "Christian," and uses religious terminology that is distinct from Muslims

- C3—A church that worships in the heart language of the people and uses local cultural forms that are deemed not too Islamic

- C4—A group that uses Muslim terminology and forms and avoid "Christian" identity; often known as followers of *Isa*

- C5—A fellowship of followers of *Isa* who consider themselves Muslim and outwardly look like their community

- C6—Individual or small groups of Muslims who are privately followers of *Isa*[6]

In more recent years the discussion and disagreement has shifted to new terminology that has grown as a missions model. Now the discussion centers around the concept of "insider movements." John Travis defines an insider movement as:

> Multiplying networks of Jesus followers in insider-led fellowships where the Bible is obeyed as the word of God, spiritual transformation occurs, and insiders remain part of the families and socioreligious communities of their birth, bearing witness to Jesus, their risen Lord and Savior.[7]

There is much in the definition that is attractive, but one word will continue to open this approach to significant problems. If "sociocultural"

5. John and Anna Travis are exemplary in their love for Muslims. I have learned a lot from them and partnered with them. John describes the C1–C6 spectrum as descriptive and it is a useful tool. However, for many it's use has legitimized C5—Muslims who love Jesus—as a legitimate, and perhaps the best, missions objective. I believe that C3–C4 approaches are the best balance of biblical soundness and cultural relevance.

6. There are numerous iterations of this spectrum, but you should see the original published form. Travis, "C1 to C6 Spectrum."

7. Travis, "Insider Movements," 9.

replaced "socioreligious," then it would be easier to steer the work between the guardrails of biblical soundness and cultural relevance. As it is, the objective of believers staying in the religious community of their birth is missiologically and biblically problematic. The tension in the definition is between the phrases "where the Bible is obeyed as the word of God" and "remain part of socioreligious communities of their birth." IM practitioners not only want disciples to stay in their sociocultural community; they want them to stay inside their religious community. All religious communities define what they believe and who is included. Giving that power over believers to a non-Christian religion is dangerous for biblical faith. Obedience will be governed by what is approved by that community. Following and declaring Jesus as Lord and Savior is in direct contradiction and conflict with every non-Christian religious system in which these insiders are trying to stay.

The insider-movement practitioners I know are godly, admirable, passionate about Jesus, and committed to reaching the nations. I praise God for every lost person they bring to personal faith in Christ. Sadly, although some seriously strive for biblical discipleship, their stated ministry objective opens the door to socioreligious solidarity trumping biblical soundness. Insider movement has become an umbrella that is inclusive of numerous approaches that deny Christ honor and may inoculate people groups from biblical faith.[8]

If remaining in socioreligious community is the goal of missions, it is simple to achieve:

- In Muslim communities, just declare *Isa* to be an unusually special prophet, avoid all references to God the Father and Jesus the Son, confess that Muhammad is now the one through whom Allah has spoken, and be faithful to the Five Pillars.

- In Buddhist communities, you can affirm Jesus to be a bodhisattva who personally achieved spiritual enlightenment and graciously stayed for a while on earth to inspire others to find their own through good works and meditation. Oh yeah, no God and no Bible!

8. The three most dangerous methods missionary friends have encountered are 1) translations or commentaries of the New Testament that take out all references to God the Father and Jesus the Son, 2) foreigners who move to a Muslim country and publicly convert to Islam to become insider witnesses, and 3) missionaries offering money to C3 and C4 believers to convert back to Islam in order to be C5. Although many IM advocates may denounce these practices, these practitioners appeal to the IM definition as a rationale.

- In Hindu society, you can devote yourself to Jesus as the tenth avatar of Vishnu and encourage people to privately worship him more than the other gods in hopes of improving their karma for the next cycle of reincarnation.

It should be obvious that each of these religious affirmations is clearly a denial of the gospel of Jesus Christ.

> Misconception 20
> Expecting Buddhists or Muslims to convert to faith in Christ is tantamount to ethnocentric cultural imperialism.

Properly separating cultural elements versus religious elements in any context is not easy, but it is one of the most important tasks for the missionary and new churches planted in that context. Paul considered cultural disagreements in the church to be disputable matters that required flexibility and freedom,[9] while at the same time adamantly contending for every facet of the core gospel message.[10] The early church made distinctions between differences in cultural expressions that allowed compromise and religious teaching which clearly did not.

The early church experienced tension between obedience to Christ and relating to their socioreligious community. Luke describes the riot in Ephesus over Paul preaching about Jesus as a full community disturbance (Acts 19). If Paul's objective was a fellowship that remained in the religious community of Artemis worship that was the majority faith and cultural identity of Ephesus, then he would have had to compromise the proclamation of the Jesus message. As it was, believers' repenting from their old religious traditions and the crowd's chanting "Great is Artemis of the Ephesians!" made it clear that both sides recognized an identifiable split in the socioreligious community. Ephesian believers still mostly dressed, talked, and ate like other Ephesians, but they were a separate religious community in terms of conviction, ritual, identity, and proclamation. Whatever religious involvement the believers had maintained of their old socioreligious life up to that point, they were convicted to

9. See Rom 14 and 1 Cor 8.

10. See Phil 1:7, 16, 27.

confess as sin and renounce. The Ephesian church was no insider movement; Paul was not an IM practitioner.

Insider movement advocates are more comfortable talking about
Hindu believers, Muslim believers, and Buddhist believers than Christian believers. There are problems with the term "Christian" in relationship to history as well as the majority of nominal Christians in America
today. However, "Christian" originally referred to devout followers of
Christ and that is still the true meaning. My ancestors were mostly Celt,
Anglo-Saxon, and Danish barbarians who mocked Christianity, robbed
and burned churches, and slaughtered many Christians. Missionaries to
those peoples were brave. When they came to Christ, they knew they
had to renounce their association with Ana, Woden, and Thor. Early
Christian kings among Celts, Saxons, and Danes had to fight battles for
survival because their pagan neighbors declared war on their faith. The
first believers among my forefathers maintained some sociocultural continuity, but not socioreligious.[11]

Historically, religious communities have tried to align formal, public religious forms with a hoped-for inner spirituality, because one supports the other. The insider movement paradigm hopes to achieve one
type of spirituality (biblical obedience) while affirming personal identity
with other religions that deny its basis. If you shared the gospel with a
young man from a strict Mormon background, would you be satisfied if
he declared his faith in Jesus but continued to insist that only Mormon
baptisms are valid and Joseph Smith was the prophet of the Restoration,
hoped one day to be exalted to godhood, and insisted that the General
Authorities of the LDS Church are prophets, seers, and revelators? That is
a believer from Mormon background (BMoB) staying within his socioreligious community.

A common argument for remaining in socioreligious community
appeals to the example of Messianic Jews. Because I admire Messianic
Jews, I have to protest equating them with *Isa* Muslims or *Jeshu Bhakt*
Hindus. For one thing, this analogy assumes that Hindu, Buddhist, Muslim (or pagan Celtic) teaching is as inspired as the Old Testament. IM advocates and practitioners share this analogy with complete seriousness,

---

11. Most early written history of England was written by and for Christians. The
best example is Bede, *Ecclesiastical History*, the primary source for even "secular" history up to that time. An interesting modern look is Fletcher, *Barbarian Conversions*.

but it sounds like a prior commitment looking for a biblical rationale, even if it does not fit.[12]

The second reason that the Messianic Muslim or Hindu analogy does not make sense is that when the gospel was proclaimed to the Jews, they were told to repent of their wickedness and come to Jesus as if they were Gentiles. Baptism was a sign of repentance and rebirth, usually reserved for Gentile converts. In other words, coming to Jesus meant acknowledging that their religious tradition was futile. The church in Jerusalem was Jewish in every sociocultural way, but the gospel demanded they acknowledge their old religious identity had no salvific value.

The cultural relevance that should partner with biblical soundness is not cultural relativity. No culture is completely good, nor even neutral. The world, the flesh, and the devil have inspired portions of every culture and religion. The missionary must learn to analyze his own culture as well as the one he/she is learning to engage with the gospel. Some missionaries in previous generations erred by assuming Muslims, Buddhists, and Hindus should mimic Europeans and enter Christendom in order to come to Jesus Christ. In contrast to such colonial ethnocentrism, it appears our generation is being swayed by deep cultural relativism/religious inclusivism to underemphasize true conversion to Christ from other religions.

Misconception 21
Buddhists, Hindus, and Muslims can love Jesus from within their own religion.

The insider movement definition includes spiritual transformation, which I know is the hope of insider movement practitioners. Coming to faith in Christ results in being born from God, sanctified, adopted into God's family, justified and forgiven of our sins, rescued from wrath to come, and redeemed from enslavement to the enemy. How does that transformation happen? It begins by repenting of our old way of life,

---

12. It is sometimes difficult to dialogue with IM advocates, partly because they use scriptural examples that do not teach what they advocate. A helpful critique of these different interpretations is Morgan and Peterson, *Faith Comes by Hearing*. Although I know of no formal connection, IM advocates use Scripture like inclusivist theologians, who believe God speaks adequately for salvation through other religions.

recognizing the futility of our religious tradition inherited from our fore-fathers, turning from our wicked ways, laying aside our futile/darkened/ignorant/hardened old self, considering our old religious life as rubbish, turning from slavery to things that by nature are not divine, and transfer-ring our allegiance from Satan to God.[13] How strange, then, to make the objective of missions remaining within that rejected religious system that was futile in attaining salvation, filled with deception, and empowered by the demonic?!

Every time I read McGavran's *Founders of the Indian Church*[14] I am overwhelmed with wonder. He tells the stories of nine people movements to Christ in South Asia during that troubled colonial period. In each case, a man heard and believed the gospel, often through the witness of a for-eigner. Then either by himself, or with a few others, the man asked to be baptized, often publicly, and was seen by his community as a traitor. Each man clearly renounced the old religious ways of his people while refusing to leave family and village. In each case, the man faced persecution and suffering, but his changed life and constant witness bore fruit until his people started to turn to Christ, usually beginning in small numbers but then growing to large numbers of believers. The stories describe *religious conversion with cultural continuity*. This is what obedience to the Bible looks like within the sociocultural community of birth for a new believer, who then becomes the seed of a movement.

The Great Commission Inside Out

There are more deeply theological works that critique the insider move-ment paradigm,[15] so I am going to focus my comments on how the para-digm reflects the Great Commission we have already considered.

Making disciples. Jesus told us to go and make disciples. This pri-marily means proclaiming the good news to the lost so they can repent of their wickedness and become followers of Jesus. The sent ones take the initiative to share the gospel and lead people to pure devotion to

---

13. See Matt 4:17; Acts 2:38; 3:19; 20:21; 26:18; Eph 4:17–24; Phil 3:8; Gal 4:8–9; and 1 Pet 1:18.

14. McGavran, *Founders of the Indian Church*. I have had the privilege to meet doz-ens of such men in contemporary movements to Christ.

15. Antonio, *Insider Church*. See also Ibrahim and Greenham, eds., *Muslim Conver-sions to Christ*; and Coleman, *Theological Analysis of the Insider Movement Paradigm*.

Christ. The goal of making disciples is both a conversion event and an ongoing process.

Every New Testament example of gospel proclamation includes both connection in the context and confrontation over the crux. Jesus consistently modeled this approach by using familiar terms and everyday examples to directly confront wrong attitudes and religious assumptions. Those most committed to their religious assumptions were the most offended by the confrontation of truth. In Acts, every gospel communication by Peter, Philip, Stephen, and Paul connected to the context of the audience and then quickly moved to confronting them with the truth about Jesus. The consistency of that approach is seen in Jewish, Samaritan, and Gentile contexts.

Baptism. In every case in Acts, the response to the gospel message was to believe and be baptized. Baptism was an outward declaration that the old way of life was nothing more than death and that in Christ the person was coming to Life. This was a high bar for both Gentiles and Jews!

For many IM practitioners, baptism is problematic and some practitioners neglect, avoid, or deny it completely. Even if they do not know much else, most non-Christians around the world view baptism as formal entry into the Christian faith and that is problematic for the IM paradigm. How can you start a movement of multiplying disciples when they have not taken the first step of obedience in discipleship? Many IM teams, who say they are starting groups of Muslims who are obedient to the Bible, have, either through confused neglect or specific intent, modeled discipleship that ignores the biblical definition of discipleship given by Jesus.

However, the problem with baptism for the IM paradigm is even deeper. Jesus stated explicitly that baptism is "in the name of the Father and the Son and the Holy Spirit" (Matt 28:19). Jesus intended initial follow-up discipleship to include affirmation of the Trinity. This is so problematic in the IM paradigm that numerous teams have attempted—some successfully—to provide a new "Muslim Idiom Translation"[16] that takes out all references to God the Father and Jesus the Son! Tragically, they are providing ammunition for coming generations of Muslim accusations that Christians have changed their Scripture. Protests from other missionaries have often been met with cool indifference by IM practitioners. As bad as this is, it is only a visible symptom of a deeper problem. I

16. Another term for these translations is "Divine Familial Terms" (DFT) translations. See Scheuermann and Smithers, *Controversies in Missions,* chs. 10–12.

certainly hope it is not universal, but some IM believers demonstrate very fuzzy confessions about Jesus.

"Teaching them to obey all that I have commanded." I do not know how widespread the practice is, but some IM teams do not actually teach. They simply give a group of local seekers a Bible—hopefully theirs, with the "true meaning" that deletes Jesus as the Son of God—and let them come to their own conclusions. Although there are times when not teaching happens by accident, it neglects the Great Commission, which commands sent ones to teach. God sent Philip miraculously into the desert to teach the Ethiopian eunuch who was already reading Isaiah. Paul sometimes spent only a few weeks planting a church, but he taught the believers night and day during that time. Teaching seekers the truth of Scripture is at the core of the mission Jesus gave us, but some now think this is unnecessary and even counterproductive.

As we have noted, the primary goal of this teaching is obedience to all that Jesus taught. In most socioreligious contexts, that will result in obvious conflict with the dominant religion unless there is compromise over what Jesus commanded us to do. Accomplishing the Great Commission requires commitment, courage, and clarity as we "speak to the people in the temple area the whole message of this Life" (Acts 5:20). Compromising the basic truths of the gospel or the obedience Jesus commanded does not honor our Master or accomplish his purpose.

An Appeal

- *To pastors and church leaders.* If you support or partner with missionaries working with Muslims, Hindus, or Buddhists, find out the strategy/approach of partner agencies and your team. Some mission agencies have declared C5 and IM to be out of bounds, so their stance is clear. If your partner agency has not done so, then ask questions and keep digging, because teams and agencies have not always been forthright about what they are doing. Conservative Christians have unknowingly sponsored such counterproductive missions projects as Bibles with no Father and Son or missions teams that move to a Muslim country and convert to Islam to be insider witnesses.

- *To mission volunteers.* If you are sensing a nudge to the nations, then prepare well theologically as well as interculturally. Do careful research about channels to help you go to the nations. Share the gospel boldly and trust God to draw hearers to himself, because it is happening all over the world.

- *To IM practitioners.* If you are already serving Christ among the nations and are surrounded by IM practitioners, then take heart and trust God. Most agencies will not require an IM approach even if it is their passion, because many sponsors would flee. I know there are sent ones in Muslim, Hindu, and Buddhist communities who are conflicted and stressed by some of the radical forms of IM ministry. Proclaim Jesus as the eternal Son of God, baptize those who believe, form congregations that only read the Bible, and affirm that their old religious tradition holds no hope for salvation. Today is the day to begin anew.

Questions to Consider

1. This chapter focuses the importance of communicating the gospel message in a way that makes sense in a particular context. Have you ever seen good examples of contextualization? What are they?

2. In your present context, what are the relevant issues most prevalent in the hearts and minds of the people around you? What are the prevalent issues in your local church, in the youth group, in your friend group, in your job, in your neighborhood, etc.? How does the gospel message speak to those things? Have you shared it that way?

3. Appropriate contextualization needs the guardrails of biblical soundness and cultural relevance. Have those guardrails been jumped in your context?

4. The following are the seven scriptural speedbumps for appropriate contextualization. Which are ones you may not have considered before? What questions do you have that you want to find more context for? Have you ever seen these speedbumps ignored?

   - Does it deny the relationship? (Matt 10:32–33)
   - Does it disguise the scandal? (1 Cor 1:17—2:2)
   - Does it depend on the wisdom of men? (1 Cor 2:4)
   - Does it deceive the audience? (2 Cor 4:2a)

- Does it distort the word? (2 Cor 4:2b)

- Does it degrade the essence? (Gal 1:6–10)

- Does it dodge appropriate persecution? (Gal 5:7–12)

5. Have you ever heard of C1–C5 or insider movements? How would you deal with this issue as a missionary?

6. Which appeal at the end of the chapter is most relevant for you? Is the Holy Spirit speaking to you about this?

Chapter 8

Indigenous Churches

How Not to Do Missions

IN THE NINETEENTH CENTURY Protestant missionaries established churches in hundreds of locations around the globe. However, there was almost no response to their approach in the Muslim world. No place illustrates this failure better than the Dutch East Indies, today's Indonesia.

The Dutch established Batavia on Java in 1619 as a base for their growing trade activities. Over the next two centuries they conquered increasingly large areas of the islands, forced the people into slave labor, built churches for themselves, and prohibited mission activity among Muslims. Carey's Baptist Missionary Society sent the first eight missionaries to reach Muslims on Java between 1813 and 1816, when Britain took administrative control of the islands during the Napoleonic Wars. When the Dutch regained control of the islands in 1816, they denied the British missionaries visas to stay and held the first printing of the Javanese Bible in a warehouse for twenty-five years, where it was eaten by termites.[1]

Finally, in the 1850s devout Dutch Christians inspired by missions activity elsewhere pressed for the founding of Dutch agencies to begin reaching the peoples of Java. These agencies sent dozens of missionaries and vast amounts of money to support their work. The missionaries were

1. Sumartana, *Mission at the Crossroads*, 9–15.

officially Dutch colonial employees and worked to bring locals into the Dutch church. They ministered paternalistically to the believers, failed to truly understand their culture, and established church life that was completely Dutch.[2] Any Muslim man who came to Christ had to become a little Dutchman—cut his hair, wear hot European clothes, change his name, and renounce most of the cultural expressions of Javanese community. Unsurprisingly, relatively few Muslims jumped that cultural chasm, and those that did were considered traitors by their people. It is also not surprising that on several occasions the Dutch mission societies publicly discussed pulling out of Java because of the lack of response among Muslims. Perhaps the Javanese were just not predestined for salvation.

Sadrach

In this historical context a little-known hero arose to pioneer a new work that is inspiring. Radin was born around 1835 in a village on the devoutly Muslim north coast of Java. It is likely that his parents starved to death during a famine caused by Dutch policies. As a young man, Radin studied traditional Javanese mysticism and became a practitioner of that folk Islamic art. Dissatisfied, he joined a Qur'anic boarding school, and eventually became an orthodox Islamic teacher with a new name, Radin Abbas. During this period, he encountered Javanese converts to Christ and began to seek more information about Jesus. He investigated a traditional Dutch church, a syncretistic Christian sect, and eventually found a Eurasian Christian to disciple him. In 1867 he was baptized and took the name of Sadrach, a courageous Old Testament hero who was faithful to God in the face of a colonizing empire! For the next three years Sadrach worked successfully as an evangelist related to the Dutch church.

In 1870 Sadrach sensed God calling him to pioneer a completely new form of ministry. He chose not to work within the Dutch church, nor to mimic the syncretistic sects he had encountered. Sadrach moved to a village and began farming a large field that had been declared haunted and cursed; this action testified to God's power and provided him steady income for fifty years. He publicly challenged imams to debate him in their mesjids and then proclaimed why *Isa* is greater than Muhammad. The usual result was the imam and his whole mesjid coming to Christ. He argued convincingly that his faith was more Javanese than Islam, because

---

2. Kraemer, *From Mission Field to Independent Church*, 90–91, 107–10.

he read the Bible and worshipped in Javanese instead of Arabic. He proclaimed *Isa* to be the long-awaited "Just Prince" of Javanese mythology, which infuriated the Dutch colonial authorities because the myth often stirred independence passions.

This, and his independent leadership, resulted in harsh persecution from the Dutch authorities, who feared what they could not control. For hundreds of years the primary religious identities known to the Javanese were Dutch Christians and Javanese Muslims, but Sadrach established a new community whose identity was a real innovation, *Kristen Jawa*. Neither Muslim nor Dutch, this C3-C4 (see previous chapter) community experienced persecution from both sides while effectively drawing thousands of Javanese to Christ.

So, while the Dutch expressed frustration that so few Javanese had joined their churches, Sadrach began a growing network of *Kristen Jawa* congregations. By the time of his death in 1924 at the age of ninety, there were approximately eighty-six congregations for a community of more than twenty thousand followers. Sadrach's work disproved the Dutch complaint that the Javanese were resistant to the gospel. They were just not interested in leaving their sociocultural life and losing their dignity by joining a foreign organization as second-class citizens. One Dutch missionary actually encouraged and assisted Sadrach, to the consternation of his countrymen. So, Sadrach was not opposed to missionaries; he was just opposed to a Dutch-dominated church. Sadrach's story exemplifies the power of autonomous indigenous churches that proclaim Christ within their own cultural context without foreign control or dependency.[3]

Indigenous Churches

In many ways Sadrach represents the objective of missions and the Dutch represent the worst model of missions. At issue is what kind of church missionaries are planting and whether it represents its local members so that they can reproduce it. The Dutch pattern is not representative of all nineteenth-century missions, however, especially its earliest stages. Carey's pioneering missionary team explained their strategy in 1805 in what has been popularly called the Serampore Covenant.[4] They pri-

3. See Partonadi, *Sadrach's Community and Its Contextual Roots*; and Guillot, *Kiai Sadrach*.

4. Serampore Trio, "Form of Agreement."

oritized learning language and culture, minimizing their own cultural offensiveness, passionately living a consistent spiritual life, translating the Bible into heart languages, proclaiming the cross of Christ in order to save the lost, investing deeply in new believers, treating Indians as equals at all times, and doing good for the people.

In light of later missions mistakes, their blueprint for planting local churches showed amazing foresight: lavish attention on raising up leaders, advise the churches in choosing their own pastors and deacons, teach the churches to support their leaders and to provide their own places of worship, expect them to take the lead in reaching their own people, look for a divine change in hearts and not cultural appropriation, and when it comes to questions regarding being biblically sound and culturally relevant, gently advise and patiently teach them as they make those decisions. How did those earlier missionaries formulate a strategy so missiologically superior to the later approach of the Dutch? Their Nonconformist ecclesiology emphasized autonomous churches without state sponsorship or outside overseers, they aimed at impacting all of India and not just planting one or two churches, and they affirmed that Scripture was their guide and Paul was their model.

Acts and Paul's epistles provide multiple glimpses into the kind of churches that he was planting. Paul personally avoided handling local funds and did not bring outside money into a local church being planted. He did raise funds to help another church during a famine, but his whole approach was designed to result in indigenous churches. Some highlights are:

- He looked to develop pastors within the church whose primary qualification was a transformed life evident to all. (Acts 14:21–23; 1 Tim 3; Titus 1:5–9)

- Churches met wherever they could afford to. (Acts 19:9; Rom 16:5, 23)

- Baptism was quickly turned over to local leaders. (1 Cor 1:14–16; 16:15)

- Churches were taught to support their pastors. (1 Cor 9:9–14; Gal 6:6; 1 Tim 5:17–18)

- Churches exercised discipline over their members. (1 Cor 5:4; 2 Cor 2:6)

- All members were expected to work to support their families, the needy, and their church. (1 Thess 4:11–12; 2 Thess 3:10–12; 1 Tim 5:8)

These are practical steps to establishing churches that trust God for their needs, stand on their own, and represent their people. It is easy to see where Carey and others learned this model of missions and church. From their day until now, wise missionaries have intentionally planted indigenous churches.

However, during the first half of the nineteenth century another mission pattern emerged that was far from this biblical model. Many missionaries went out from state churches to minister in colonial areas ruled by their nation; new churches were viewed as a part of the state church back home. Soon churches were being planted around the world with subsidy and control that undermined indigeneity. Missionaries often lived in compounds that might include their homes, a church, a school, and perhaps a clinic that hired new converts and pulled them from their villages. Non-reproducing churches usually resulted when missionaries served long-term as the pastor or financially supported a local pastor. It did not take long to see that this model was resulting in cut-off Christian enclaves and long-term dependency rather than reproduction of churches.

> Misconception 22
> The best way to plant healthy churches cross-culturally is for foreigners to maintain control because of superior training and gifting.

By the 1850s missions leaders responded to this subsidized approach by advocating planting indigenous churches with three defining characteristics: self-supporting (is not dependent on outside funding), self-governing (makes its own decisions), and self-propagating (shares the gospel and start other churches from their own giftings and resources).[5]

---

5. Englishman Henry Venn wrote, "Every convert should be instructed from his conversion in the duty of laboring for his self-support, and for the support of Missions to his Countrymen, and to lay himself out as Missionary among his relations and friends to bring them to truth." Warren, *To Apply the Gospel*, 64.

American Rufus Anderson stated, "As soon as the mission church has a native

It might not be the fastest way to get to a church, but it is the only way to get to a non-dependent church and to a hundred or a thousand churches. One insightful missionary in China said, "Christianity has been introduced into the world as a plant which will thrive best confronting and contending with all the forces of its environment; not as a feeble exotic which can only live when nursed and sheltered. All unnecessary nursing will do it harm."[6]

During the colonial period missionaries were divided between these two conflicting approaches to subsidy. Many saw their heavily subsidized approach as an initial phase of work, but, sadly, history proved it difficult to change the ingrained pattern.[7] Tragically, missions records from the 1920s to 30s indicate that the majority of Protestant missions work was still heavily subsidized. In postcolonial missions, these practical insights about indigeneity were rediscovered.

Misconception 23
Established partner churches should generously support and help in any way they can the newer, and often poorer, churches begun from missions efforts.

---

pastor, the responsibilities of self-government should be devolved upon it . . . The salary of the native pastor should be based on the Christianized ideas of living acquired by his people; and the church should be self-supporting at the earliest possible date. It should also be self-propagating from the very first. Such, churches, and only such, are the life, strength, and glory of missions." Beaver, *To Advance the Gospel*, 98.

6. Nevius. *Planting and Development of Missionary Churches*, 26. First published in 1885, reprinted multiple times. This is a classic critique of the subsidized approach to missions. See also Allen, *Missionary Methods: St. Paul's or Ours?* Both men saw Chinese churches dominated by foreign men and money to the detriment of Chinese churches supporting, governing, and propagating themselves while depending on God alone. Subsidy destroyed local initiative and responsibility, kept the church too foreign, and severely limited the ability to reach the nation.

7. At the height of the colonial period, the International Missionary Council met in Madras, India in 1938. The two following quotes represent the frustration with subsidized church-planting methods that caused dependency even after fifty to one hundred years:"It is futile to expect a Church to develop more than a flabby, uncertain life on the basis of a generation of external support, as to expect a strong man or woman to result from a similar course of treatment" ("Psychology of Self-Support," 136)."Dependence on alien money violates the most elemental principles of self-respect and patriotism and forfeits the esteem of better-class neighbors in an oriental community" ("Psychology of Self-Support," 142).

However, in recent years these precious lessons are frequently ignored in the mishmash of missions misconceptions. In brief, some contemporary practices are likely to result in non-indigenous churches that are dependent on outside resources and have little chance of reproducing so that the gospel spreads through their people:

- Planting churches in other cultures that have the DNA of our church back home,

- sending money to overseas churches instead of missionaries to the lost,

- forming a team to serve as complete staff for a new church overseas, and

- international church planting that looks like planting across town.

Faith and Finance (Including Foreign)

Christians from more advanced economies are often unaware that their money can undermine indigenous Christianity in other cultures just as deeply as colonialism did. This is especially true when the scale of the respective economies is dramatically different. What seems like a small amount of money to the giver may be more than enough to cause dependency or discourage local giving in the other.

Coming to faith in Christ can have a dramatic impact on the finances of a family, sometimes for the worse. I have seen new believers lose their jobs, be publicly disinherited by their family, thrown out of their home, cheated by their employers, and offered such difficult work for minimal pay that they would likely work themselves to physical breakdown. Faithfulness and courage in the face of such treatment is the first test of new believers' faith before the jury of their unbelieving peers.

In spite of such persecution, it is common for redeemed families to slowly rise economically as faith transforms lives and priorities. Real Jesus followers work hard and reprioritize spending. Biblical values such as working as an expression of devotion to God, living morally, taking care of family and community, honesty in business dealings, not being dependent on others, and the importance of education for children contribute to family and societal economic health. German sociologist Max Weber recognized this pattern as the "Protestant work ethic"[8] that contributed to the economic advancement of Protestant countries beginning with the Reformation.

One of the most compelling contemporary accounts of the economic benefits of Protestant faith comes from Niall Ferguson, a preeminent contemporary historian who happens to be an atheist. Ferguson agrees with Weber that Protestant faith has transformed personal and community economies. For Ferguson, it is not only the biblical value of work and savings, but literacy, high trust in other believers, and the concept of judgment inspiring honesty, all of which are economically beneficial qualities. He renamed this the "Protestant word ethic."[9] Ferguson cites China as a recent example of Christianity transforming economics. He connects China's recent economic rise with the rapid growth of Christianity, which added stable hard-working labor and more honest Christian businessmen. These benefits of Christian faith arise from within the lives of those who believe and not from outside resources.

Donald McGavran, one of the most influential missiologists of the twentieth century, studied large movements to Christ in South Asia and noted that new Christian communities often experienced a rise in economic status. However, McGavran described an important difference between 1) the "redemption" of family finances, which comes from deep faith in Christ and is as infinitely reproducible as the gospel, and 2) "lift," which he defined as the benefits offered to new believers in terms of social services, education, and employment. Unlike redemption, lift is limited by the budget of outside funding.[10] Lift can also undermine the reproducibility of redemption in two ways: a) it often separates the believers from their community, which shuts down evangelism, and b) it can subvert pure faith if worldly benefits are too closely linked to people coming to Christ.

It is amazing that an early German sociologist analyzing Reformation Europe, a Scottish historian looking at contemporary China, and an American missions scholar looking at what caused churches to grow

---

8. Max Weber is the father of modern sociology and coined this phrase in 1905. His insight into how Protestantism influenced the growth of the economy is his most important contribution. Weber, *Protestant Ethic and the Spirit of Capitalism*.

9. Ferguson, *Civilization*, 256–88. Ferguson is not a Christian, but as an economist and historian he is certain that Protestant faith inspires economic growth. Ferguson identifies six "killer apps" that were critical to the rise of the West, but states that the Protestant ethic was the "glue" that held them all together (pp. 12–13).

10. McGavran, *Understanding Church Growth*, 296–97.

in South Asia= all saw the same economic reality. *Strong Protestant faith often enhances the socioeconomic status of new believers.*

Misconception 24
In spite of minor complications, outside funding does more good than harm.

One trigger for such change is often the radical impact of hearing the gospel and being called to a personal decision that transforms new believers' lives. Rejecting fatalism, new believers realize their decisions do make a difference, including how they make a living and spend their money. Evidently, *the increase in dignity and self-reliance in the life of new believers is how God intended for his church to support itself within every language and people on the planet.* Unfortunately, no matter how well intentioned, unwisely used outside funding short-circuits this spiritual process. Tragically, it is difficult to rewire a short-circuited Christian community that has lost its spiritual dynamic to reach its own people. In the eighteenth century the English term "rice Christians" was coined from an earlier Portuguese expression to describe the poor who were given a bag of rice for attending church. Giving rice often increased attendance, but, except in the case of disaster, generally undermined sincere faith and made planting an indigenous church less likely.

Today the issue of indigenous churches is still relevant because the majority of global Christians and the unreached are not wealthy. Believers from more advanced economies need to be sensitive to common consequences of outside money used in missions. These are unintended consequences of outside funding (OF) that are common around the world:

1. OF unintentionally stimulates materialism instead of Christianity.

2. OF steals shepherds from their sheep and sometimes the whole flock.

3. OF can make poor, but happy, people begin to feel dissatisfied.

4. OF often corrupts pure motives of people who were already serving with joy.

5. OF can draw men's faith away from God and toward other men.

6. OF steals dignity and initiative from local believers.

7. OF, whether in large or small amounts, can hinder spiritual reproduction.

8. OF creates denominational hierarchies based on fundraising rather than spiritual life.

9. OF can put churches on welfare that results in learned dependence and helplessness.

10. OF sometimes undermines true spiritual service and partnership.

11. OF often ruins good relationships between the givers and recipients.

12. OF causes intense jealousy between the recipients and their neighbors.

13. OF may upend indigenous ministry in the surrounding area.

14. OF hardens the local community that suspects local believers sold out for money.

Outside givers are often unaware of these consequences and walk away feeling satisfied that they were able to help.

Carefully Consider What You Are Communicating

My coworker Steve and I were visiting a creative access country to explore opportunities to expand our agency's ministry. For several years, colleagues had been visiting the country looking for partners and visa options and some of their new friends had asked to meet with us. We sat down to drink tea with six wonderful brothers in Christ that morning, one older gentleman and five of his protégés.

The older man was the "founder," who began to tell us the story of their network of churches. As a young man he had gone to America to get a missions-focused education, then returned to his homeland and began to do evangelism, discipleship, and church planting. For two decades the work progressed into multiplication. Tens of thousands of Buddhist/animists professed faith in Christ and were baptized into hundreds of new churches. This humble servant of God captivated us for almost an hour as he recounted his fruitful life and the work of God in their midst. Here was a wonderful example of an Asian network of churches that grew up completely on local resources and dependence on God.

As he talked about the churches, the younger men showed us growth graphs so we could visualize it. We saw that the steep upward growth curve ended suddenly several decades earlier. Since then, the chart showed a plateau and more recently a decline. The chart itself was silently screaming the question, so I asked, "Sir, what happened the year the growth stopped abruptly?" The silence in the room was deafening until he told us a group of foreign pastors had visited and pledged to provide pastoral support to supplement the income pastors got from their poor churches. Then he explained that from that day they could not keep planting churches and training new pastors because the pastoral support did not increase. They quit growing because they lacked more foreign subsidy.

We had been quietly listening to the story, but at this point I had to ask another obvious question: "What exactly did you lack when you were growing so fast without foreign subsidy?" I do not think that anyone had asked that question, because the founder hesitated a moment before looking up and answering firmly, "Absolutely nothing. We lacked absolutely nothing." As he bowed his head in grief, I saw relief in the eyes of the younger men.

As we continued to talk, they asked us two important questions. The first question was whether they needed to change their name to "Baptist" in order for us to work with them. We assured them that, although their beliefs were very similar, they did not need to change their name. The second question would have been surprising if we had not heard their story. They asked us if we could work alongside them without offering them money. Steve and I assured them that we knew the danger of outside funding and that we would not attempt to subsidize their churches. Our hope was to be spiritual partners who, if anything, help them get back on their own feet to bring the good news to their people and the surrounding ethnic groups.

Steve and I had previously seen subsidy steal initiative, destroy dignity, and develop dependency. The foreign pastors who graciously offered to send pastoral subsidy meant well but had no idea of unintended eternal consequences. This is why all of us involved in international missions should learn to think carefully about the messages we are sending when we use outside funding or other forms of assistance.

Analyzing Our Confused Message

Let's practice analyzing messages sent in real life mission examples.

- How about those volunteers building houses in Mexico? I have asked numerous people about the message this sends and usually hear, "They know we really love them." OK for that family, perhaps, but what about the neighborhood or village? If the person getting a new house is a Christian, then the neighbors know they might get a house too if they join the local church. If the person is not a believer but is told the gospel while the house is going up, then the neighbors might also be open to hearing if you build them a house! Do the volunteers intend to make evangelism in that place far more difficult?

- A volunteer team did a humanitarian project in a Buddhist country without clearly declaring why they were doing it. They hoped to show the people God's love, but the community was not thinking about the foreign concepts of God or selfless love. My missionary friend asked some neighbors what the volunteers were doing and the answer was, "These are very good people who are earning better karma for their next life." Did the volunteers intend to show those people that they are good Buddhists?

- A team of foreigners came to construct a church building in Asia. The volunteers, the materials, and the design all came from outside. The sweating volunteers assumed they were exemplifying Christ's love to the community. However, numerous men watching the proceedings openly complained that these foreigners were very selfish, because at that time in the agricultural cycle most of them would have helped raise the building for a thirty-cent rice meal. Did they intend to culturally appear so selfish and to segregate the village from the project and the church?

- A successful Asian Christian businessman asked me if it was true that pastors in a neighboring country were only paid $25 a month. When I affirmed that this might be true for many, he graciously offered to provide a higher salary to twenty or more of them. I asked him two questions: a) What if $25 is the average income of the members of those churches and, if so, do you think the pastor should be the richest man among them? b) What if a foreigner attended our church next Sunday and offered to provide our pastor with a $150,000 salary? He was so incensed by that question that with a flushed face he declared that our church should support our own pastor. After I said nothing and let his own words sink in, he nodded in agreement.

- A group of house churches doubled every year for five straight years, resulting in several hundred churches and thousands of new believers and baptisms. A missionary unconnected to the work sought out several of the pastors and told them that house churches are not legitimate because they do not have church buildings and a fully supported pastor. He raised funds from his supporting churches and "bought" forty churches by constructing cement buildings and giving $1,000 per year per pastor. The message his church back home got was that he was an amazing missionary who could report forty churches in his first term. The message those forty pastors got was that they now had a new patron. Most importantly, the message that the large group of reproducing house churches got was to stop reproducing, which they successfully accomplished immediately.

- A respected foreign pastor was invited to teach a conference overseas for leaders in a growing network of new churches. He used the same style of scholarly explanation and original-language word studies that his well-educated congregation loved back home. He was excited to use his teaching gift in missions; the local leaders were awed by his unique knowledge. However, he did not like the simple meeting facilities, so he asked his church to sponsor the next meeting. They paid each participant's transportation and housed and fed them in a hotel they could have never afforded. By the second year, this annual conference was the only training the local pastors wanted to attend. Other trainings by national leaders have dried up for lack of interest, but every year the foreigner is encouraged by the big crowd at his conference. Did the pastor intend to undermine the process of raising up national network leadership that does not have the resources to financially compete with him?

Misconception 25
As long as our intentions are good we do not have to worry about unintended consequences from our mission efforts.

- A group of missions volunteers serve for a week alongside a local pastor in a developing country. They are impressed by his sincere devotion to his church and the simplicity of his life. In the van on the way to the airport, the volunteers come up with an excess $2,400 they do not need to get home. As they say goodbye to their newly beloved pastor friend, they hand him the money as a love gift. The gift roughly equals the annual amount his church sacrificially raises to support him. On the way home, he begins to plan for multiple teams, which will take approximately 50 percent of his ministry time in the coming years. Did the volunteers intend to make him "their" pastor and contaminate the qualities that impressed them while also discouraging his church from sacrificially supporting him?

- A gracious, godly Asian mission leader asked me to breakfast to hear about their missionaries serving in a part of the world far away. He opened his laptop to show me photos of two large buildings and explained that one was a new $1,000,000 building for the first church they established in that country. He explained that the local people would not be able to provide such an impressive edifice for many years, so his church and other partners did it for them. Then he explained that the second building was the new seminary, constructed for another $1,000,000, to train ministry students in that country. He added, however, with a little frustration, that the people are so poor that his church had to provide full support to coax students to even attend the school and there were still so few because they could not qualify educationally. So, how do you tell this dear brother in Christ that extra-biblical assumptions such as that a church has to have a nice building and leaders must have formal theological education will undermine the planting of reproducing indigenous churches?

Good Stewards

All Christians are called to be good stewards of what God has entrusted to us, and the more we have, the more we are held responsible. Tragically, there are a lot of well-intentioned missions misconceptions related to the use of outside funding that are counterproductive. As noted, integrating humanitarian work with clear gospel witness is a powerful model of cross-cultural evangelism. However, ongoing support of communities, churches, and ministries will harm the spiritual health and ministry focus of those groups. There is a growing stream of contemporary missions that is committed to sending our money instead of sending our messengers to the nations. Hundreds of millions of dollars flow each year to ministries in less developed nations.[11] That flow is making it harder in many countries for missionaries to find local partners who want to establish reproducing indigenous churches. ("Supporting an indigenous church or leader" is an oxymoron). I have fostered relationships with potential partners who could not get over expectations of financial support, which I take as a clear sign to look elsewhere. Just as some countries develop a "helpless beggar" mentality, so do some Christian communities.[12]

Here are some considerations and recommendations about stewardship of what God has given us.

1. Outsiders, including Westerners, often assume that the people they are ministering to are poor and lack resources. It may be that their socioeconomic status is closer to the global average than the missions team's. Local people who look poor to us almost always have great expertise to live and function in their context. When we begin with the assumptions that our wealth, technology, organizational ability, and amazing spirituality are the answer to their problems, it is most likely we are going to do more harm than good, no matter how we go about it.[13] Be careful that your team does not come home feeling great because you raised yourselves by lowering the people you "served."

2. There are constant crises around the world such as war, famine, drought, flood, earthquake, typhoon, etc. Crisis victims need immediate help, but this aid is benefited by expertise and good preparation. When someone is hungry by their standards and not ours, we should feed them, if possible. However, within a short period of time we need to get beyond the crisis mode and work *with* them

11. Recent reports and lawsuits have raised public awareness that hundreds of millions of dollars given for this purpose through a famous channel of funds to Asia have likely not been spent as promised.

12. Lederleitner, *Cross-Cultural Partnerships* deals with the misunderstandings, different expectations, conflict, and broken relationships that arise from outside funding of ministries around the world. The great disappointment to me is that many Christians now equate international kingdom partnerships with financial relationships.

13. Palmer, *So You Want to Dig a Well in Africa?* analyzes common myths about service projects.

to empower them to feed themselves. Otherwise, we do long-term harm by creating dependency that both sides will eventually despise.[14]

3. If you want to help a community that is relatively poor, then prioritize high-value projects that can help willing families or the whole community. If the community does not have clean water close by, then that should be a high priority. Clean water is vital to health and growth. There are also simple ways to train people to produce better food for their families by growing gardens or raising small animals when there is natural feed available. If there is a high rate of illiteracy, then teaching people to read opens the door to helpful information. This is especially powerful if you teach mothers to read using basic public health information.

4. One of the best ways to help a community is to help them build capital to escape the domination of the wealthy (Prov 22:7). In many cases, $25–100 can supply key equipment or free people from middlemen, which empowers them to meet their needs and increase family income. However, doing this involves training, working closely with local people over time, and developing a locally governed organization that is responsible for the resources. Some have been successful with small loans paid back to the community, while others have found savings groups to be more effective in assisting people in making a living while avoiding deeper dependence. Don't overlook the possibility that women may be better at participating in this kind of program than men. When done well, savings groups or micro-loans break dependency, build dignity, and empower the people to meet their own needs.

5. Never subsidize a local church. Paying the pastor or giving relief to the congregation, except in an emergency, will certainly result in a weakened church that may not sustain itself and reproduce. Subsidy sometimes results in increased numbers, but it almost always prevents the thirty-, sixty-, and one-hundred-fold multiplication of believers and churches that God intends to reach whole nations (Matt 13:8).[15]

14. Corbett and Fickert, *When Helping Hurts*; see pp. 103–22 for a helpful overview of "Relief, Rehabilitation, and Development."

15. I believe that it is biblically legitimate to support overseas cross-cultural missionaries from other people groups, but many of those who receive such support are

Remember that love—informed and tough rather than sentimental—is far better for guiding mercy ministries than guilt. Guilt just dumps cash and walks away relieved, even if it adds to the problems. Love demands that we know the people, study methods of helping, and do what empowers them to help themselves. Real love should build dignity and self-reliance in the lives of those receiving it.

Pioneer churches that are a) functionally indigenous, b) spiritually dynamic, c) biblically sound, d) culturally relevant, and e) organizationally reproducible are most likely to glorify God by impacting their people. Paul's warning about the love of money causing all kinds of evil (1 Tim 6:5–10) is relevant to overseas church planting because outside funding often destroys indigeneity, draws dependence away from God, distracts from biblical truth, smells of foreignness, and often adds extra-biblical elements that make church reproduction unlikely.

Questions to Consider

1. Have you ever considered the difference in an autonomous indigenous church (self-supporting, self-governing, self-propagating) versus a church supported, led, and run by cultural outsiders? How does this important distinction affect the way that missions is done?

2. This chapter discusses how outside funding given with sincere hearts to help can sometimes be a hindrance to new believers and/ or indigenous churches. The difference between redemption and lift is discussed. How does this understanding impact the perspective you have on the ways that missions is supported and done?

3. There are multiple places in this chapter where different dangerous practices for supporting indigenous churches are identified. Do any of these examples ring close to home for you? Is there anything that you might need to reconsider through the content of this chapter?

4. Consider what messages you, as an individual or as a local church, want to pass on to those you are supporting and partnering with in other cultural contexts. Is there anything that needs to change in order for that message to be more clearly expressed?

---

actually local church pastors instead of pioneer cross-cultural gospel missionaries. That is not missions; it is subsidy.

5. Some real-life missions examples are included that should be analyzed regarding the confused messages given. Which of these examples stands out the most to you? Why?

6. Of the considerations and recommendations given at the end of the chapter, which do you need to respond to in order to love indigenous churches well? What is a short-term immediate response? What is a long-term response? Whom can you share this with for accountability?

Chapter 9

Movements to Christ

SADRACH'S MINISTRY RESULTED IN tens of thousands of Muslims turning to Christ and gathering into churches from 1870 to 1920. He used an indigenous social network among Quranic teachers to get the gospel quickly to thousands of people, then kept connection with the growing network of churches through visits, letters, and leadership conferences every thirty-five days. Churches built their own meeting places (and often rebuilt them when they were burned down) and had bivocational, informally trained pastors. Sadrach's unusual gifting as an evangelist, teacher, and leader was important, but the whole community was sharing their faith in ever-expanding social circles. Sadrach's network was the best movement among Muslims in the first 150 years of the Protestant missions movement. His work exhibited many characteristics of movements to Christ throughout history because believers, disciples, and churches were reproducing themselves. In this chapter, a "movement" is the rapid reproduction of believers, disciples, and churches within a particular socioethnic group.[1]

In order to facilitate such movements, missionaries may need to prioritize the pioneer evangelizing and discipling that was evident in

1. This kind of reproducing Christianity has been called a "people movement" (because the gospel spreads quickest through social relationships within a particular socioethnic group), a "discipleship movement" (because disciples making disciples is how it occurs), and a "church-planting movement" (because biblical disciples are gathered into churches).

the nine movements from individual converts that McGavran described (mentioned in chapter 7). Another pattern of missionary involvement happens when the missionary finds a group of churches that have not reproduced in generations, but with the right training and encouragement then multiply to reach hundreds or thousands of churches. There are multiple examples of this approach taking place around the world today.

Kingdom Growth and Our Response

Jesus used parables to describe the mysterious growth potential of God's kingdom. Mark 4 is primarily composed of three of those parables. The Parable of the Soils (vv. 1–25) explains that kingdom seed can multiply a hundred-fold, but it has to fall in the right soil. The Parable of the Seed (vv. 26–29) emphasizes that seeds grow in ways we do not understand or control, but that can produce a large harvest in time. The Parable of the Mustard Seed (vv. 30–32) emphasizes that even a small seed has potential to grow into a large plant that provides shade for many. As God created seeds to mysteriously grow and produce something much larger than their seminal stage, his kingdom was intended to grow in the same way. We should be delighted when kingdom seeds multiply into much fruit!

Misconception 26
Missions reports of amazing response are likely unsubstantiated and the result of shoddy methods.

It is not unusual for Christians in established churches, even those that are the legacy of a movement, to express skepticism and criticism of reports about such rapid growth. We are hesitant to believe in something we have not experienced ourselves. Common objections are a) that reports seem to imply that clever human techniques can produce spiritual results, b) that reporters must be lax or untruthful in reporting numbers of believers and churches, and c) that missionaries appear to be neglectful of church health and pastoral preparation, assuming those things take a very long time. The overall assumption is that something that happens quickly must be badly done. It is ironic that in biology rapid reproduction is viewed as a sign of health, but in ecclesiology it is suspected to be a sign of illness.

Lessons Learned from Early Surveys of Mass Movements

These objections and questions are not new; they have been surfacing for over a century as large movements to Christ have been reported, especially in India. Indian Christians, missions agencies, donors, and even newly appointed missionaries have raised objections or skepticism about any work that produced abundant fruit! Partly in response to such criticism, the National Christian Council worked with missions agencies to carry out the "first critical survey of mass movements," beginning in 1928.[2] The survey was done with technical research expertise and involved both Indian Christians and veteran missionaries. Ten different movements composed of people from the lower half of Indian society, representing numerous languages and castes, who came to Christ through the ministry of various denominations were chosen for study. The movements ranged in size from a few thousand to over 250,000 believers. Surveyors conducted intensive interviews of thousands of Christian families regarding their social, economic, and spiritual lives before and after becoming Christians. The researchers found undeniable proof that these movements were not only real, but they represented 80 percent of the fruit of Protestant missions in the country.[3]

Believers coming to Christ in large social groups within a single identifiable caste or social segment is the norm for Indian Christianity. Not only are they the norm, but these believers exhibited a stronger Christian influence in their lives than those Christians who came to Christ as individuals and had been extracted from their sociocultural community. Movement converts had a deeper understanding of biblical faith, experienced social transformation, improved their economic life, were viewed as less Western by their neighbors, were healthier, were more often financially independent, were more likely sending children to school, and their churches were more often self-supporting.[4] Those

---

2. Pickett, *Christian Mass Movements in India*, 5.

3. Pickett, *Christian Mass Movements in India*, 303. After forty years of studying movements, McGavran declared that the majority of Christians in Asia, Africa, and Oceania are the descendants of mass movement believers. McGavran, *Understanding Church Growth*, 336. My own family's Christian heritage developed from movements among Celts, Anglo-Saxons, and Danes over a thousand years ago and by Protestant movements over the last four hundred years.

4. Picket, *Christian Mass Movements in India*. This summary is taken from over three hundred pages of information and analysis found in the book, which deserves a

are overwhelming signs that movement believers were more mature and deeper in their faith than other believers in India at that time.

Misconception 27
Believers in fast-growing movements are more likely to be shallow in their faith and spiritually immature.

The initial survey was followed by another slightly different study in early 1936. A large survey project studied missions results across middle India by including both areas of rapid growth and those with very little growth. Statistics showed that 134 mission "stations" in this large area were growing about as fast as the birthrate—12 percent per year. However, eleven stations were growing at an average of 200 percent, mostly from multiple adult baptisms. This time the purpose of the study was not just to describe movements, but to try to identify why some ministries were so much more fruitful.[5]

The study showed that the number and faithfulness of the missionaries had little influence on whether a movement began or not. However, *how the missionaries carried out their mission was critical.* For instance, beginning with primary schools or with famine relief was actually a negative factor in facilitating a movement. Helping extract converts physically or financially from their villages was a definite negative factor because every movement studied began with an individual or small group who believed, was baptized, and then stayed in community to share their faith. Sometimes it took years of witness, but eventually the believers began to see large numbers of their people turn to Christ from their testimony.

Misconception 28
How we go about the missions task has little effect on the eventual results.

---

full reading.

5. Pickett, McGavran, and Singh, *Christian Missions in Mid India*, 1–3. One reason these studies are so valuable is that most movements today occur in sensitive places, which increases difficulty, although contemporary in-depth assessments are being done.

The study affirmed that missionaries should view every believer as a miracle of God who can be equipped to share the gospel immediately with his/her people. Gospel witness should focus on the people or segment from which believers are coming. All ministries should focus on establishing reproducing local churches. Witnessing should be a basic expectation of discipleship, even before baptism. When a small group of believers exists, special attention should be given to their immediate discipleship and to their witness. The most important factor in their discipleship is to establish a new pattern of life and corporate worship within the first month after baptism![6]

Sadly, the majority of missions teams working in that part of India had carried out their mission in some way that appeared to have undercut such gospel saturation and church reproduction.

1. Providing houses, jobs, or financial assistance to new believers to help them escape from their angry community may seem to be compassionate, but it effectively cut off relationships and evangelism. In fact, this made it much harder to win more of that people group.

Misconception 29
It takes years of development before local believers can significantly contribute to the ministry of their church.

---

2. Most missions teams did not equip, empower, and encourage believers from the lower rungs of society to win their people to Christ, even when the evidence clearly showed them to be the most responsive. Many missionaries, mostly from the upper levels of society back home, hoped to win more upper-caste people to Christ and were worried the lower classes would offend them. There was also a tendency to depend on professional local and foreign evangelists instead of the new believers to share their faith. Ironically, these

---

6. Pickett, *Christian Mass Movements in India*, 240. "Probably the most critical month with most mass-movement groups is that immediately following baptism. Successful pastors and superintendents told us that they can do more to establish Christian worship and standards of conduct in that month than in any subsequent year, and that if the opportunity is not seized then, the task becomes increasingly difficult the longer it is neglected."

approaches failed to bring in both the upper caste and the lower castes to Christ. The greatest number of high-caste people to believe were in places where lower-caste people were being transformed by Christ in large numbers.

3. Colonial missionaries and their paid Christian partners often viewed their poor, formally uneducated converts as helpless people who needed to be "nursed" or "coddled." It was commonly assumed they needed many years of being ministered to before they could contribute significantly to ministry.[7] The study showed this attitude created dependency and helplessness, which shackled the simple, powerful, Spirit-directed ministry of transformed believers that is the engine of every movement.

4. Missionaries who introduced extra-biblical elements or traditions from church models back home were likely to spoil reproduction in their work. New churches composed of new believers must provide their own places to meet and need to be led by their own people instead of more experienced outsiders.[8]

Spontaneous Expansion

These precious missiological lessons were not only evident in India. Missionary Roland Allen wrote about the mission patterns and response in China that he saw around the year 1900. He noted that Spirit-directed, unorganized, and unsanctioned witness by unpaid local believers, the irresistible attraction of the transformed community, and the resulting new churches were a "spontaneous expansion" of the church in China that was healthier and more reproducible than what resulted from traditional

7. This is still a major point of contention among established churches where men prepare for years before entering formal leadership. Paul's instruction to not confirm a new convert as a leader (1 Tim 3:6) was given for a context where the Ephesian church may have been a decade old. In his instructions to Titus on Crete, Paul left out this qualification, perhaps because the church there was composed of newer converts (Titus 1:7–9). When Paul and Barnabas appointed elders in Lystra, Iconium, and Antioch (Acts 14:23), the most mature of those leaders were probably younger in their faith than a year. Paul only ministered in Thessalonica for three to eight weeks, but when he wrote the believers there, he considered them a church (1 Thess 1:1). That church may not yet have had a pastor and may have been functioning with informal local leaders that were very young in their faith. It seems the principle was to look to the most mature local believers available, even in the earliest stage of the church.

8. Pickett, *Christian Missions in Mid India*, 99–111.

missions work.[9] Allen described two theories or approaches to mission that are familiar even now.

> Misconception 30
> The best way to win the nations is to start fewer, purer, and more mature churches like ours back home.

a. Develop a very established, organized, and educated church that will later begin to expand and reproduce. This usually resulted in a "complete absence of any zeal for the conversion of others." If it is thought that the church can only function and grow through this established model, then it must go through a long period of education. Allen noted that where formal education had gone on the longest, the zeal of the church for propagation of the gospel was weakest.

b. The spontaneous propagation of the gospel must be the work of local believers from the very beginning. Churches must be indigenous from the beginning, or else how will they plant new churches? These new churches must have their own leaders and must worship and observe the ordinances from the beginning. The churches should be simple, without complicated organization, if they are to reproduce.[10]

Allen observed that spontaneous expansion is actually hindered by missionaries when they assume new believers need their constant "nursing," hesitate to entrust the sharing of the gospel to those without formal training, bring in more outside teachers instead of training local believers to read and teach, and give the impression that the church is dependent on outside financial or personnel resources and cannot function and grow on its own.[11]

It is striking that missionaries working in such disparate contexts came to the same clear conclusions about common approaches to missions.

---

9. Allen, *Spontaneous Expansion*, 6–17.

10. Allen, *Spontaneous Expansion*, 18–31.

11. Allen, *Spontaneous Expansion*, 32–40.

Recent Observations Regarding Contemporary Movements

In June 2018 I joined five other SBC seminary professors to spend nine days alongside missionaries to observe work in an Asian setting where multiple movements have occurred with many thousands of reproducing churches. Our objective was to see for ourselves the kind of work that had raised so much skepticism and objection back home. After a couple of days of orientation, we broke into three separate teams to observe new churches in different areas/networks and hear testimonies from about fifty local church planters and network leaders.

It was inspiring and humbling to hear the testimonies of men, women, and teenagers transformed by the gospel and being so fruitful in their new faith. Many heard the gospel for the first time, quickly recognized the gift of God and believed, were baptized, and joined in Bible reading and worship with others. They immediately started sharing their faith with friends and family, which often necessitated their discipling newer believers within a few weeks of their own conversion, and then gathered those believers into churches according to the pattern of Acts.

At the end of our trip, the six theological educators summarized our findings (in bold below):

- **We collectively witnessed an extraordinary movement of God in different locations**.

  - This resulted in prevalent ethos/DNA of indigenous churches multiplying at different rates.

  - We heard multiple testimonies of healings and miracles.

- **We were privileged to witness foreign/local servants exercising God-called ministries**. Regarding the character of workers observed:

  - Local leaders exhibited transformed lives, dedication to the task, and spiritual fruitfulness.

  - Missionaries exhibited a patient urgency, teachability, and dependence on God to cause growth.

- **There was clear evidence in diverse contexts of the Bible displayed as the ultimate authority for faith and practice.**

  - Church worship services were centered around a biblical text.

  - Local leaders develop doctrinal statements as needed based on exploring Scripture together.

- **Leaders show commitment to evaluate and work toward biblical ecclesiology (healthy church).**

  - Both missionaries and local leaders use practical diagnostic tools and maps to track and coach the churches.

  - Beyond the fourth generation, leaders check/coach to strengthen the DNA of new churches.

- **Missionaries have significant personal investment (mentoring) throughout all phases of the core missionary task.**

  - Missionaries spend extensive time mentoring local leaders, from the local house church leaders up to large network leaders. This was often sixty to ninety days a year.

- **Missionaries and network leaders give specific attention to train emerging pastors to be able 1) to teach and 2) to refute false teaching/beliefs.**

  - "Foundations" training involves bringing new and potential pastors together to study biblical passages and practice teaching them.[12]

  - "Confessions" is a process used to answer contextual doctrinal questions through intensive group study of relevant passages. Network leaders use the resulting doctrinal statements to coach house church leaders to counter false teachings.[13]

---

12. See *Foundations for Emerging Leaders.*
13. See *Confessing the Faith within Church Planting Movements.*

- **Both locals and foreigners desire various approaches to theological education (2 Tim 2:15). There is an emerging aspiration for indigenous theological leaders.**

  - Missionaries are focused on starting churches and movements but are also committed to strengthening.

  - Some networks are exploring training from national theological programs for their better-educated leaders.

- **There is expectation, practice, and accountability leading to intentional evangelistic witness and disciple-making.**

  - New believers are trained to share their faith with multiple family members and friends from the beginning.

  - In group settings there is accountability for sharing that makes evangelism a core ethos.

  - The broad multiplication of believers, witnesses, and disciplers is the driving force behind these movements.

- **There is evidence of cross-cultural engagement and mission (unreached people groups [UPGs]/unengaged unreached people groups [UUPGs].**

  - Some believers from one religious background are trained and engaging other religious groups.

  - Several young networks are sacrificially supporting their own international missionaries.

My personal observation from this trip and other glimpses into movements is that they are powered by the gospel, especially where it is both *news* and *good*. Hearers realize that Jesus is a treasure hidden in a field and gladly sell all they have to buy in (Matt 13:44). This kingdom analogy explains so much of what subsequently happens to produce a movement, especially when the treasure finders don't keep it to themselves. New believers in the network I visited are trained to share their faith with twenty relatives and friends within the first months of faith. More witnesses, disciples, and simple churches sprout from that massive seed sowing. I honestly wonder what exactly critics back home want to stop![14]

14. Two outstanding resources about contemporary church planting movements

From Bottom to Top of the Pyramid

Some critics of movements have a hard time envisioning how something could multiply like a movement because they only know their own context, where Christianity has been long established. They assume movements function like church life as they know it, so they try to imagine such multiplication planned and budgeted from the top down. Power within a movement comes from heaven, but it mostly moves from bottom to top. Strong leadership and vision are imperative, but we use the word "movement" to describe a growing pattern of radically changed lives at the grassroots level. It is like a rising tide—wise missionaries are not pumping the water; they are working hard to not block up the flow and to ride the wave.[15] In the figure below, the left side of the triangle lists tasks that missionaries work on, but quickly turn over to local partners as well.

Working "up" a movement:

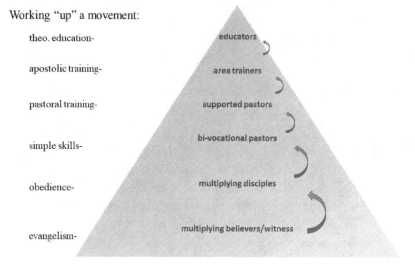

theo. education-

apostolic training-

pastoral training-

simple skills-

obedience-

evangelism-

educators

area trainers

supported pastors

bi-vocational pastors

multiplying disciples

multiplying believers/witness

Movement Triangle

---

are: Garrison, *Church Planting Movements*; and John and Coles, *Bhojpuri Breakthrough*.

15. To visualize a common critical mistake, place your hand over the portion of the pyramid just below the words "supported pastors." When the missionaries or local believers act as if the lower half of the pyramid is not legitimately church, then the work will not multiply into a movement.

Not Just Whether, but How We Do Missions

How we do missions is an important factor in the results we get. Yes, choosing to obey Christ and join God in his mission to the nations is a critical decision. Yes, staying focused on the core mission task of evangelism, discipleship, and church planting is essential. However, we have seen that committed missionaries who focus on the core mission task might tweak their methods in a way that aligns them with God's purpose to multiply believers, disciples, and churches. So, how can we tweak our efforts to maximize the potential for facilitating a movement to Christ?

1. *Pray intensely.* The foundation of a movement methodology should be continual, intense prayer by the missionaries, their local co-workers, and their partners. This task is God's task and only he can convict of sin, transform new believers, call and raise up leaders, and start the process over again. Everything eternal is from God, but missionaries often exhibit a pragmatic activism. Their busyness can be an excuse for not spending hours in prayer. Where God is moving miraculously, his servants are praying fervently. They need to regularly entrust their lives and ministry into his hands. They need to seek God's presence and align with how he is working at the moment.

2. *Sow immensely.* "How can they believe in one of whom they have not even heard?" (Rom 10:14, NIV). It is no accident that Jesus described the sent ones as declaring good news to the whole world. A common missions mistake is to settle for planting seeds in a small plot. Yes, we should do that, but we should not be content when only a few hear. Seed can be broadcast through multiplying personal witness in multiple social networks among a people, through the use of powerful films about Jesus, and through the use of tracts, SD cards, and other media that are easily distributed. Paul's words used in another context still seem appropriate here: "He who sows sparingly will also reap sparingly" (2 Cor 9:6). It is powerful when the gospel becomes common gossip.

3. *Harvest intentionally.* This seems so obvious that we forget it has been neglected in missions history. When the gospel is broadcast widely, the sowers should be looking for any sign of responsiveness and focus attention there. If you stumble on a vein of gold, even in an unexpected place, then dig deep to follow the vein. The

responsive are usually not the English-speaking globalized minority, but regular people and the lowly. Equip new believers to share the gospel with everyone they know! Learn from them how the gospel has impacted them, so you can be more effective in bringing in the harvest.

4. *Disciple infectiously.* Failure here is one of the most common factors in undermining a movement. Discipleship should be immediate, intense, and empowering. When new believers lead their family and neighbors to Christ, in most cases they should be the ones who do much of the discipling, even when they are only a few weeks or months ahead in their own faith. If disciples are not discipling, then they are not really disciples, are they? So, discipleship must be simple and reproducible. Believers should immediately obey the Lord by reading the Bible (or hearing stories), sharing their faith, and gathering for worship on their own. This is the opposite of how established churches usually do it, but the lack of fruit from those usual methods is often obvious.[16]

5. *Congregate immediately.* This is counterintuitive for those who grew up in large, established churches. Teach about the church quickly and get the believers, even if only a few, to start acting like church (Acts 2). These groups meet wherever they can and are led from within because outsiders are equipping them to do so. At this point, leadership is shared and functional, not positional or professional. That means it needs coaching but is reproducing. I do not count two or three as a church, but they should begin acting like the church they can grow into.[17]

6. *Function indigenously.* The resources for space, leadership, decision-making, outreach, and ongoing support are within the new community of faith. The resources are in the harvest! Outsiders may advise and coach, but the new believers should see this as their church. History shows that outside resources poured in early do not usually result in indigenous reproducing churches later. The primary

16. Dent, "Decisive Discipleship."

17. In Matt 18:15–20 Jesus speaks about his presence with two or three gathered together in his name. He also makes some distinction between taking an issue to two or three witnesses and taking it to the whole church. Although there are similarities between two or three gathered in his name and the church, Jesus assumes the church is larger.

resources are the Bible and the Holy Spirit, which these believers have already. Missionaries and national partners must avoid passing on extra-biblical expectations, values, and models of church.

7. *Lead inconspicuously.* This is difficult if the missionary loves to be at the forefront, is motivated by public acclaim, or simply has an overbearing personality. Facilitating a movement is hard work, and often comes at personal cost. It is usually harder to coach others to teach Romans or speak at a network gathering than to do it yourself. This does not mean missionaries have to be invisible, but they must prioritize equipping and encouraging national partners from beginning to end. Movements begin to mature when local leaders are training the workers and other trainers.

8. *Equip inspirationally.* Equip leaders at their level of need and ability, rather than yours. Setting up a seminary too soon for a few leaders may deflate the vast majority of potential leaders who cannot attend for a variety of reasons. Equip for practical skills that empower them to lead worship, share the gospel, coach a discipler, etc. Use a discovery Bible teaching method that results in their increased confidence in the Bible and the Holy Spirit rather than awe in an outsider's great knowledge or gifting! Expect every leader to pass on what they are learning rather than keeping it to protect their position.

9. *Reproduce infinitely.* Making believers, disciples, and churches as quickly and as broadly as possible has eternal implications for the nations. Leaders may get tired, or the wrong influences can enter the networks, or social conditions may change, so urgency and focus are important. Some missionaries, and even local leaders, may advocate for slowing it all down. If that happens, inertia often makes it difficult to get back to rapid multiplication. If we hope tomorrow is the day of salvation, we will likely miss part of the harvest. The longer a movement continues within a people group, the greater the percentage of that people who become believers. That should be impetus enough for all to run the race with endurance.

10. *Encourage indefinitely.* Missionaries working with such dynamic local leaders will likely need to change their own priorities and ministry roles over time. This may also result in less direct involvement in the movement as it grows. I advise missionaries in that situation to keep contact and continue to encourage the local leaders, because

there will never be another influence like them. Encouragement is a primary task from the beginning until the movement is quite developed. Paul maintained contact with churches over time and watched to make sure that false teachings did not penetrate the work.

Keeping the End in Mind

One of my favorite hobbies is kayak fishing. It is fifty-two miles from my garage to the little beach on the Pacific where I push out my kayak. I have to prepare the equipment that makes it more likely my journey will end with fish such as kelp bass, halibut, or shark. When I leave home, there are thousands of potential turns that could lead me away from the water. In fact, if I take a wrong turn one mile from my house, I wind up high and dry in the desert. I have learned I should leave home by 4:30 a.m. if I want to beat rush-hour standstills. I have to keep the end in mind while loading the car, driving to the beach, and all the time I am out in my 'yak.

Sometimes when I get there, the fish do not seem to be biting. I cannot control that, but I try to make the most of the opportunity, because I may need to switch bait, peddle another mile, or patiently fish until the bite picks up. It is my intention to minimize my mistakes and to be ready for fish at any time, while trusting God for the actual results. *I do know that we will not catch fish if we don't have bait in the water.* It is important to decide I am going fishing, but how I go about this task is absolutely critical to the results, even if I do not have control over all the variables. The primary thing that kayak fishing and facilitating a movement have in common is the necessity of keeping the end in mind, working intentionally, and trusting God for the bite.

Jesus told us to proclaim the good news to all creation and to make disciples of all the nations. That is the end we must keep in mind. It took from Genesis 2 to about AD 1800 for the human population to reach one billion, and another 125 years to reach two billion. We are now past eight billion and it only takes about twelve years to add another billion people who need to hear! We may have a higher percentage (10 percent) of earth's population that are evangelical Christians today than at any time in history, but we also have far more lost people to reach than ever before. That is why it is so critical that missions efforts focus on sharing the gospel broadly, discipling more disciplers, and planting reproducing churches. Although outside "sent ones" are critical to getting the process started, there is no doubt that most of the resources for bringing in the harvest are in the harvest now.

Let's say we go overseas and successfully make four disciples (or plant four churches) in a year. If we keep adding four more each year, then at the end of the decade we will have reached forty. Wow, parties in heaven for faithful service! Hopefully, some of those results will reproduce. However, it is possible that we will be further behind than when we started, unless the potential of those new disciples or churches is maximized. In contrast, if we make four reproducing disciples or churches, then the results are breathtakingly different: 4 x 4 x 4 x 4 x 4 x 4 x 4 x 4 x 4 x 4 = 1,048,576. Multiplication quickly outpaces addition, so spiritual fruit that reproduces abundantly is absolutely necessary to accomplish the Great Commission.

The Trapdoor Churches

Years ago a spark ignited kindling when the Bible became available for the first time in the heart language of a large people group. As they read it for the first time, some became dissatisfied with their traditional religious life and began to dream of personal faith in Christ and its communal expression they saw described in the Bible. Some of these new believers boldly proclaimed their faith and began to influence their neighbors. Small groups arose spontaneously that shared this new faith and began to meet secretly as churches. These young churches illegally published and distributed their biblical convictions, even clandestinely tacking them up for public display where they lived. Some leaders further spread awareness of their convictions through public debates with traditional religious leaders.

Not surprisingly, community leaders pushed back hard on this underground movement by mocking the unsophisticated group with no sanctioned worship sites and bivocational pastors with little formal education. Mocking eventually turned into punishing the believers for spreading their biblical message. Persecution focused on the pastors of the underground churches, based on the assumption that the movement would die if they were in prison. A large percentage of pastors in the first generation of the movement died young in dark dungeons from disease and malnutrition.

The threat to pastors resulted in an emphasis on personal Bible study and participation in worship for every believer. Like churches in multiple places around the world today, these persecuted churches quickly learned to keep a low profile by moving their meetings around, arriving individually from different directions, and wearing work clothes when they walked to meetings. Churches assisted pastors in avoiding capture by placing lookouts nearby, building hidden trapdoors for quick escape, meeting in one small home while the pastor taught through the window of an adjacent home, and meeting outside in remote locations. It helped if the pastors were young and spry!

In spite of these difficulties, the number of "trapdoor churches" grew from one to more than fifty in forty years. This nascent movement sounds a lot like movements in various parts of the world today, some of which are growing even faster. These trapdoor churches arose in England in the first half of the 1600s and by the end of that period were beginning to be referred to as "Baptists."

These churches continued to grow over the next one hundred years, but some churches were especially successful in spreading the movement. For instance, in the mid-1700s eight families led by Shubal Stearns moved to the American frontier to establish a new church with sixteen adult members. This group had been deeply impacted by the revivalist, moderately Calvinist, spontaneous, emotionally expressive, and passionately evangelistic First Great Awakening. The church quickly grew to six hundred members in their rural location and members were taught and trained to be on mission. Over the next seventeen years, which included the bloody Seven Years' War, this church established new churches for hundreds of miles in every direction. In fact, by 1772 there were forty-two daughter, grand-daughter, and great-granddaughter churches, which produced 125 preachers sent out as itinerant evangelists or pastors for groups of families relocating to plant another church. The passion and vision of this one church maximized the harvest on the frontier while most wealthier and better-educated churches missed it. A great number of churches today are a living legacy of this movement and others like it.[18]

18. For further reading on this movement, see McBeth, *Baptist Heritage*, 21–69, 113–22, 227–35; Finke and Stark, *Churching of America*; and Kidd and Hankins, *Baptists in America*, 77.

Misconception 31
My church is well established, so it could not be a
legacy from a movement.

Growth continued at breathtaking speed as approximately ten thousand believers in 1776 grew to one hundred thousand by century's end and then grew again to almost one million by 1850! I cite this story not because those churches were exceptional, but because they are exemplary. Many denominations around the world have had a movement phase in their history. This story exemplifies that a large portion of Christians today have such a movement in their spiritual heritage, even if they do not realize it. A majority of the world's ethnic groups are still waiting for their own.

Questions to Consider

1. The seminary professors interviewed new believers who were sharing their faith: "they immediately started sharing their faith with friends and family, which often necessitated their discipling newer believers within a few weeks of their own conversion, and then gathered those believers into churches according to the pattern of Acts." Respond to the immediacy of these new believers' witness and sharing. Is that something that you do or do not see in your local context? Why or why not? What would it look like to disciple new believers you know with an intentional immediacy to share their faith?

2. The observation is made that in movements, "hearers realize that Jesus is a treasure hidden in a field and gladly sell all they have to buy in." What has it meant in your own life to recognize the treasure of the gospel? In what areas of your life have you not bought in?

3. How does recognizing the power of a "working 'up' movement" change your perspective and potentially your strategy for missions? See the figure on page [X-REF].

4. How we do missions matters. Ten things are included in this chapter for how we can tweak our efforts. Consider the list below and which

areas of your life God might want to work in you so that you can walk in these things more effectively when given the opportunity.

1. Pray intensely

2. Sow immensely

3. Harvest intentionally

4. Disciple infectiously

5. Congregate immediately

6. Function indigenously

7. Lead inconspicuously

8. Equip inspirationally

9. Reproduce infinitely

10. Encourage indefinitely

5. "Jesus told us to proclaim the good news to all creation and to make disciples of all the nations. That is the end we must keep in mind." In what ways are you keeping the end in mind?

Section 3

Missions in God's Power

GOD INVITES US TO *join him on mission, because he is the only one who can empower us to accomplish it. This mission is a spiritual struggle that cannot be won primarily through our endeavor.*

The five Great Commission statements all end with the promise that we are joining him on this mission and that his power is with us.

- "and lo, I am with you always, even to the end of the age." (Matt 28:20)

- "These signs will accompany those who have believed: in My name they will cast out demons; they will speak with new tongues; they will pick up serpents, and if they drink any deadly poison, it will not hurt them; they will lay hands on the sick, and they will recover." (Mark 16:17–18)

- "And behold, I am sending forth the promise of My Father upon you, but you are to stay in the city until you are clothed with power from on high." (Luke 24:49)

- "And when He had said this, He breathed on them and said to them, 'Receive the Holy Spirit.'" (John 20:22)

- "You will be baptized with the Holy Spirit not many days from now . . . but you will receive power when the Holy Spirit has come upon you." (Acts 1:5, 8)

The three chapters in this section explore who it is that leads and empowers missions. Although missions requires bold steps and decisive action on the part of Christ's followers, it is only possible in God's power. We might be tempted to abstain because we know our weakness and limitations, but in reality the important issue is who God is, not us.

Chapter 10—Power for Sowing

Jesus promised that his Presence—the Holy Spirit—and power will accompany those who go to redeem the nations. The Spirit's power is essential to overcome Satan's resistance in the heart of the potential witness and in the heart of potential believers.

Chapter 11—Discipling in Primal Contexts

Acts provides several examples of how the early church dealt with spiritual challenges in the power of God. These examples can guide missionaries today who disciple new believers in power contexts like those of the early church.

Chapter 12—God's Presence in Missions

Those sent to the nations will likely face obstacles and great difficulties. They can work in confidence that Jesus faced such painful difficulties and that God will never forsake them.

Chapter 10

Power for Sowing

TEN SEMINARY STUDENTS AND I arrived in a Muslim megacity and began acclimating to our surroundings. The team went to bed after our first full day still tired from the flight. The plan for the next morning was to make a formal visit to an Islamic university and spend time with students who wanted to practice English.

The next morning the team gathered for a breakfast of cornflakes, ramen noodles with egg, fruit, and instant coffee. Jon and Fred were rooming together and began to share with the team their experience from the previous night in the room next door to mine. They had talked and prayed for a few minutes before going to sleep, but in the middle of the night they were both awakened at the same time. They described sensing an intruder in their room and having the most overwhelming feeling of alarm and terror. They turned on the light and were surprised there was no visible person, but the unseen spiritual presence was still palpable. They read Scripture and prayed until eventually the spirit left the room. I knew these young men to be level-headed and courageous, but they confessed that it was the most surprising and frightening experience of their lives. I was not completely surprised, because I had previously experienced something similar and I knew demonic attacks commonly happened to missionaries serving in that country.

During our prayer time, the team thanked God for his grace and asked him to protect and lead us during our visit to the university. When we arrived, the English program dean, several professors, and fifty students greeted us warmly. The young university imam also attended just to make sure everything was OK. After some greetings and introductions, each of my students took a group of university students for two and a half hours of English dialogue. As they shared about their lives, I could see that each naturally got to their testimony within fifteen to twenty minutes and conversationally shared the gospel. Not only were these Muslim students not offended, but their facial expressions reflected interest and delight with the experience. Since the majority of local students were female, Jon and Fred wound up alone with the young imam, who was also interested in improving his English.

After the visit, the team debriefed the experience and shared their excitement about what had transpired. Each group had gotten to know each other, with a lot of smiles and laughter interspersed with extensive dialogue about the most important thing in the lives of my students, Jesus. There were many questions and answers and nobody seemed to be offended or angry. Jon and Fred shared that the young imam, Abdullah, was interested to hear what Christians actually believe and expressed complete surprise to hear their explanation of the death and resurrection of *Isa Al Masih*. We all praised God and turned our attention to new ministry opportunities.

Two days later Jon and Fred reported over breakfast another visitation by a spirit intruder to their room. Once again, they both awakened to a presence that brought initial fear, but they rose once more to pray and read Scripture together and the presence departed a second time. As we were getting ready to pray together, Jon got a phone call from Abdullah asking whether they were free to come meet him again. We released them to go back to meet their new friend and prayed that God would speak through them to his heart. Later that day we learned Abdullah told them he could not forget their testimony and wanted to ask more questions because the gospel had caught him off guard. So, Jon and Fred spent several hours with this young influential Muslim leader sharing more details of the good news with him. Abdullah was cautious but showed true interest in this surprisingly compelling gospel message. As we debriefed the day's events later that afternoon, it became obvious that Satan had tried to intimidate the two guys just hours before they had these opportunities to openly share Christ with this now intrigued imam. We praised the Lord and asked him to grow the seed planted in Abdullah's heart.

Several other students had unusual spiritual encounters during that trip like nothing they had experienced before. My family and I had experienced similar encounters over the years and I recognized this common form of attack on potential witness in that unreached environment. Satan does not like to let loose those he holds under his thumb. His power is manifested in different ways in various contexts, but he is always working against the purpose of God in our lives. This story may seem dramatic, and a bit crazy to some,[1] but it reflects an important reality about sharing the gospel with the whole world. Satan will go to great lengths to intimidate and hinder the witnesses.

The Heart of the Witness Is the First Battlefield for the Lost

I came to faith in Christ at the age of sixteen and quickly sensed the Holy Spirit prompting me to talk about Jesus with my classmates. My first couple of attempts to share about Jesus surprised me because there was an unseen barrier that was difficult to cross, as opposed to talking about anything else, including church. Those were my first experiences with the struggle against the enemy for the souls of men. I learned that in order to cross that barrier of doubt, fear, and hesitation, I needed to be spiritually prepared, breath a prayer of submission to God, and by faith jump into the topic of God's love in Christ. Once I'd jumped, the barrier fell behind and I would quickly sense God's power to declare the truth of Jesus, but I did not share as often as I should have because the pushback intimidated me.

Most Christians know they have a responsibility to make disciples, be witnesses, and share the good news with the world. However, many Christians feel the pushback from the enemy, conclude that witness is not their thing, and then rarely, if ever, talk openly about Jesus again. Sadly, that means they learn to ignore the Spirit's prompting in their lives. For me personally, evangelism is not my most prominent gifting, but as one sent to the nations it is an essential part of my calling. This is why

1. It is common for Western believers today to be as influenced by scientific naturalism as the Christian worldview of biblical theism. Biblical theism affirms the following: 1) God is creator and sustainer of all things. 2) Angels and demons interact with humans. 3) God is concerned and involved in our lives. 4) Physical, emotional, mental, and spiritual elements of our lives are all intertwined. 5) God cannot be manipulated or ultimately ignored. 5) Satan is our enemy, but God is greater. It is from this worldview that we must be ready to battle an enemy that lies, blinds, and deceives us and our audience.

connecting to the divine power God provides for sowing the gospel is absolutely essential to the missions task.

In Matthew 16:13–20 Jesus states that the confession that he is "the Christ, the Son of the Living God" is a truth revealed by God himself and is the foundation of the church. He also ties such confession to the spiritual battle between the reign of God and the gates of hell. When Jesus said the gates of hell cannot overcome the church built upon that clear confession, the disciples had no idea that in a short time Jesus himself would burst through those gates on Easter Sunday. All subsequent victories at those gates are possible because Christ won that eternal victory. The gates of hell can neither destroy the church nor continue holding captive those within who hear the confession and come to faith in Christ. When we share Jesus with those under the power of the enemy, we are storming the gates of hell. In fact, it is the Holy Spirit who is fighting this battle; our participation is not the strength or will of man, but gentleness, submission, and courage in the Holy Spirit.

That does not mean Satan will not put up a fight over that confession. When Satan successfully obstructs Christians from being witnesses, then further battles are avoided. He wins in the lives of those who do not hear. Lost people are held in the status quo of spiritual death and submission to the god of this world. This battle in the hearts and minds of believers has eternal consequences daily for the majority of lost people on earth. This spiritual struggle is one reason so many Christians believe the confession personally but rarely share it with others. Satan uses every scheme he can to limit the witness of believers.

Many believers are unprepared for this struggle because they signed on for peace and love and are unaware they are called to be warriors. They may not realize that there are no neutrals in this war and that everyone is either struggling against the reign of Christ or of Satan. Many believers seem unaware of the divine resource God has provided for this battle for the souls of men. Jesus promised that those who take on his Great Commission would not go alone; Jesus would always be with them, the Holy Spirit would come upon them, and divine power would result from that presence. When the Holy Spirit came upon the disciples, their doubts and confusion were transformed to conviction and courageous confession.

> O, do not pray for easy lives. Pray to be stronger men! Do not pray for tasks equal to your powers. Pray for powers equal to your tasks! Then the doing of your work shall be no miracle. But you shall be a miracle. Every day you shall wonder at

yourself, at the richness of life which has come in you by the grace of God.[2]

None of us are saved without the Holy Spirit preparing our hearts and drawing us to Christ. At the moment we believed, our inner new birth was the work of the Holy Spirit. He teaches us the truth about Christ and he bears testimony about Jesus as Lord. He guides us in what to say when our faith is on trial.[3] He is also producing the fruit of the Spirit[4] in our lives that makes our witness attractive in any setting. When a Christian fails to confess Jesus verbally, it is because he has stifled the Holy Spirit who lives within.

In contrast to that failure and our common timidity, Acts describes the early believers as characterized by an interesting quality called *parrhesia*. *Parrhesia* is an ancient Greek compound word that literally means "to say it all." Its earliest usage was to describe the right/freedom/confidence of a citizen of a democratic Greek city to openly speak his opinion when the citizens were gathered (*ekklesia*) to discuss an issue or make a decision. In that sense, it is similar to the concept of "freedom of speech." This quality characterized full citizens in contrast to slaves, foreigners, and visitors, who had no such right.

The confidence "to say it all" developed a different connotation when there was disagreement, open opposition, and negative consequences. In those situations, it conveys more than freedom; it emphasizes courage and boldness to speak out in the face of opposition. It is in that sense that the word appears repeatedly in Acts.[5]

In Acts 4:13, the Jewish leaders were surprised by the apostles' boldness because they were common, uneducated men, but were changed by their time with Jesus. In 4:29–31, the whole church was empowered to declare God's message boldly in the face of a threat because they asked God for courage and were filled with the Holy Spirit. In 14:3 Paul and Barnabas spoke boldly for a long period in Iconium because they sensed a battle at the gates with great response and hostile opposition. These verses show that boldness comes from being with Jesus, depending on his

---

2. Brooks, *Visions and Tasks*, 330. Brooks was a famous nineteenth-century American preacher and author of "O Little Town of Bethlehem."

3. Titus 3:5; John 14:26,;15:26–27; Luke 12:11–12.

4. See Gal 5:22–23. Love, joy, peace, patience, kindness, goodness, faithfulness, gentleness, and self-control are admirable and attractive character traits in every cultural context.

5. Hahn, "Openness, Frankness, Boldness."

strength, and the Holy Spirit taking control of the witness. In fact, the primary sign of the Spirit's influence in Acts is boldness to speak about Jesus. This theme is so prominent in Acts that the book ends with a statement about Paul continuing to proclaim the gospel with unhindered boldness.

Both Paul (Acts 9:27–28) and Apollos (Acts 18:26) began to proclaim Jesus boldly as soon as they came to faith. Neither had spent time with Jesus on earth, but they received the Spirit, who empowered them to courageously declare their new conviction. Perhaps you can remember that initial flame in your heart when you first believed that brought joy, peace, and the awareness of God's presence. It probably lasted until you disobeyed his leading or simply neglected to stay connected to his presence. Think back to the last time you knew the Holy Spirit was leading you and identify when and how that experience came to an end. That is a good place to start resubmitting yourself to the Holy Spirit.

Paul described being filled with the Holy Spirit (Eph 5:18) as an obligation that should be experienced continuously. Although we receive the Holy Spirit the moment we believe, the Christian life means submitting to his leadership repeatedly each day. It is not that we need more of the Holy Spirit, who was poured on us richly (Titus 3:5–6), but that the Holy Spirit needs more of us.

Misconception 32
People without the gift of gab or the spiritual gift of evangelism are unlikely candidates for effective mission proclamation.

The resulting pattern of bold witness is not an expression of unusual personality or even spiritual gifting. *Courageous witness is the direct result of the believer submitting to the leadership and power of the Holy Spirit within him/her.* It probably looks a bit different for an extravert than an introvert, but both find ways to boldly declare the good news of God's love in Jesus Christ. It is available to every believer who seeks to be obedient. It seems likely that Timothy was a bit timid, perhaps because of his youth, but in 2 Timothy 1:7 Paul reminds him that "God has not given us a spirit of timidity, but of power and love and discipline." This bold Spirit empowers the use of our spiritual gifts in ministry. Potential witnesses should prepare for and practice sharing the gospel, identify any demonic lies that hold their tongue, ask the Lord to help them create opportunities, and then obey the Spirit when he prompts them to share.

In a passage about sharing their faith, Paul encourages the Colossians with these words:

> Devote yourselves to prayer, keeping alert in it with an attitude of thanksgiving; praying at the same time for us as well, that God will open to us a door for the word, so that we may speak forth the mystery of Christ, for which I have also been imprisoned; that I may make it clear in the way I ought to speak. Conduct yourselves with wisdom towards outsiders, making the most of the opportunity. Let your speech always be with grace, as though seasoned with salt, so that you will know how you should respond to each person. (Col 4:2–6)

Peter's instructions about witness include some of the same themes:

> Who is there to harm you if you prove zealous for what is good? But even if you should suffer for the sake of righteousness, you are blessed. And do not fear their intimidation, and do not be troubled, but sanctify Christ as Lord in your hearts, always being ready to make a defense to everyone who asks you to give an account for the hope that is in you, yet with gentleness and reverence; and keep a good conscience so that in the thing in which you are slandered, those who revile your good behavior in Christ will be put to shame. (1 Pet 3:13–16)

It is evident from these prominent early church leaders that all believers should submit themselves to the leading of the Lord, expect opposition to their witness, pray for opportunities from God, share their faith in daily life, and accept the risk for doing so.

Lessons from the Sower

Jesus described God as like a sower who goes out to broadcast the seed of the word so that it falls on various types of soil (Luke 8:4–15). Numerous commentators note that in this parable God seems to be wasting seeds on bad soil. The comment is based on misconceptions about 1) the sower and 2) the seeds.

First, we have already seen that God has a universal intention in his redemptive plan and that he has directed the church to spread the gospel to all nations and even to all creation. God knows which soil will produce a good crop, but his plan is for all to hear of his compassion in Christ and then their response proves the worth of the soil. Some from every ethnolinguistic "field" will believe and follow Christ. We join the sower in casting gospel seed to every corner of the field and to every field on earth. So, the good news of the parable is that the sower has a universal intention and calls us to join him in broadcasting the seed lavishly, and there will be an amazing harvest that results!

Second, God is not like earthly farmers, who have limited amounts of seed to spread. The gospel message spread under the influence of the Holy Spirit is infinitely reproducible. Faithful witnesses will not run out of seed this year because they have shared the gospel too often. We could speak of nothing else for the rest of our lives to an ever-growing circle of hearers, and we would not run low on seeds.

Misconception 33
It is a waste to spread the gospel on hard ground, so we should be careful to focus on the right kind of people.

So, how do we join the sower in this work?

1. *The sower sows indiscriminately and lavishly and so should we.* So, if we are called to sow a field that has not been sown before, then we should focus on that field and sow lavishly. God knows what soil will produce fruit, but we do not. *A common mission mistake is to spend too much time inspecting soil rather than simply sowing seed.* In my lifetime, multiple unreached peoples that most of the church thought were impossible to reach have proven to be the most responsive peoples in this generation.

2. One of the most common mistakes of mission strategies is that *too small a garden is getting seed and potentially missing responsive soil not far away!* We must start with our own personal verbal witness but take strategic action to get the good news out beyond our personal circle through multiplying witnesses and the use of various forms of media.

3. *Some people will not respond to the gospel until they have heard it several times* or had time for it to sink deep into their hearts. New believers from UPGs have often mentioned to me that they had

more than one encounter with the gospel before they believed. Sharing the gospel should always include an invitation to believe; then immediately ask the person when you can talk again about these things. Gospel conversations often need to occur over months or years, but should include that invitation to believe, even if you mention it dozens of times. One of the most important ministry lessons I learned was to prioritize my time with those who were most open to hear the gospel and consider that invitation.

4. *Our witness should be natural and conversational.* Explain and appeal like a friend, not a pulpiteer. Ask them questions and invite questions from them. Share gospel stories that are relevant to their life situation and experience. You may need to "re-spiritualize" your witness to free it of the naturalistic bondage of modern culture. Of course, share with your present friends, but intentionally start multiple relationships with people that are based around gospel conversations.

The Heart of the Hearers Is the Second Battlefield for the Lost

When the believer accepts his/her responsibility to share the gospel broadly and seeks the power of the Holy Spirit to carry it out, then he/she has entered into the second battlefield for the lost. When the Holy Spirit works in the heart of the believer to inspire verbal declaration of the gospel, he also works in the hearts of the hearers, where another phase of the battle rages. Satan does not want the hearers to bear fruit even if they hear the gospel.

The Parable of the Sower describes four potential responses to the seed being sown:

- On hard ground, the seed is "snatched up."

- On rocky ground, the seed may immediately sprout, but later "withers away" in the heat.

- On thorny ground, the seed may seem OK, but is eventually "choked out" by the competition from thorns.

- The good soil is where the seed enters an "honest and good heart," "holds fast," endures heat and thorns, and bears much fruit (Luke 8:15).

I once thought that three out of four soils were OK, but then I realized that farmers only count the fruit and everything else is burned as chaff. I think other people make that same mistake by assuming the kingdom includes even those one-week sprouts and withered stalks whose life is choked out.

Snatched Up

The image of birds picking up seeds off the hard ground is a clear and haunting image. An enemy steals the seed before it has a chance to impact the field at all. This enemy is the "evil one" (Matt 13:19), "Satan" (Mark 4:15), "the devil" (Luke 8:12). There can be no mistaking that the battle won in the believer's heart is followed by spiritual warfare in the heart of the hearer. In an unreached context, the newness of the message can be either a hindrance or an incredibly interesting innovation.

By praying and proclaiming, we sow seeds with faith that some will stick. We pray for opportunities with those in whom God is already preparing a hearing. We pray that what we have shared will not be eaten up by the lies of the enemy. We share so that our message is sticky, at least long enough for the person to consider its meaning. We experiment with different language, stories, times, places, and aspects of the gospel in order to increase the likelihood that the seed has time to interact with the person's heart.

Withered Away

This image of quickly sprouted blades withering in the heat without deep roots is easy to imagine. This type of person hears something good in the message that is attractive and shows interest without conviction or commitment. This is human, fleshly response to the promise of love, peace, joy, and a room in the big palace. Who would not raise a hand to show interest in such things? However, it may be shallow response that cannot handle a little heat and light. As soon as there is any difficulty, this fleeting interest dies away.

Misconception 34
We can do nothing to influence how the soil receives
the seed.

In some places this is less of a problem, because hearers know they will pay a price for following Jesus. In fact, because of that knowledge, they will not take too seriously any witness that only talks about the good things. The time to introduce hardship and suffering into the message is the first time you share about Jesus being crucified and then ask them to take up their cross to follow him. From that point in time the message should be a mix of amazing promise and real cost. This is why Jesus, Paul, and Peter talked so openly about persecution before it arrived. The worst thing is for a new believer to be surprised by the heat and to lose confidence in the message.

So, we pray for spiritual conviction that counts the cost and follows Jesus in suffering. Our message is not just a list of advantages; it acknowledges hardships and affirms Jesus is worth it. Pray that you will continue to speak boldly in the Spirit, because Satan will certainly accuse you of not loving your audience, who will experience pain from hearing. Then pray for new believers to have deep roots and be courageous in their witness and response to suffering to come.

Choked Out

This pattern is so common we may not notice it. The world system, influenced by Satan and appealing to our human fleshly nature, can easily choke out faith. It doesn't even have to look like a direct confrontation; it just patiently crowds out the nutrients necessary for healthy faith. This is a common profile of Christianity in some parts of the world. Christians may be barely hanging on to life in the midst of their personal briar patch. They may not have given up much of the world for Jesus and spend much time and energy choked with worldly worries and chasing pleasures. In a pioneer setting, it should be plain if people are not ready to give up traditional worldly pursuits for a focused life of following Christ.

So, this is why we preach repentance for forgiveness of sins as Jesus commanded. Turning to Jesus means turning away from the world. We must call men and women to faith that prioritizes seeking God's kingdom first and valuing the treasure above all other things. Following Jesus begins with denying yourself and taking up your cross. Our prayer for our audience is that the Holy Spirit will show them these things and that our life and words will clarify it.

Sin, Righteousness, and Judgment

So, now the battle in the hearts of the hearers is laid out. Satan, our own selfish nature, and the world conspire to make the seed fruitless in the life of the hearers. However, the same powerful divine presence that can free believers "to say it all" is also working in the hearts of the lost, drawing them to real faith in Christ. We should listen to the Holy Spirit within us in order to work consciously in harmony with what the Holy Spirit is doing in them.

> But I tell you the truth, it is to your advantage that I go away; for if I do not go away, the Helper will not come to you; but if I go, I will send Him to you. And He, when He comes, will convict the world concerning sin and righteousness and judgment; concerning sin, because they do not believe in Me; and concerning righteousness, because I go to the Father and you no longer see Me; and concerning judgment, because the ruler of this world has been judged. (John 16:7–11)

The Holy Spirit is working in the deepest part of the hearts of those who hear the gospel in order to bring about true conviction and conversion. He is cross-examining them about three critical spiritual questions:

1. Am I OK in relation to God? The Spirit says, "No, you are a guilty sinner."

2. Can I work this out by myself? The Spirit says, "No, you cannot be righteous on your own."

3. Will I be held accountable for my life choices? The Spirit says, "Yes, you will be judged by Jesus, who determines your eternity, so be ready."

Only this kind of deep conviction can draw lost men and women to Christ, so our message must be clearly in harmony with what the Holy Spirit is doing in those who hear.

It is the Holy Spirit who makes the work of evangelizing the unreached possible and eventually inevitable. When the gospel seed is patiently cast broadly, a harvest will come. Some faithful sowers work for
decades awaiting that time, but the time is coming. A Spirit-empowered
witness sows the seed in a good heart prepared by the Spirit, where it
holds fast and takes root, withstands the hot sun, and overcomes thorny
competition, so that it bears much fruit. That seed falls to the earth again
and dies, so that it can become the foundation of the church among that
people. Yes, this foolish hope is the faith of those who are called to share
Jesus with those who have never heard.

Unlikely Harvest?

I smiled when he introduced himself as Imran Khan, because his name
is shared with one of the most prominent men in the Muslim world—a
sports hero and influential politician. In his country, this name usually signifies that the person is a descendant of early Muslim kings. When we met
him, Anne and I were staying in the apartment of friends who were briefly
visiting the US and Imran was the new guard for their apartment building.

We often stopped and chatted in his language, a new one for us that
we were trying to learn in our fifties. Imran seemed pleased, perhaps
because the other residents were distanced by religious concerns and
prejudices. One day around New Year's, Imran asked if we knew about
those "sweet biscuits" that Christians made during the celebration of the
birth of the Prophet *Isa*. He reminisced about visiting a neighboring village as a child and receiving Christmas cookies from the only Christian
families within walking distance of his home. One look at Anne gave me
permission to tell him "we" would make some special for him. So, the next
day I delivered a plate full of Christmas cookies to our new friend, who
was surprised at the simple gesture. The following day there was a midday
knock on our door, and there stood Imran with a heaping plate of steam-
ing biryani, one of my favorite foods. That exchange began a cycle of trading cookies for spicy biryani every few days for the next couple of weeks.

When our friends Brian and Karen returned from the US, we were
able to talk more in depth with Imran. We mentioned God's love and
his special revelation to mankind through our holy book, which Imran
had heard about. When we offered to give him a Bible to read, Imran
became very excited. Several days later we gave him a New Testament in

his dialect and Imran began to read. At that point, I thought it best to let him read for a few days and prayed the Holy Spirit would speak directly to his heart through Scripture. So, every day as Imran guarded the gate, he spent hours reading that New Testament. In fact, when I checked back with him a little over a week later, he was beginning his third reading of it. Over the next few weeks, we chatted with Imran briefly every day or two, but still waited on any extensive teaching because he was already hooked on reading our holy book. He quickly showed real understanding and we noticed Imran explaining what he was learning to the other residents of the building.

We entered the gate one day and Imran stopped us to excitedly share what he could no longer hold inside. He stood up, held the New Testament in one hand, used his other hand to emphasize every point, and with a joyous smile said:

> The holy book says that God has declared that we are guilty before him because of our sins. He sent *Isa* to be a sacrifice for our sin and then he rose from the grave so that we can be right with God again. But we cannot do works to cause this change; we only need to have faith in *Isa*, who died and came back to life. When we have faith, God changes us and makes us family. He gives us the task of telling everyone about the truth so that all may have faith in him.

His words took my breath and tears welled up in my eyes. I knew other Muslims who trusted Christ primarily from reading Scripture and listening to the gentle voice of the Spirit. Imran's simple summary of the good news was powerful and as clear as a bell! Imran had never heard a Christian sermon, but he almost looked and sounded like a preacher. I admit, although I had been praying for him daily, I was not expecting the clarity of his declaration.

I asked Imran if this was what he personally believed and he assured me he believed in *Isa* and he asked about baptism. It was clear that Imran had already walked through the process of Romans 10:9–10, believing in his heart and confessing with his mouth. We made plans to start reading Scripture together and talk about what it means, although I saw no hint of error in his confession. The next morning when I looked for him, Imran was not at his usual place beside the gate, and later I found a new guard there. Imran had been transferred to another location in order to quell angry complaints from our Hindu neighbors that he was preaching Jesus to them. We never saw Imran again, but I have prayed for him many times. I do know that he left that post with faith from simply reading a Bible he had taken with him. Scripture and the Holy Spirit in a hungry heart are a powerful combination. I am confident I will see him again because his heart was good soil just waiting on the seed, which he quickly recognized as good news.

Misconception 35
Miracles were normal during Bible times, but today they are extremely rare and play no role in God's mission.

Signs of God's Power

This chapter has focused on the normal expression of divine power in evangelism within the heart of the witness and the heart of the hearer. I must mention one other expression of God's power in evangelism. Especially in unreached contexts where the gospel is quite new and there is not a redeemed community to reflect the transforming power of that message, miracles often occur as signs pointing the lost to the gospel. Miracles can make this new message a little bit sticky so that more hearers take time to seriously consider it. However, just as in the ministry of Jesus and the early church, miracles may result in anger and rejection in some people while drawing others into the sphere of gospel influence. The two responses may be evident in the same village or household.

I know of contemporary cases of every type of miracle reported in the New Testament. Neither Satan nor God has stopped working, often in the same patterns we see in the New Testament. Transformed lives are the best miraculous sign pointing to the gospel message, so it appears that other miracles often taper off as the redeemed community develops and takes on their role of indigenous witness. So, we should focus on prayer and proclamation while not being surprised by Satan's opposition or God's demonstration of power.

I was visiting and sharing the gospel with a Muslim family one day and as I got up to leave, I realized there was a man lying on a cot in the corner of the room. He had not moved or made a sound in the ninety minutes I had been there. The family told me he had been sick for some time, had nothing to eat or drink for many days, and had been completely unresponsive for three days. I went over to pray for him[6] and realized that his bloated body was likely the result of his system shutting down and fluid building up. His breathing was very shallow and difficult. So, I prayed for God to heal him and left the village.

Two weeks later I returned to that home and noticed the man was not lying in the corner and assumed he had died. We had a good conversation again about Jesus and this time there were even additional family members. As I got up to leave, an older man who had been very attentive to our gospel dialogue mentioned that I did not seem to recognize him. He thanked me for my prayer for him and said that he was completely well within two days of my prayer. I was so shocked to realize he was the man I assumed was already dead that I smiled but was almost speechless. Sadly, though I had cited the power of Jesus Christ as I prayed, I did not immediately declare God's claim on his life in response to this healing.

Friends, do not make my mistake! Proclaim Jesus and do pray for God's blessing on people. Yes, and be prepared to proclaim even more boldly when God performs a miracle among those who hear.

Holy Spirit, guide my heart and mind today. Lead me to those you are preparing to hear the gospel and fill my heart with your love for them. Give me courage to speak boldly and naturally. Guide me to share effectively and empower the words I speak. Convince my lost friends to believe the truth and follow Jesus. Amen.

Questions to Consider

1. Do you think your worldview aligns with a biblical worldview on the work of the enemy and the power of the Holy Spirit? If not, what areas do you need to ask God to influence so that you are better able to take part in the battle?

2. Have you made excuses not to share the gospel because of your personality or spiritual gifting? How can your spiritual gifts and

---

6. I often prayed in the name of Jesus, or *Isa*, and never sensed that Muslims were not appreciative. In fact, most knew that Jesus regularly performed miracles such as healing, while "their" prophet never did. So, they often were excited to have a Christian pray for them in the power of Jesus.

personality posture you for sharing the gospel? What role does obedience play?

3. Have you ever experienced the unseen barrier talked about when trying to share your faith? Have you ever jumped that unseen barrier with the help of the Holy Spirit and experienced the boldness he offers in sharing your faith? Acts 4 shows that "boldness comes from being with Jesus, depending on his strength, and the Holy Spirit taking control of the witness." Are you willing to prepare for future opportunities?

4. "Potential witnesses should prepare for and practice sharing the gospel, identify any demonic lies that hold their tongue, ask the Lord to help them create opportunities, and then obey the Spirit when he prompts them to share." How can you prepare to share the gospel? How can you practice sharing the gospel? How can you work to identify any demonic lies that hold your tongue? What Scripture responds to those lies? How can you prepare yourself to recognize the Spirit's prompting and obey it?

5. The Sower invites us to join in the work. Are you sowing broadly? Are you planting seeds in too small of a garden? Do you share repeatedly with an invitation? Is your witness natural and conversational? If you responded "no" to any of these questions, what would it take for you to be able to respond "yes"?

6. As you share and disciple, how is your witness in harmony with the Holy Spirit in the three critical questions central to the human experience?: 1) Am I Ok in relation to God? 2) Can I work this out by myself? 3) Will I be held accountable for my life choices?

7. What do you think would happen if you were to boldly pray the prayer included at the end of this chapter? Would you consider praying this prayer regularly over the next month?

> Holy Spirit, guide my heart and mind today. Lead me to those you are preparing to hear the gospel and fill my heart with your love for them. Give me courage to speak boldly and naturally. Guide me to share effectively and empower the words I speak. Convince my lost friends to believe the truth in any way that brings You glory. Amen.

Chapter 11

Discipling in Primal Contexts

DURING A RECENT TRIP overseas, I encountered several examples of the conflict between the powers of darkness and Light in the lives of those who have heard the gospel. These cases occurred in a three-day period in a neighborhood cultural context where spiritual power is a part of everyday life, so for some of us from a more naturalistic culture, they may seem fantastic.[1] These examples are of real people in the midst of real conflict, so please pray for them by name.

Case #1

Rak and Soni had owned a popular neighborhood temple with a large imposing idol in their home, but they had felt constant spiritual oppression that caused major stress in the family. So, when they heard about Jesus, they decided to become Christians. They got rid of the idol, closed the temple, and lost income. They immediately faced persecution for their new faith, but stood firm in their decision to follow Christ. However, the spiritual oppression did not completely stop and we dropped in to pray and counsel them. Soon after we began talking about Jesus, Soni

---

1. These experiences, and others, were concentrated into a few days in 2019 because I joined workers who were actively engaged in pushing back the darkness and storming the gates of hell. I include them here not because they are neatly resolved, but because they are sometimes messy, like discipling among the unreached.

began to sneeze, yawn uncontrollably, and make a clicking sound with her tongue, which I suspected was a physical struggle against a demon. Both the timing of the episode and similar previous experiences raised my suspicion. She backed into another room and when we later checked on her, she was in an altered state of consciousness and catatonic on the floor. Only after we prayed for twenty minutes was she able to sit up and start to come out of it. This family knew that Jesus could bring peace, but they continued to be attacked. Efforts to train them in discipleship and standing in God's armor as a family proved fruitless, as they continued to follow their old cultural habit of seeking holy men (now pastors) to come fix their spirit problem each week. It appears that the "house" got swept repeatedly (Matt 12:44–45), but demons kept entering the "back door."

Case #2

I met Bal and Av, two adult male cousins, on the way to a house in the village where we were going to worship. The men worked construction and, like most men they knew, as young adults had become alcoholics and abusive at home. When they had heard the gospel the previous year, Jesus set them free from alcohol and quickly brought peace and joy to their families. I smiled when their wives described their "new" husbands. I learned the family had moved out of this village house two years earlier because they were constantly oppressed by spirits there.

When we arrived, the two men went through the house and took down every idol, picture, and amulet that had been used to connect the home to their old religious life. They put it all in a sack and left the house, so I followed out of curiosity. We walked about half a mile and without comment they dumped the sack into a swiftly flowing river and walked home. We then worshiped the Lord and dedicated the house to his purpose. The cousins declared that this house, which the village knew had been infested with spirits, would now become the center of witness about Jesus.

Five women among those who joined us for worship were family members who were curious about Christ. One young wife named Dee had been frequently bothered by spirits at night, so I asked her to read the verses of the "Roman Road" story to the group and tell us what they said. She replied that she could not read a "holy book," but I assured her that God would speak to her. After she read the first few verses, she looked up at us with tears in her eyes, and exclaimed, "I can understand!" Over the next few minutes, she simultaneously read, understood, and explained the good news about Jesus to the whole group. Then Dee declared her desire to follow him and was joined by four more members of the family.

Case #3

Sister Raj asked our partner pastor to bring us by her home for prayer, where she shared her story over tea and cookies. She had heard the gospel and believed two years earlier and shared her faith with her husband's extended family in the home where they lived. They immediately abused her and threatened her if she did not recant. When she stood firm, they denied her a place at the table and her husband cut off all assistance, so Raj became an unacknowledged "ghost" living in the house. She realized she had to fight for her two young children, whom she hoped would trust Christ as well. The family consulted lawyers for advice on taking the children away and priests who carried out ritual curses on her. Raj probably weighed seventy pounds when she believed, and quickly was growing weaker. She took a bold step downward from their middle-class status and found jobs in the neighborhood cleaning houses for food.

In telling her story, there was no hint of anger or envy in her voice, only gratitude to Jesus and concern for her children—and a flash of joy in her smile! I have never been so humbled to pray for such a courageous sister in Christ, who is fighting a spiritual, legal, emotional, social, and physical battle of life and death.

Six Exemplary Stories from Acts—How the Early Church Responded to Spiritual Power

Primal religion, animism, spiritism, and folk religion are just some of the names of the popular worldview that emphasizes manipulating spiritual power, whatever its source. In some cultures this is the primary religion, but for billions of people it is the foundational worldview underneath a formal religion such as Islam, Buddhism, Hinduism, or even Christianity. Animists do not love their spirits and gods; they fear them. They hope to appease them to avoid some catastrophe or to bargain for something they want. This view of reality is sometimes categorized as a power orientation, because power is central to life.

Misconception 36
The Acts stories about demons and strange events are not applicable to challenges Jesus followers face in our world.

The book of Acts includes six passages about spiritual power that many Westerners hardly notice. The passages provide examples of the spiritual conflict between darkness and light. Some Western commentators stumble through these passages; because they are uncomfortable with how God acts, they explore naturalistic explanations of the divine and demonic demonstrations of power, or they wish the stories answered more of their questions. In contrast, when missionaries read Acts with believers coming out of animism, these passages often create excitement because they address real issues these believers face. The point is that a) God had specific reasons for inspiring these passages, so we should strive to learn the lessons he intended, and b) in regard to spiritual power Western culture is more alienated from biblical contexts than most other cultures around the world.

So, this chapter is built on these six passages to prepare for appropriately discipling those coming from power-orientation worldviews. When missionaries do not assist new believers in dealing with the kinds of problems that arise in these passages, especially when the outsiders discount them as superstition, the believers are left with their old ways to deal with them. Syncretism often results from such half-blind discipleship. Numerous missionaries have asked me what they should do when they have unexpected spiritual encounters, and I give them the only answer that makes sense: "Do what the early church did." That begins with trusting the Holy Spirit's power and guidance in those moments. If we were pushing back the darkness with our abilities, we really should be intimidated and doubtful. When in the power of the Holy Spirit we face anything that Satan throws at us or the believers we work with, then we do so with absolute confidence in our Companion. As you look at these passages, take time to read each specific biblical story before reading that section of the chapter.

Story 1: Acts 5:1–11—Ananias and Sapphira Struck Down for Fraud

Ananias and Sapphira were obviously well-off members of the church who desired to enhance their own reputation by making a generous gift to the community. They were not obligated to sell their property or to give all the proceeds to the church, but they were obligated to tell the truth. The couple conspired to lie to the church, and to God, about the percentage they were dedicating to God. This was selfish and deceptive, but the worst part of their sin was to bring the influence of Satan into a church full of the Holy Spirit. In fact, they were "filled with Satan," which is reminiscent of Satan entering Judas to betray Jesus (Luke 22:3). Their sin contrasts with Luke's use of the phrase "filled with the Holy Spirit" in the previous chapter to describe the Jerusalem church. Pretending to be more pious than they actually were, they conspired to commit "financial fraud"[2] and bring the lie of Satan into a community filled with the truth of God. They may not have realized they were essentially lying to God himself.

This story has obvious parallels with Joshua 7:1, where Achan "kept back" for himself some of the banned riches of Jericho and received the death penalty from God and Israel. In fact, the rare Greek word for "kept back," *enosphisato*, is used to describe the sin in both accounts. In both cases, Satan attacked the new community of faith by inciting a member to do a selfish act and to cover it up. In both cases, God's judgment fell on the guilty party and reverent fear of God fell on the community. Luke's language clearly points to God striking them down.[3]

The story does not clearly state whether the couple were truly Christians, although they were obviously baptized members of the Jerusalem church. Likely they were Christians, for several reasons: 1) they were struck dead, but not pronounced to be cursed in eternity; and 2) if they were only faking their faith, then it would have been simpler to expel them from the fellowship of the church. That non-believers would lie to God is not shocking, but this sin was grievous because it was Christians, members of the church, who lied to him.

So, is it possible for believers to become so deceived that they are filled with Satan? The common theological objection is that Satan cannot possess, or own, someone who belongs to God. However, this objection is

---

2. Bock, *Acts of the Apostles*, 221.

3. The only times in Acts we find the word *ekpsycho*, which describes God striking a person down, is with the deaths of Ananias, Sapphira, and Herod Aggripa (Acts 12:23).

not helpful because the common word used in the New Testament means to be demonized, which does not imply ownership, but influence; not possession, but obsession and oppression.[4]

New Testament writers warned believers that Satan is a real threat:

- Jesus taught his disciples to pray (Matt 6:13) by instructing them to ask God "to lead us not into temptation, but deliver us from the evil one" (NIV). That is a strange prayer if Satan is really no threat to believers.

- Paul warned the Ephesian believers against giving the devil space or room in their lives (Eph 4:26–27). Why warn against something that is not possible?

- Paul was attacked by a demon and asked the Lord repeatedly to take it away, but God decided to allow the demon to painfully torment Paul to humble him (2 Cor 12:7–9). "The verb 'to torment' (*kolaphizein*, 'abuse,' 'batter') implies humiliating violence—being slapped around; and the present tense suggests that it was persistent—something that happens over and over again."[5] We must acknowledge that even faithful believers can experience painful, prolonged attacks from the enemy.

Misconception 37
For the Christian who has Jesus in his life, Satan can be no more than a minor inconvenience.

The harsh judgment on the couple could actually have had a redemptive element. Paul talked about turning over an unrepentant believer to Satan with a hope that the person might be saved or be taught not to blaspheme (see 1 Cor 5:5 and 1 Tim 1:20). Although they were struck down by God as a testimony to all who heard about it, the couple may have still entered heaven by grace.

There are several powerful lessons in this story. Believers can be so deceived by Satan that they bring his lies into the church. Do not trifle

---

4. See Arnold, *Three Crucial Questions*, where this topic is the second question addressed in the book.

5. Garland, *2 Corinthians*, 522.

with God or play him for a fool. When church leaders become aware of such issues, they should directly confront the lie of Satan as a warning to the perpetrators and the church.

Story 2: Acts 8:4–25—Simon the Magician Offers Money for Power

The second example in Acts is perhaps less disturbing than the first, but far more confusing. Philip had preached the gospel in Samaria and performed great miracles of exorcism and healed those with long-term disabilities. The whole city was filled with joy that such a good thing had come to their place.

For some time before Philip arrived, a man named Simon had been practicing miraculous magical arts in the city. Simon was not a modern visual illusionist; he was a manipulator of, and manipulated by, demonic spiritual power. The people had never seen such wonders and were mesmerized by Simon's power. Simon loved the attention the whole city lavished on him. The Samaritans blended deep animism with some acknowledgement of the legacy of worship of God, so Simon declared that his animistic, dark power was from God. In an animistic context such syncretism may seem normal.[6] We should avoid assuming Simon's power was based on simple visual tricks, but assume they were instead inspired by spirits, just not the one leading Philip!

Once Philip started preaching the gospel with signs and wonders occurring, the city shifted its attention to him instead of Simon. Many Samaritans believed in the name of Jesus and were baptized, confirming what Jesus had predicted in Acts 1:8. Simon also believed, was baptized, and began to follow Philip. Simon was amazed and attracted by Philip's miracles, which would be the expected response from a new Christian or an old magician.

When the Samaritans believed, they did not receive the Holy Spirit. That event took place when Peter and John arrived and prayed for the believers. In the context of Acts, where belief and reception of the Holy Spirit are normally simultaneous, this separation seems to have been for the benefit of the church in Jerusalem, so there would be no question that

---

6. In the Christian worldview where spiritual power comes from is the critical question. In animistic contexts the source is not so important, but what the power can do is the critical question. In Western culture fascination with spiritual power of any kind is growing as we become more postmodern.

salvation had been extended to the Samaritans. When Simon saw the apostles laying their hands on the Samaritans to receive the Holy Spirit with visible signs, he immediately offered money to join them. This is where the two cultures of theistic faith and animistic practice clashed!

From a biblical worldview, to treat divine power as a commodity should be unthinkable. God alone has such power and he grants it to those he chooses. Simon, although a believer, still held cultural assumptions that power exists as an entity that can be manipulated. Practitioners of magical power usually seek and pay for new empowerments like Simon attempted to. Although Simon had believed and was trying to follow Jesus, he had dragged along some desires and assumptions from his old way of life.

Once again, we wish that Luke had clarified Simon's spiritual status because we don't understand the syncretism that Peter denounced so strongly. Peter proclaimed that Simon needed to repent, if that were possible, from desiring the attention he once enjoyed and for attempting to manipulate God's power. Simon, whom Luke describes as a baptized believer, was still in bondage to his old sins. Luke does not answer how that is possible; he just reports the example of how the early church dealt with it. The leaders immediately confronted and warned him.

Simon's response surprises us. He asks the apostles to intercede for him so that he can be forgiven. The church has often judged Simon harshly for what may have been a refusal to personally repent.[7] Was Simon unrepentant, or sincerely asking these men who were closer to Christ to intercede for him? Contemporary scholars hold different views.[8] That Simon, who once aggrandized himself, would humble himself and ask them to pray for him because he accepted their rebuke and acknowledged their closeness to God makes sense in the context of the story.

Either way, for those who disciple men and women coming from animistic backgrounds, this story is a reminder that discipleship is an ongoing process that requires vigilance against the old way of life. The apostles immediately rebuked Simon the sinner and called him to repent

7. There were several myths in the early church that blamed Simon for numerous problems that arose. Most scholars agree that he could not be guilty of all of them, if he was guilty of any. For our purposes we are only focusing on Luke's account and not later myths.

8. See Bock, *Acts of the Apostles*, 335–36. Bock believes that Simon was dismissive of Peter's warning. Keener, on the other hand, states: "it remains possible that by recognizing the apostles' superiority to himself in the matter of prayer (contrast Acts 8:18–19), Simon may indicate repentance." Keener, *Acts*, 1533.

and turn back to the Lord. The gospel seed had sprouted in his heart, but it may have still been too early to know whether it might get crowded out by thorns and never produce fruit.

Story 3: Acts 12:1–24—Herod Oppresses the Church

Acts 12 tells the story of Herod Agrippa opposing the purpose of God by oppressing the church and accepting glory that belongs to God alone.[9] He was responsible for the first execution of a church leader, James the brother of John. He imprisoned Peter with the intention of trying him publicly, which clarifies his motivation to please the Jews who were angry about the growth of the Jesus movement. The church in Jerusalem gathered to pray for Peter and God sent an angel to miraculously set him free. Ironically, when Peter showed up at the gate where the church was praying, they did not believe it could be him. Peter then snuck away to continue his ministry.

Sometime later, Herod spoke to the people of Tyre and Sidon regarding a misunderstanding and the crowds exclaimed that they had heard the voice of a god and not a mere man. When Herod accepted this praise, an angel from God struck him, so that he died of worms a few days later. Luke tells us that the gospel kept spreading and multiplying after this event.

Modern sensitivities may cause us concern about Almighty God striking down a political leader who opposes his purpose, but this is a fairly clear and clean account. Modern people sometimes want to ask, "Who does God think that he is?" Obviously, God knows that he is God and it is completely right for him to judge and strike down such a rebellious leader.

The lesson for the church is that persecution may come from higher authorities and the correct response is to turn to God in prayer. In response to those prayers, God sent an angel twice—once to save Peter and once to strike down Herod. Both are appropriate actions by God when he so chooses, although even in Acts these are not common occurrences. However, the church in pioneer settings should be ready for persecution from non-believing authorities and should be appealing to God for help.

---

9. His uncle Herod Antipas condemned John the Baptist and participated in the trial of Jesus. His grandfather was Herod the Great, who murdered babies who might have been born Messiah in Bethlehem.

And the church should not be surprised when an angel or a released leader shows up.

I once visited a Christian community that had recently come out from under such oppression. There had been Christian churches among that tribal people for many decades, but they had in recent years sensed God calling them to complete the task of evangelizing their own people. As their leader—appropriately named Paul—led them toward more aggressive sharing of the gospel, a traditional non–Christian religious leader publicly stated that he would not allow them to accomplish this mission. He verbally and physically attacked Paul to stop the evangelizing he was actively pursuing. However, within a few weeks, that prominent religious leader was attacked and killed by a tiger—a first in several decades in that district. When word of his death spread through the people group, both Christians and many non-believers acknowledged that this was the hand of God. The result was like Acts 12:24; the gospel spread and multiplied until the number of churches had increased tenfold.

Story 4: Acts 13:6–12—Elymas the Magician Struck Blind

Paul and Barnabas preached their way across Cyprus, but Luke chose to summarize the results in this one story. Their ministry got the attention of the Roman proconsul, Sergius Paulus. Sergius is described as an intelligent man, perhaps because he was open to the truth of their message. However, his counselor, Elymas, a Jewish magician, opposed the message and distracted him from clearly hearing Paul's message.[10] As a magician, Elymas likely advised Sergius by interpreting events and forecasting the future through ritual contact with spirits and astrology.[11] His intention was to bait the proconsul and twist the truth.

Paul may have been offended that a Jewish magician and false prophet was opposing the message of the Jewish Messiah. He accused Elymas of being a son of the devil rather than a son of Jesus (Bar-Jesus), a reference again to the conflict between two kingdoms. This was not a competition between Paul and a political counselor; it was a conflict between the Holy Spirit and the spirits behind the magic. Paul, filled with the Holy Spirit, recognized the spirits empowering Elymas and

---

10. Polhill, *Acts*, 292–95. Polhill explains there were many Roman officials with the name Paulus, like Saul, and that officials often took on fortune-telling counselors and considered Jews to have connection with a great religion.

11. Witherington, *Acts of the Apostles*, 396.

confronted him. Paul "cursed" him with temporary blindness, which shut him up.

Sergius was curious and attracted to the gospel, and on seeing this miracle he quickly believed. The proclamation of truth combined with this power encounter to stop a detractor resulted in faith on the part of this important Roman official.

If you were sharing the gospel with a new friend and someone present constantly interfered with the message in spite of your polite appeals, would you ever confront the spirit thwarting God's purpose?

Story 5: Acts 16:6–34—Slave Girl Released from Demonic Possession

A slave girl exploited to make money for her owners enters the story in Philippi. She had been following Paul's band for several days and was causing a disturbance by her comments. In fact, Paul reacted from a deeply disturbed soul only after multiple encounters. Paul was not focused primarily on exorcising demons; he was proclaiming the gospel and training disciples. As he did that, however, this demon reacted to his presence and ministry. Missionaries should emulate this priority— preach Jesus, make disciples, and respond to demons who interfere in pushing back the darkness.

The spirit that inhabited the girl is described as a "python" spirit, which means a fortune-telling spirit. In Greek culture Apollo was probably the most popular and influential god. One of his roles was to forecast the future, so the famous oracle of Delphi forecast the fortunes of Greece with inspiration from Apollo, who was embodied in a python. The spirit of Apollo entered the oracle, who then forecast the future in a different voice.[12]

The whole idea seems crazy and fantastic to us today, but Anne and I encountered a shocking parallel during our first year overseas. Not far down the road from our apartment in modern Singapore was a temple with two large cages out front. We eventually realized the cages held huge pythons that laid there for months between feedings. It was a spirit-medium temple and on auspicious days a medium would come and wrap a python around himself. The spirit in the python would then possess the medium, who made a lot of money for the temple by telling fortunes for

12. Witherington, *Acts of the Apostles*, 493–94.

hundreds of inquirers. Two thousand years and seven thousand miles separated the contemporary parallel to this biblical story about a python spirit. Satan is still up to the same old tricks.

The girl was crying out, "These men are bond-servants of the Most High God, who are proclaiming to you a way of salvation." So, why was Paul so disturbed by this seemingly positive testimony that he cast out the demon? I suggest two major reasons:

1. The message was filled with half-lies/half-truths.

   a. "Most High God" is interesting in light of Luke 8:28, where "Legion" cries out to Jesus as the "Son of the Most High God." Demons acknowledge who God the Father and God the Son are, but in terms that avoid voluntary submission. In Jewish contexts this phrase pointed to Yahweh as the only true God among the gods. However, in Greek contexts like Philippi it would have been heard as an acknowledgement of Zeus or Apollo as the first among many gods.

   b. "A way of salvation." The girl's statement does not acknowledge Jesus as *the* way of salvation. It states that their message is *a* way of salvation, and even salvation in this context would be most likely understood as health and a good life, not eternal life with God.

2. Paul was concerned about the gospel becoming wrongly associated with false ideas and practices.

   a. He did not want the message from God to be associated in any way with the demon making the announcement. Jesus responded the same way to demonic testimony.

   b. He did not want their ministry and reputation connected in any way to the horrific exploitation of this slave girl.

So, when this demon interfered with evangelism and teaching, Paul confronted the spirit and cast it out of the girl. She was immediately freed from her demonic tormentor, but not her human ones. Paul may have expected the exorcism to cause trouble in the city, largely because she was a source of great income, but he acted boldly on behalf of the girl and the gospel anyway.

Story 6: Acts 19:8–20—Sons of Sceva Try to Manipulate the
Name of Jesus

The sons of Sceva were Jewish exorcists who recognized that there was
unusual power in the name of Jesus. So, as spirit practitioners they attempted to manipulate his name as they did with other spirits. The painful
and embarrassing lesson was that the Son of God will not be manipulated
or managed like created spirits can be. As Simon learned, Jesus's power is
connected to relationship and his gracious choice, not a name to attach
to incantations. The same spirits who would have fled from the power
of Jesus wielded by a Holy Spirit–empowered believer were incensed by
his name being spoken by non-believers who were not connected to his
power. Non-believers should not attempt to play with God or manipulate
divine power. The whole city of Ephesus heard this story and grew in
respect for the name of the Lord Jesus.

It is interesting that the Ephesian believers also learned an important lesson from this event, although from a different point than the sons
of Sceva. The event convinced them that mixing old magic with new
faith in Jesus is extremely dangerous. The two sources of power are in
conflict, so it is possible to get burned by either. Luke tells us the believers began to confess their involvement in magic and to destroy hidden
paraphernalia of their old practices. After coming to faith in Jesus, they
had clandestinely continued their involvement in magic, fortune-telling,
incantations, etc., but burning the guidebooks was a final renunciation of
that way of life. Discipling believers from this background should start
with renunciation of other powers and practices and requires continued
vigilance against falling back into old patterns of belief/behavior.

A Biblical Pattern for Contemporary Discipling

Disciplers who work among the least reached peoples will likely find challenges similar to these faced by the early church. The cultures of many
unreached peoples today involve power-oriented, animistic worldviews.
Disciplers must rely on the Holy Spirit to guide and empower them, focus
on scriptural truth as the norm, and pray for the transforming power
of the Holy Spirit to address these issues in the hearts of their disciples.
They must also watch and respond consistently and courageously to the
twisting and interfering work of Satan.

If we look carefully at these six passages, there is one other major element of this ministry that should be mentioned here. In some of these events, the disciples got into trouble with the community or authorities. Sometimes that cannot be avoided when we are faithful to the Holy Spirit's leading. However, in every single case Acts tells us that one spiritual result of confronting the enemy was the advance of the gospel and faith.

- "Multitudes of men and women were constantly added to their number" (Acts 5:14).
- They were "preaching the gospel to many villages" (Acts 8:25).
- "The word of the Lord continued to grow and be multiplied" (Acts12:24).
- "[T]he proconsul believed when he saw what had happened" (Acts 13:12).
- "[I]mmediately he was baptized, he and all his household" (Acts 16:33).
- "[S]o the word of the Lord was growing mightily and prevailing" (Acts 19:20).

Early Church Responses to Challenges of Spiritual Power				
Passage	Person	Manifestation	Problem	Ministry response
Acts 5:1–16	Ananias and Sapphira	Deception entered the church for the first time.	Church members are filled by Satan and lie to the church and God.	Leaders confronted the sinners and God struck them down.
Acts 8:9–24	Simon	Mesmerizing spirit amazes and astonishes the crowd.	New believer wanted to manipulate divine power.	Truth encounter from leaders to rebuke the ex-magician
Acts 12:1–24	Herod	Political leader stands against God's purpose and glory.	Non-believer acts against the gospel, the church, and God himself.	Believers pray. God sends angels to free Peter and later to strike Herod down.
Act 13:4–12	Elymas	Deceiving spirit blinds and makes dull the mind of a lost person hearing the gospel.	Demonic influence to interfere with an unbeliever hearing and believing	Power encounter to shut up the demon empowered influencer
Acts 16:16–21	Slave girl	Fortune-telling spirit possesses the girl and speaks out.	Demonized unbeliever confuses the proclamation of the gospel.	Exorcised the demon from the girl
Acts 19:11–20	Sons of Sceva	Overpowering spirit attacks non-believing exorcists.	Non-believers try to manipulate the name of Jesus.	Believers renounce/ repent of animistic practices and destroy paraphernalia.

Unexpected Opposition and Victory

I had been meeting weekly with Eli and Yuni in their home for several weeks. Eli professed to be a Christian and Yuni was his Muslim wife. This certainly looked like an open door to share the gospel with both of them, but I was especially excited about sharing the gospel with Yuni.

However, by the third session of looking at what the Bible says about Jesus, a disturbing pattern had developed. Yuni sometimes raised questions that were really objections to Christian faith, as I half-expected her to do. However, as I answered her questions and we read the Gospels together, she began to ask questions for better understanding. That is when the unexpected spiritual interference raised its head.

Eli had told me his family were traditional Christians from another island. He was proud of this religious heritage and repeatedly stated how much better Christianity was than Islam. His spiritual condition was very concerning, however. He boasted that he had slept with a different coed each day for three years of college and that his pastor uncle had facilitated it all by giving him a magical incantation to seduce the one thousand girls he had been with. At the end of three years, Eli had gotten sick and flunked out of school. Years later, he continued to express anger towards God for letting him down! He married Yuni because he had gotten her pregnant and I cringed at the Christian testimony she had received from her husband. Now, each time Yuni showed openness to the gospel, Eli would jump into the conversation with strong pronouncements or by steering it in another direction.

I had prayed for wisdom and for Eli to be more sensitive to what the Holy Spirit was doing in Yuni's heart. The next time we met, Yuni once again showed openness to the gospel and Eli responded by raising his voice and waving his hands while making random declarations. I sensed the Spirit's prompt to ask him about the incantations he had mentioned, so I did. Eli got up and pulled out of a Bible two pieces of paper with writings on them. With pride he again explained how they were really powerful magic. I prayed under my breath and asked the Holy Spirit to intervene so that Yuni could hear unencumbered and come to faith. I asked Eli if, in the name of Christ, he was willing to destroy the incantations. Honestly, I was a bit surprised when he quickly agreed to do so. He tore them into pieces and burned them on a plate, then we prayed for God's blessing on their home.

The atmosphere of our Bible study changed immediately. Yuni began openly to consider what turning to Christ would mean for her and asked thoughtful questions to truly understand what Christ had done for us. Eli remained mostly silent over the next few weeks and when he did talk, it was not too disruptive. After several more sessions, Yuni declared she had decided to follow Christ and trust him as Savior. Her prayer to him was simple, but heartfelt.

Two weeks later Yuni visited her family on a holiday. Family members were expressing anger about some family slight and Yuni stated they would all be better off if they learned to forgive. Someone responded by sarcastically asking, "What, have you become one of those Christians too?" Although she had not planned to do so, she could not deny the Savior in her life now, so she said, "Yes, I have." Family members began shouting angrily at her and then her father quieted the group with these words: "You are no longer my daughter and will never be welcome in this home again. Tomorrow I will announce in the newspaper that we have disinherited you and that no one should treat you as a member of our family."

Later, on their way home, Eli and Yuni stopped by for a visit. Yuni teared up as she talked about her family's reaction to her new faith. Then, with a big smile, she said that in spite of the grief she felt from separation from her family, she had never experienced such overwhelming joy and peace as she sensed God's presence comfort her heart. She had found the treasure hidden in a field and joyfully sold everything she had to buy it.

Questions to Consider

Story 1: Acts 5:1–11 Is it possible that believers can become so deceived that they are filled with Satan and start working against God's purpose? What implications do you see for your personal walk with the Lord? What implications are there for ministering in your fellowship?

Story 2: Acts 8:4–25 Have you seen divine power from the Holy Spirit being treated like a commodity by Christians? How should believers respond to such a practice?

Story 3: Acts 12:1–24 How would you respond if a higher authority began to persecute the church where you live? What would be the best humble and courageous response to such pressure?

Story 4: Acts 13:6–12 If you were in a context where the spread of the gospel was being slowed down by someone like Elymas, who was empowered by enemy spirits, would you be ready to respond with confrontation alongside your proclamation of the truth?

Story 5: Acts 16:6–34 What would you do if it was obvious that a demon was manifesting through someone you had contact with?

Story 6: Acts 19:8–20 Is it likely for believers in your setting to be involved in magic or other animistic practices? If discipling believers needs to start with renunciation of old patterns of belief/behavior related to these things, how does that happen? Is it possible there are some old experiences or habits that you need to address?

Chapter 12

God's Presence in Missions

MY FIRST VIVID MEMORY about Christ's cry of desolation, "*Eli, Eli, lama sabachthani?*" was hearing a physician describe the physiology of the crucified when I was a teenager. I was struck by how little I appreciated the great sacrifice Jesus had made for me. As a young preacher I occasionally spoke on Matthew's crucifixion account, highlighted by an experience in my first ministry position while a college student. On Palm Sunday 1978, I was privileged to preach the morning sermon at Ridgecrest Baptist Church in Jackson, Mississippi.

I attempted to describe the crucifixion in gory detail, including the flesh-tearing scourging, the spasms of pain from iron spikes driven against the nerves between the bones of his hands and feet, and the terrifying, panic-inducing process of slow asphyxiation. The sermon climaxed with Matthew 27:46 as I dramatized the Father turning his back on the Son in the midst of his agony so that Jesus cried, "My God, my God, why have You forsaken me?" My graphic description combined with the humid heat resulted in two sweet elderly ladies passing out during the sermon. They were helped to the foyer by the deacons and revived with hand fans and cold water, while I continued to press our disregard for the price Jesus paid for our sin. As I drove back to school after the service, I was excited to have reached a higher level of power in my preaching. For the next fifteen years I had a favorite sermon for evangelism and discipleship.

In the Context of Muslim Apologetics

In 1992 my family and I were living in Indonesia. My task was training Christian leaders while also reaching out to one of the largest Muslim unreached people groups in the world. My greatest missions challenge was learning to share the gospel with Muslim neighbors, including many young men who came to visit our home. Some were simply curious about a foreigner who spoke their language, but frequently young men came who were being trained in anti-Christian apologetics in their mosque and were testing their training on me. Those conversations were challenging and enlightening, and honed my presentation of the gospel to my new Muslim friends.

My missionary friend Kent was about to move to another city and called to tell me that he had met a young man with many questions and had suggested he come talk to me. Several days later, I opened the front door to meet a handsome twenty-two-year-old Javanese man who introduced himself as "Lucky." We chatted about his life and family and I eventually mentioned that I suspected he had a question for me. He immediately asked, "*Apa maksudnya 'Eli, Eli, lama sabachthani?'*" The first words were a common question we used daily in conversation—"What does it mean?" The second phrase of his question was familiar, but I was momentarily confused because I did not recognize any Indonesian words or grammatical construction. When I realized after a few seconds that he was quoting Matthew, two things immediately dawned on me: 1) he was not the average drop-in guest but an Islamic apologist-in-training, and 2) I had a contextual challenge to my long-held explanation of "*Eli, Eli, lama sabachthani.*"

Almost weekly I had been conversing with Muslim friends about two issues related to Jesus: 1) why the Trinity is not tri-theism, and 2) how God could allow his special envoy to be killed so dishonorably. One of the most common objections to the gospel I heard from Muslim friends was that Christians are polytheists. In Islamic teaching Christians are guilty of *shirk* or associating something or someone with the one true God. As radical monotheists, many Muslims believe this is the one unpardonable sin that cannot be overlooked by a merciful *Allah*. So, a common Islamic challenge to Christian faith has been to confuse Christians who stumble over explaining the Trinity. I realized that if I explained that God the Father had abandoned God the Son when he was on the cross, Lucky would immediately ask how God could abandon himself.

Most Muslim cultures place a high value on honor, and it makes no sense to Muslims that Allah could dishonor and shame *Nabi Isa*, the great prophet sent as the Word of *Allah*. Muslims believe their theology shows more honor to Jesus than does ours. I intended to explain that Jesus was sent to be the Lamb who takes away the sin of the world, but Lucky's question challenged me to go again to the scripture to explore whether the atonement truly included the Father abandoning the Son. So, I invited Lucky to come back the following week for a longer discussion and spent the rest of the afternoon reading Matthew 27 and the passage Jesus quoted in Psalm 22.

The question confronting me was whether in reality the Father abandoned the Son. This question challenges us to affirm both a clearly substitutionary atonement and the essential, eternal unity of the triune God. I was not, and am not, questioning whether Jesus was the Suffering Servant who was "smitten of God, and afflicted," "pierced" and "crushed" for our transgressions, and the atoning sacrifice who was "displayed publicly as a propitiation" for our sins.[1] The issue is whether the Bible teaches that the Father abandoned the Son while he took this distinctive action of dying for our sins.

That afternoon in response to this missional challenge, I began the process of testing my preunderstandings against the biblical text, which has resulted in a years-long hermeneutical spiral.[2]

In the Context of Psalm 22

As soon as Lucky was out the door, I went to my study and reread Matthew 27. I then turned to Psalm 22 because it is the source of the "*Eli, Eli . . .*" quote. I remembered that the Qur'an affirms that David was one of the four greatest prophets who were given a revealed book by *Allah*.[3] Although I had read Psalm 22 before, I admit that it felt like I was reading it for the first time as I pondered this question.

As I studied the psalm that afternoon, five observations struck me deeply:

1. See Isa 53:4, 5, 10; Rom 3:25; 1 John 2:2.

2. Klein, Blomberg, and Hubbard, *Introduction to Biblical Interpretation*, 240–42.

3. Al Qur'an, Surah 17 (Al-Isra'), verse 55. This quranic affirmation does not legitimize Psalms for the Christian, but it does point to a potential bridge for sharing revealed truth with Muslims. The four books are the Taurat given to Musa, Zabur given to Daud, Injil given to Isa, and Al Qur'an given to Muhammad.

1. I was surprised that the first affirmation of God's faithfulness is found in verses 3–5, immediately after the cry of desolation.

2. The three cycles of complaint seem to describe three aspects of the suffering—emotional anguish, social antagonism, and physical agony. This seemed to be the most specific prophecy of the crucifixion I had read in the Old Testament.

3. The psalmist continues to talk to God as if he were present and hearing him.

4. The first section of praise, especially verse 24, specifically states that God did not forsake the sufferer. I reread the verse several times to make sure I was seeing it correctly.

5. The final section of praise states that all the families of the nations will know and worship God—reminiscent of the covenant to Abraham in Genesis 12:3.

In light of Lucky's question, I could think of no good reason to ignore the full context of Psalm 22 while interpreting Matthew 27:46; my hermeneutical spiral took a ninety-degree turn. The insights I gained that afternoon form the basis of my understanding. Here is how I see the psalm in outline form.

Psalm 22

Section 1: Protest of Personal Suffering to God (vv. 1–21)

Consists of three cycles of complaint and hope, with each expression of hope beginning with an emphatic "But you" to highlight God's character and appeal to him.

    a. First cycle of complaint and affirmation—emotional anguish (vv. 1–5)

        1. Cry of desperation regarding abandonment, distance, and no answer (vv. 1–2)

        2. Affirmation of God's holiness, power, and trustworthiness (vv. 3–5)

b. Second cycle of complaint and affirmation—social antagonism (vv. 6–11)

   1. Cry of shame regarding being abandoned to his antagonists (vv. 6–8)

   2. Affirmation of God's constant presence and first request for help (vv. 9–11)

c. Third cycle of complaint and appeal—physical agony (vv. 12–21)

   1. Cry of pain regarding physical torment (vv. 12–18)

   2. Appeal to God for assistance and confidence in the answer (vv. 19–21)

Section 2: Celebration of God's Answer and Victory (vv. 22–31)

This is the most extended and victorious praise hymn in all the protest psalms.

a. Celebration in the assembly that God has not abandoned the sufferer (vv. 22–26)

b. All nations and future generations will turn to the Lord and worship (vv. 27–31).

Over the next month Lucky did return, and we spent hours together reading Matthew 27 and Psalm 22. Lucky was moved by the descriptions of the suffering we read but found it difficult to accept that God had allowed such a horrible tragedy. During our third afternoon together, Lucky looked up at me in surprise when we read Psalm 22:24 and said, "God did not leave him!" As we continued reading, Lucky saw that there was a reason for the suffering—that all nations would be blessed. I then showed him the promise to Abraham in Genesis 12 and emphasized the connection between *Taurat, Zabur,* and *Injil* (Torah, Psalms, and Gospels) that explains why *Isa* died to honor God and to bring us salvation.[4] There in my study Lucky thanked God for these revealed words and asked God to forgive him through *Isa's* sacrifice.

4. I have used Gen 12:1–3; Ps 22; and Matt 20:25–28; 27 multiple times since then to show Muslim friends the long-term purpose of God to bless the nations through the sacrifice of *Isa* as expressed in three books they acknowledge as revealed.

In the Context of Protest Psalms

Recent scholars refer to Psalm 22 as an *individual protest psalm*, because "protests voice deep suffering but assume that the crisis can be resolved by God's intervention. Psalm 22 is an "excellent example of a protest psalm."[5] The psalm does express some of the most agonizing cries of pain and despair found in the Bible, but they are interspersed with unusual affirmations of hope and victory. In fact, Psalm 22 includes thirteen verses of complaint to God and eighteen verses of hope, request, and celebration. Psalm 22 is a lament in which the "thank-offering" is so prominent that "it is hard to know whether the thanks or the lament is the predominant feature."[6]

Because protest psalms often swing dramatically between absolute despair and resolute faith, we must be careful not to take specific statements out of the context of the psalm.[7] This is especially true because the cries of despair are often hyperbolic. Psalm 22 includes several examples; "It stretches the literal truth for the sake of emotional impact . . . the psalmist's entire skeleton did not really get out of joint nor did his heart suddenly become melted wax."[8]

The cry of desolation that begins Psalm 22 is part of a two-verse complaint in which two realities are addressed. First, the psalmist addresses Yahweh three times as *Eli*, "my God." The complaint is an act of faith and an acknowledgment of whom the psalmist addresses. In spite of his pain, Yahweh is still his God. Secondly, these verses are a cry of despair that *Eli* is not acting like "my God." The Hebrews did not view their relationship with Yahweh like us moderns, focused on our own inner faith and experience. God chose them and answered their prayers in practical ways, so they trusted him. His presence was fully expected to result in concrete actions. God had abandoned the psalmist not in the sense of withdrawing his presence, but in the fact that God's answer had

---

5. Klein, Blomberg, and Hubbard, *Introduction to Biblical Interpretation*, 452.

6. Gillingham, *Poems and Psalms of the Hebrew Bible*, 223.

7. Klein, Blomberg, Hubbard, *Introduction to Biblical Interpretation*, 461. "Individual protest psalms speak to situations of individual suffering and may be applied accordingly . . . At least initially, the student should be wary of extracting instant devotional applications rather than pausing, first, to ponder seriously the text within its original context."

8. Klein, Blomberg, and Hubbard, *Introduction to Biblical Interpretation*, 404–5.

not delivered him from his distress. The decision to not deliver Jesus from suffering and death is the "abandonment," rather than punitive wrath.[9]

In the Context of First-Century Judaism

Scholar N.T. Wright explores Jesus' self-understanding and his messianic mission within the religious community of first-century Judaism.[10] According to Wright, "There is no debate . . . on the place of the Psalter in forming the worldview and expectation of second-Temple Judaism."[11] Pilgrim psalms were recited or sung on the way to Jerusalem and on festival days the festive psalms were used. The Psalms kept Israel's hope alive in the promise of God to David about a future kingdom. The protest psalms were also used regularly in worship to "speak again and again of the suffering of the people of YHWH, and of their trust in him to vindicate and deliver them." First-century Jews, like David, cried out to God to complain about their depressing circumstances, i.e., Roman occupation, while also affirming their trust that God hears and will eventually answer their prayer for help.

> Misconception 38
> When Jesus cried, "My God, my God," he did not know it was the first line of Psalm 22 that clearly affirmed God did not abandon the speaker.

Wright builds from Dodd's observation that New Testament evidence overwhelmingly shows the earliest disciples of Jesus had a specific

9. Goldingay, *Psalms*, 342–47. "God is still identified with Jesus and is steadfastly watching him on the cross, totally identified with what Jesus is doing. In Christ, God is reconciling the world (2 Cor. 5:19). But God is holding back from acting to deliver Jesus and thus from gaining the relief that God as well as Jesus wants from the pain of this moment."

10. Wright, *Jesus and the Victory of God*, 593. Wright argues that "we can credibly reconstruct a mindset in which a first-century Jew could come to believe that YHWH would act through the suffering of a particular individual in whom Israel's sufferings were focused; that this suffering would carry redemptive significance; and that this individual would be himself. And I propose that we can plausibly suggest that this was the mindset of Jesus himself."

11. This quotation and the following paragraph from Wright, *Jesus and the Victory of God*, 586.

view of certain Old Testament passages to explain the ministry of Jesus.[12] He also commented that Jesus himself is the most likely source of that view (see Luke 24:27). Jesus, then, developed his understanding of his mission to suffer to restore Israel as a blessing to the nations from key passages in Isaiah, Daniel, Zechariah, and the Psalms. Wright argues Jesus intimately knew Psalm 22 because it mirrored so closely his own self-understanding of suffering and eventual victory. "From the historical point of view there is no reason why Jesus should not have carried Psalm 22 (and a good many others) in his head, and why he should not have prayed its first verse as he underwent the agony of crucifixion."[13] If Wright is correct, Psalm 22 informed the self-understanding of Jesus and was on his mind during the crucifixion, so it seems likely he quoted verse 1 with reference to the whole psalm. This was likely the primary view of the early church.

In the Context of Matthew's Account

Psalm 22 is the most frequently quoted psalm in the New Testament, always in connection to the suffering and victory of Jesus. Of the thirty-one verses in the psalm, eleven are cited in the New Testament. All four Gospels quote or make allusions to it.

Matthew's crucifixion account is of particular interest regarding Psalm 22. Matthew shares with Mark's Gospel the cry of desolation and no other sayings from the cross. The most important element of Matthew's account for interpreting "*Eli, Eli . . .*" is the unique way that he tells the crucifixion story. The cry of desperation in verse 46 is the fourth time Matthew uses Psalm 22 to describe what happened at the cross!

- Matt 27:35 references Ps 22:18—"divided up His garments."

- Matt 27:39 references Ps 22:7—"wagging their heads."

- Matt 27:43 references Ps 22:8—"let Him deliver him."

12. Dodd, *According to the Scriptures*, 108–10. In short, Dodd states:"At the earliest period of Church history to which we can gain access, we find in being the rudiments of an original, coherent, and flexible method of biblical exegesis which was already beginning to yield results . . . This is a piece of genuinely creative thinking. Who was responsible for it? . . . But the New Testament itself avers that it was Jesus Christ himself who first directed the minds of His followers to certain parts of the scriptures as those in which they might find illumination upon the meaning of his mission and destiny."

13. Wright, *Jesus and the Victory of God*, 596–604.

- Matt 27:46 references Ps 22:1—"My God, my God, why . . . ?"

The whole structure of the account is built on Psalm 22 because Matthew saw the events in light of this psalm. He interpreted the suffering of Jesus, including the cry of desolation, in the context of the whole psalm. In fact, Matthew may point to his source of this understanding in the account of Jesus' arrest (Matt 26:52–54), where Jesus explained to the disciples that he could "appeal to My Father" to immediately stop the suffering, but that he did not because Jesus was consciously fulfilling Scripture. Matthew understood Jesus' meaning to include Psalm 22.[14] If Jesus quoted Psalm 22:1 with no thought to the entire psalm, it was in contrast to how Matthew described the event.

In the Context of the Seven Last Words

As noted, Matthew and Mark include the cry of desolation, while Luke and John do not include it but do include three other sayings of Jesus from the cross. Certainly, we should consider Jesus' cry of Psalm 22:1 in light of the other six sayings.

This chronological listing and the designations for these Seven Words are traditional and common:

First Word: "Forgiveness"—Luke 23:34

"Father, forgive them; for they do not know what they are doing."

Second Word: "Salvation"—Luke 23:43

"Truly I say to you, today you will be with Me in Paradise."

Third Word: "Affection"—John 19:25–27

"Woman, behold your son!. . . "Behold, your mother!"

Fourth Word: "Anguish"—Matthew 27:46

"My God, my God, why have you forsaken Me?"

Fifth Word: "Suffering"—John 19:28

"I am thirsty."

14. Witherington, *Psalms Old and New*, 69. "Jesus himself seems to have provided the impetus for the use of some of the rest of this psalm to describe and explain the crucifixion of Jesus and its surrounding circumstances . . . In fact, the Matthean crucifixion narrative is deliberately cast in light of Psalm 22, showing how the end of Jesus's life fulfilled this psalm."

Sixth Word: "Victory"—John 19:30

"It is finished."

Seventh Word: "Contentment"—Luke 23:46

"Father, into your hands I commit my spirit."

Two observations are particularly relevant. First, the initial word and the last word are prayers Jesus addressed to his "Father." This signifies the intimate relationship that the Son had with the Father throughout his ministry. In fact, every prayer of Jesus in the Gospel accounts is addressed this way, unless we read the cry of desolation as a prayer instead of a quotation. In Matthew's account, "Father" is not only a way to address God, but "my Father" is used by Jesus to teach his disciples about this close relationship.

So, Jesus expressed intimacy with God and seemed to expect a hearing from the beginning to the end of his crucifixion. The two prayers were addressed to the only one who could answer for God alone can forgive sin and receive Jesus' spirit. If indeed the Father abandoned the Son on the cross, either Jesus was mistaken to appeal to him or the abandonment took place only in the midday hours. What effect could abandonment bring if it did not last until the end?

Second, the Gospels portray Jesus quoting the Psalms several times during the passion and especially during his crucifixion. As we have seen, protest psalms include a complaint to God, an appeal for help, and praise for his answer. It is striking that Jesus quoted three protest psalms attributed to his forefather David in his Seven Last Words from the cross.[15] So, in addition to the fourth word, which quotes Psalm 22:1, the fifth word alludes to Psalm 69:21 and the seventh word quotes Psalm 31:5. There is also another possible allusion to Psalm 22:31 ("He has performed it") in the sixth word, "It is finished." So, the pattern we saw in Psalm 22, of complaint combined with confidence in God's help, is confirmed twice more from the cross. Perhaps this is coincidence, but the repeating pattern is striking.

- Psalm 22:24—"For He has not despised nor abhorred the affliction of the afflicted; Nor has He hidden his face from him; But when he cried to Him for help, He heard."

---

15. Mays, "Prayer and Christology," 322.

- Psalm 69:33—"The humble have seen it and are glad; You who seek God, let your heart revive. For the Lord hears the needy and does not despise His who are prisoners."

- Psalm 31:5, 22—"Into your hand I commit my spirit; You have ransomed me, O Lord, God of truth . . . I am cut off from before Your eyes, nevertheless You heard the voice of my supplications when I cried to You."

It seems unlikely that Jesus did not know all of Psalm 22 and quoted verse 1 without reference to the rest of the psalm. Jesus choosing three Davidic protest psalms that all clearly affirm God's continued help, and quoting them out of context seems unbelievable. Jesus was thinking of and quoting psalms that speak of suffering and God's faithful care for his servant in that suffering.

In the Context of Jesus' Statements about His Coming Suffering

All four Gospel writers include statements Jesus made about the suffering that he was to endure. The Synoptics share similar warnings that Jesus would go to Jerusalem, be rejected by the religious leaders, and suffer and die there (Matt 16:21; Mark 8:31; Luke 9:22). Jesus warned that he would suffer at the hands of men, and there is no mention of the Father forsaking him.

John's Gospel includes two statements of particular interest, because Jesus clearly stated his expectation that the Father would be with him during his suffering. John 8:12–30 is a conversation that Jesus had with Jewish leaders about being sent by his Father and returning to his Father.

> So, Jesus said, "When you lift up the Son of Man, then you will know that I am He, and I do nothing on My own initiative, but I speak these things as the Father taught Me. And He who sent Me is with Me; He has not left me alone, for I always do the things that are pleasing to Him." (John 8:28–29)

"Lifted up" here probably means both the cross and the glory that it would bring. John affirms that Jesus knew the one who sent him on mission would be with him as he accomplished it. "God does not and will not forsake His messenger. Jesus is not abandoned."[16] Jesus was telling those

16. Morris, *Gospel According to John*, 452. See also Borchert, *John 1–11*, 301. Jesus

who would eventually wag their heads and taunt him at Golgotha that the Father would be there also.

Jesus' words in John 16 are not directed to his antagonists, but to his disciples. Jesus stated, "A little while, and you will no longer see me, and again a little while, and you will see me" (v. 16). The disciples were confused and concerned about this "little while." Jesus warned them that they would mourn and rejoice over the things that were coming. In verse 32 he told them, "Behold, an hour is coming, and has already come, for you to be scattered, each to his own home, and to leave Me alone, and yet I am not alone, because the Father is with Me."

The disciples were clearly worried that Jesus would abandon them, but he countered their question by informing them that they would abandon him. But Jesus would not be completely abandoned, because "this text makes clear that the *Father did not abandon his Son!*"[17]

So, on two occasions Jesus confirmed his expectation that the Father would be with him in his suffering. If John is the same "beloved disciple" who stood at the cross, he had a front-row view to see the fulfillment of the religious leaders lifting up Jesus and the scattering of the disciples. Whether it was at that moment or later when John recalled this promise, it must have been a powerful moment.

Summary of Evidence

It is commonly acknowledged that the first line of a psalm, such as "*Eli, Eli, lama sabachthani?*," was at times used as a designation for the whole psalm in Second Temple Judaism. That was a practical necessity when the psalms had no numbers and the reader literally scrolled down to find the reading. Douglas Moo, however, questions whether that applies to Jesus' cry of desolation: "Rabbinic sources indicate that the first verse of a psalm could be used as a title of the whole, but all of these references occur in liturgical settings in which opening verses would easily become titles (as in our hymns)."[18]

"exhibited a firm conviction that the one who sent him on mission had not abandoned him."

17. Borchert, *John 12–21*, 180–81. Morris adds, "The present tenses, which Jesus uses of the Father's presence with Him, are natural for abiding reality. Always the Father is with Him." See also Morris, *Gospel According to John*, 713–14.

18. Moo, *Old Testament in the Gospel Passion Narratives*, 271.

Based on the Scriptures, should we not describe the cry of desolation in Matthew 27:46 as "liturgical use" of Psalm 22? During Passover week on a hill outside the Holy City, the Great High Priest offered up himself as the Lamb of God for the sins of the world. In excruciating pain and with desperate gasps for breath, Jesus offered up prayers from three liturgical psalms, which the Father heard because of Jesus' piety. Although the cluster of grieving women, the sneering crowd, and the unsuspecting powers of darkness did not realize it, it was the most important "liturgical" moment in his story and in ours. This cosmic act of worship, consisting of a sacrificial offering and prayers lifted up to God, is the source of eternal salvation that now results in praise to the Lord that extends to all nations and future generations.

Biblical interpretation begins with reading a word, verse, or passage within its context. So, the popular understanding of Godforsakenness related to Matthew 27:46 appears to hang from a thin hermeneutical thread. It is built primarily on one verse, which must be interpreted out of context:

- out of the context of Ps 22,
- out of the context of individual protest psalms,
- out of the context of the religious environment in which Jesus lived,
- out of the context of the first disciples, who could not tell the crucifixion story without referencing this psalm,
- out of the context of the recorded sayings of Jesus from the cross,
- out of the context of what Jesus said beforehand about his coming suffering.

Now let's return to my friend Lucky. Several years ago, he reached out to me through social media after no contact for twenty-three years and asked if I was the same Mr. Don who had spent those afternoons with him that left an indelible impression in both our lives. You see, you can't read Scripture in a different context without being changed by it. My continued study of this passage has strengthened my confidence that I did not mishandle Scripture when I answered his question. Jesus was not referring to some break or disruption in the Trinity. His death was dishonorable to society, but not disgusting to God. It was the most supreme act of self-giving sacrifice to obey and accomplish God's purpose.

God's Constant Presence with Those He Sends

There is an important implication from this passage for missions today. We need to remember God's presence has always been a key element in his purpose for mankind and even our joining him in it. The first two chapters of the Bible portray God's presence with Adam and Eve in the garden before the fall and the final two chapters of the Bible emphasize his presence with the redeemed in the New Jerusalem. Everything between Genesis 3 and Revelation 20 is an account of God's purpose worked out across centuries to reestablish the relationship that binds his presence with fallen mankind. The Father planned this redemption before the world began, and it did not include withdrawing his presence at the most critical moment.

> Misconception 40
> Missions service and life can be hard and sometimes the missionary will just have to tough it out alone.

Jesus promised his disciples, "As the Father has sent me, I also send you" (John 20:21). Such a promise would not give much peace if at the most painful moment of Jesus' mission, the Father abandoned him to suffer alone. No, the Father who sent him was with Jesus, and Jesus is always with those he sends to the nations. Those who are pushed to the nations know how personally important this reality is for their life and ministry.

"Those who seek Him will praise the Lord.
Let your heart live forever!
All the ends of the earth will remember and turn to the Lord,
And all the families of the nations will worship before You.
For the Kingdom is the Lord's
And He rules over the nations." (Ps 22:26–28)

Questions to Consider

1. How have you understood the cry that Jesus gave from the cross, "My God, my God, why have you forsaken me?" Is this something that you have studied on your own or has this been taught to you? How did this chapter confirm or push back on that perspective?

2. Have you ever had an experience where you cried out to the Lord a cry of desolation while also crying out in affirmation that God is present and working? What was the relationship of those two seemingly contradictory things?

3. Read Psalm 22. Where do you see specific support for the observations made in this chapter about this passage? What stands out to you as you look at this passage?

   a. God's faithfulness is affirmed after a cry of desolation.

   b. There are three cycles of complaint describing emotional anguish, social antagonism, and physical agony. Identify these and consider them in light of Jesus' death.

   c. The psalmist talks to God as though he is present and hearing him even though he begins with the phrase "why have you forsaken me?"

   d. It is stated that God does not forsake the sufferer.

   e. Praise that acknowledges God's heart for the nations is given.

4. Now read Matthew 27, keeping the following pairs in mind:

   a. Matthew 27:35 references Ps 22:18—dividing his garments

   b. Matthew 27:39 references Psalm 22:7—"wag their heads."

   c. Matthew 27:43 references Psalm 22:8—"let Him deliver him."

   d. Matthew 27:46 references Psalm 22:1—"My God, my God, why . . . ?"

5. Had you noticed the two statements in John 8:12–30 and 16:32 about God's continued presence during the suffering of Jesus?

6. Why is it important for you personally and for your ministry moving forward to know that God did not abandon his Son and will not abandon his people?

7. In light of the whole book, discuss some of your big takeaways and how you will put deeper or new knowledge to action. What would you like to learn more about?

Bibliography

Allen, Roland. *Missionary Methods: St. Paul's or Ours?* First published in 1912, reprinted multiple times.

———. *The Spontaneous Expansion of the Church: And the Causes Which Hinder It.* Eugene, OR: Wipf & Stock, 1997. First published in 1927.

Antonio, S. T. *Insider Church: Ekklesia and the Insider Paradigm.* Pasadena, CA: William Carey Library, 2020.

Arnold, Clinton. *Three Crucial Question about Spiritual Warfare.* Grand Rapids: Baker Academic, 1997.

Barna Group. "Competing Worldviews Influence Today's Christians." 2017. https// www.barna.com/research/competing-worldviews-influence-todays-christians.

———. "Survey Reveals That Fewer Adults Have a Biblical Worldview Now than Two Years ago." October 18, 2018. Worldview Study. https://www.georgebarna.com/ research/7622/survey-reveals-that-fewer-adults-have-a-biblical-worldview-now-than-two-years-ago.

Beaver, R. Pearce, ed. *To Advance the Gospel: Selections from the Writings of Rufus Anderson.* Grand Rapids: Eerdmans, 1967.

Bede. *Ecclesiastical History of the English People.* Edited by D. H. Farmer, translated by Leo Sherley-Price. Rev. ed. New York: Penguin Classics, 1991.

Bock, Darrell. *Acts of the Apostles.* BECNT. Grand Rapids: Baker Academic, 2007.

Borchert, Gerald. *John 1–11.* New American Commentary 25A. Nashville: Broadman & Holman, 1996.

Brady, David. *Not Forgotten: Inspiring Missionary Pioneers.* Maitland, FL: Xulon, 2018.

Brooks, James. *Mark.* New American Commentary 23. Nashville: Broadman & Holman, 1991.

Brooks, Phillips. "Going Up to Jerusalem." In *Visions and Tasks, and Other Sermons.* Phillips Brooks's Sermons, Fourth Series. New York: E. P. Dutton, 1886.

Coleman, Doug. *A Theological Analysis of the Insider Movement Paradigm from Four Perspectives.* Pasadena, CA: William Carey Library, 2011.

Confessing the Faith within Church Planting Movements. http://noplaceleft.net/wp-content/uploads/2017/08/Confessions-2.pdf.

Corbett, Steve, and Brian Fickert. *When Helping Hurts: How to Alleviate Poverty without Hurting the Poor. . . and Yourself.* Chicago: Moody, 2009.

Cranfield, C. E. B. "Who Are Christ's Brothers?" In *On Romans and Other New Testament Essays*, 125–36. Edinburgh: T. & T. Clark, 1998.

Crawford, Mary. *The Shantung Revival*. 1933. Reprinted by Randy Clark, Mechanicsville, PA: Global Awakening, 2005.

Dent, Don. "Decisive Discipleship: Why Rapid Discipleship Is Preferable and How It Is Possible." *Global Missiology*, October 2015, 1–21.

———. *The Ongoing Role of Apostles in Missions*. Bloomington, IN: Westbow, 2019.

DeYoung, Kevin, and Greg Gilbert. *What Is the Mission of the Church?: Making Sense of Social Justice, Shalom, and the Great Commission*. Wheaton, IL: Crossway, 2011.

Dodd, C. H. *According to the Scriptures: The Sub-Structure of New Testament Theology*. London: Nisbet, 1952.

Duckworth, Angela. *Grit: The Power of Passion and Perseverance*. New York: Scribner, 2016.

Ferguson, Niall. *Civilization: The West and the Rest*. New York: Penguin, 2011.

Fidler, Preston. *1000 Cups of Tea: Gospel Fluency across Cultures*. Middleton, DL: n.p., 2020.

Finke, Roger, and Rodney Stark. *The Churching of America, 1776–2005: Winners and Losers in Our Religious Economy*. Brunswick, NJ: Rutgers University Press, 2008.

Fletcher, Richard A. *The Barbarian Conversions: From Paganism to Christianity*. New York: Henry Holt, 1998.

Foundations for Emerging Leaders. http://noplaceleft.net/wp-content/uploads/2016/02/Foundations-Training-Overview-8-25-15.docx_.pdf.

France, R. T. *Matthew*. Tyndale New Testament Commentaries. Downers Grove, IL: IVP Academic, 1985.

Garland, David. E. *2 Corinthians*. New American Commentary 29. Nashville: Broadman & Holman, 1999.

Garrison, David. *Church Planting Movements: How God Is Redeeming a Lost World*. Midlothian, VA: Wigtake, 2004.

Gillingham, S. E. *The Poems and Psalms of the Hebrew Bible*. Oxford: Oxford University Press, 1994.

Gladwell, Malcolm. *Outliers: The Story of Success*. New York: Penguin, 2008.

Goldingay, John. *Psalms*. Vol. 1. Baker Commentary on the Old Testament. Grand Rapids: Baker Academic, 2006.

Gray, Sherman. *The Least of My Brothers: Matthew 25:31–46: A History of Interpretation*. Atlanta: Scholars, 1989.

Green, H. Benedict. *The Gospel According to Matthew*. Oxford: Oxford University Press, 1975.

Guillot, C. *Kiai Sadrach: Riwayat Kristenisasi di Jawa*. Jakarta: Grafiti Pers, 1985.

Gutierrez, Gustavo. "Toward a Theology of Liberation (1968)." In *Liberation Theology: A Documentary History*, edited by Alfred T. Hennelly, 62–74. Maryknoll, NY: Orbis, 1990.

Hahn, H. C. "Openness, Frankness, Boldness." In *The New International Dictionary of New Testament Theology*, edited by Colin Brown, 2:734–37. Grand Rapids: Zondervan, 1986.

Hagner, Donald. *Matthew 14–28*. Word Biblical Commentary 33B. Dallas: Word, 1995.

Hay, Rob, Valerie Lim, et al. *Worth Keeping: Global Perspectives on Best Practice in Missionary Retention*. Pasadena, CA: William Carey Library, 2007.

Hesselgrave, David. *Paradigms in Conflict*. Edited by Keith Eitel. 2nd ed. Grand Rapids: Kregel Academic, 2018.

Ibrahim, Ayman, and Ant Greenham, eds. *Muslim Conversions to Christ: A Critique of Insider Movements in Islamic Contexts*. New York: Peter Lang, 2018.

John, Victor, and David Coles, *Bhojpuri Breakthrough: A Movement That Keeps Multiplying*. Midlothian, VA: Wigtake, 2019.

Keener, Craig. *Acts: An Exegetical Commentary*. Vol. 2. Grand Rapids: Baker Academic, 2013.

——. *Matthew*. IVP New Testament Commentary. Downers Grove, IL: IVP Academic, 1997.

Kidd, Thomas, and Barry Hankins. *Baptists in America: A History*. New York: Oxford University Press, 2015.

Klein, William, Craig Blomberg, and Robert Hubbard. *Introduction to Biblical Interpretation*. 3rd ed. Grand Rapids: Zondervan, 2017.

Kraemer, Hendrick. *From Mission Field to Independent Church*. The Hague: Boekencentrum, 1958.

Lai, Patrick. *Tentmaking: Business as Missions*. Waynesboro, GA: Authentic Media, 2005.

——. "Tentmaking Uncovered." In *Business as Mission: From Impoverished to Empowered*, edited by Tom Steffen and Mike Barnett, 79–100. Pasadena, CA: William Carey Library, 2006.

Lawrence, Una Roberts. *Lottie Moon*. Nashville: Baptist Sunday School Board, 1927.

Lederleitner, Mary. *Cross-Cultural Partnerships: Navigating the Complexities of Money and Mission*. Downers Grove, IL: InterVarsity, 2010.

Lupton, Robert D. *Toxic Charity: How Churches and Charities Hurt Those They Help*. New York: Harper One, 2011.

Mays, James. "Prayer and Christology: Psalm 22 as Perspective on the Passion." *Theology Today* 48:3 (Oct 1985) 322–31.

McBeth, Leon. *The Baptist Heritage*. Nashville: Broadman, 1987.

McGavran, Donald. *The Founders of the Indian Church*. Chennai: Church Growth Association of India, 1998.

——. *Understanding Church Growth*. Rev. ed. Grand Rapids: Eerdmans, 1980.

Moo, Douglas. *The Old Testament in the Gospel Passion Narratives*. Sheffield, UK: Almond, 1983.

Morgan, Christopher, and Robert Peterson, ed. *Faith Comes by Hearing: A Response to Inclusiveness*. Downers Grove, IL: IVP Academic, 2008.

Morris, Leon. *The Gospel According to John*. NICNT. Grand Rapids: Eerdmans, 1971.

Nevius, John. *Planting and Development of Missionary Churches*. First published in 1885, reprinted multiple times.

Palmer, Jeff. *So You Want to Dig a Well in Africa?* Bloomington, IN: Westbow, 2020.

Partonadi. Sutarman. *Sadrach's Community and Its Contextual Roots: A Nineteenth-Century Javanese Expression of Christianity*. Amsterdam: University of Amsterdam Press, 1988.

Pickett, J. Wascom. *Christian Mass Movements in India*. Lucknow, India: Lucknowb, 1969. First published in 1933.

Pickett, J. Wascom, Donald McGavran, and G. H. Singh. *Christian Missions in Mid India: A Study of Nine Areas with Special Reference to Mass Movements*. New Delhi: Isha, 2013. First published in 1938.

Polhill, John. *Acts*. New American Commentary 26. Nashville: Broadman, 1992.

"The Psychology of Self-Support." In *The Economic Basis of the Church*, edited by J. Merle Davis, 136–66. Tambaran Series 5. Oxford: Oxford University Press, 1939.

Rauschenbush, Walter. *Christianizing the Social Order*. Boston: Pilgrim, 1912.

Rundle, Steve, and Tom Steffen. *Great Commission Companies*. Downers Grove, IL: InterVarsity, 2011.

Scheuermann, Rochelle, and Edward Smithers, eds. *Controversies in Missions: Theology, People, and Practice of Mission in the 21st Century*. P Pasadena, CA: William Carey Library, 2016

Schnabel, Eckhard. *Mark*. Tyndale New Testament Commentaries 2. Downers Grove, IL: IVP Academic, 2017.

Serampore Trio. "Form of Agreement." 1805. https://www.wholesomewords.org/missions/bcarey13.html.

Sherman, Bill. "Only 17% of serious Christians have biblical worldview, a new poll from evangelical group finds." *Tulsa World*, June 23, 2017. https://tulsaworld.com/lifestyles/only-17-percent-of-serious-christians-have-biblical-worldview-new-poll-from-evangelical-group-finds/article_bd3b367d-2889-502d-9919-498e60cdcf66.html.

Southern Baptists and Their Far Eastern Missions. Richmond, VA: Southern Baptist Convention Foreign Mission Board, 1925.

Stevens, Marty. *Temples, Tithes, and Taxes: The Temple and the Economic Life of Ancient Israel*. Peabody, MA: Hendrickson, 2006.

Sumartana. *Mission at the Crossroads*. Jakarta: Gunung Mulia, 1993.

Third World Bishops. "A Letter to the Peoples of the Third World." Dated August 15, 1967. In *Liberation Theology: A Documentary History*, edited by Alfred Hennelly, 48–57. Maryknoll, NY: Orbis, 1990.

Travis, John. "The C1 to C6 Spectrum: A Practical Tool for Defining Six Types of 'Christ-Centered Communities' Found in the Muslim Context." *Evangelical Missions Quarterly* 34:4 (1998) 407–8.

———. "Insider Movements: Coming to Terms with Terms." In *Understanding Insider Movements: Disciples of Jesus within Diverse Religious Communities*, edited by Harley Talman and John Travis, 7–10. Pasadena, CA: William Carey Library, 2015.

Warren, Max, ed. *To Apply the Gospel: Selections from the Writings of Henry Venn*. Grand Rapids: Eerdmans, 1971.

Weber, Max. *The Protestant Ethic and the Spirit of Capitalism*. 1920. Translated by Stephen Kalbert. Oxford: Oxford University Press, 2010.

Winter, Ralph. "The New Macedonia: A Revolutionary New Era in Mission Begins." In *Perspectives on the World Christian Movement*, edited by Ralph Winter and Steven Hawthorn, eds. 3rd ed. Pasadena, CA: William Carey Library, 1999.

Witherington, Ben, III. *The Acts of the Apostles: A Socio-Rhetorical Commentary*. Grand Rapids: Eerdmans, 1998.

———. *Psalms Old and New: Exegesis, Intertextuality, and Hermeneutics*. Minneapolis: Fortress, 2017.

Woodberry, Robert D. "The Missionary Roots of Liberal Democracy." *American Political Science Review* 106:2 (May 2012) 244–74.

Wright, N. T. *Jesus and the Victory of God*. Christian Origins and the Question of God 2. Minneapolis: Fortress, 1996.